Of the press, by the press, for the press, and others, too

A critical study
of the inside workings
of the news business.
From the news pages,
editorials, columns
and internal staff memos of
𝕿𝖍𝖊 𝖂𝖆𝖘𝖍𝖎𝖓𝖌𝖙𝖔𝖓 𝕻𝖔𝖘𝖙

Edited by Laura Longley Babb
Washington Post Writers Group

HOUGHTON MIFFLIN/BOSTON
Atlanta   Dallas   Geneva, Ill.   Hopewell, N.J.   Palo Alto   London

Washington Post Writers Group
William B. Dickinson Jr., Editorial Director
Laura Longley Babb, Associate Editor/Books

Cover photograph by David Sharpe

PN
4867
·04

948258

Contents

Introduction

By Philip L. Geyelin

Barbara Walters: Do you think the President should be impeached?
*Martha Mitchell: That I don't know. But I think one thing is inter-
esting. The* Washington Post *came out yesterday with a wonderful editorial, and I was so proud of them, "For Your Information," one of
these initials "F.Y.I."*
Walters: F.Y.I.?
*Martha Mitchell: But anyway, it cleared up Jerry Ford in his state-
ment about the President's impeachment—of which he was a prosecutor on the committee, or something, when they tried to prosecute
Douglas?*
Walters: Jerry Ford . . . wanted to have Justice Douglas (impeached).
*Martha Mitchell: All right. Now he came out with this statement—
remember?—about why and how a President should be impeached.
Well, instead of the press taking the whole statement, they only took
part of it. And yesterday the* Washington Post *cleared up the whole
thing in an editorial which I think is great . . .*
*Walters: But do you think the President should be impeached,
Martha?*
—From an interview with Martha Mitchell on the NBC-TV
"Today" show, March 12, 1974.

Thank you, Mrs. Mitchell; we needed that. It is about seven years now that
the *Washington Post,* in a number of different ways, has been engaged in
the difficult and sometimes even dangerous business of subjecting itself
and the rest of the news media to the sort of analysis and criticism that it
regularly directs at just about everything else, and frankly it has not always been joyous work; the response from some quarters has been, at best,
flat.

You will observe, for example, from the above exchange that Barbara
Walters does not entirely share Martha Mitchell's enthusiasm for, or even
comprehension of, the value of a newspaper editorial devoted to the purpose of straightening out a popular misconception deriving from a persis-
tent misquotation of a public official by the press.

This is easily understandable; Mrs. Mitchell is controversial enough a
public figure to welcome even a faint sign of contrition, or even simple
humanity, on the part of the press. Barbara Walters, being a media figure,
is naturally more concerned with the question of, say, whether President
Nixon should be impeached. Moreover, as we have discovered within our
own ranks, news people are people, only more so—which is to say that they

i

fiercely cherish their First Amendment protections and take great pride in their own particular contributions to the freest possible flow of information and opinion with the least possible interference from anybody — including their own editors.

Walter Lippmann, who has probably thought longer and harder and to better effect about the problems of the press than any man, put the matter very well in a column entitled "Criticism of the Press," written in March of 1947 in response to the report of the Commission on Freedom of the Press which proposed, among other things, "that the members of the press engage in vigorous, mutual criticism." Lippmann replied:

> *They are talking about newspapermen criticizing other newspapermen in their newspapers. We are all tempted, and now and then we indulge, but on the whole we refrain. And the reasons are good reasons. They are the same reasons which make it very rare indeed that a lawyer or a doctor or an actor or a professor will speak out publicly and say how badly the lawyer argued his case, how inexpertly the doctor diagnosed the disease, how lamely the actor performed, how dull was the professor's lecture.*
>
> *For there is a fellowship among newspapermen as there is in other crafts and professions. They are not lone wolves. They have to see each other, meet together and work together, and life would become intolerable, as it would in a university faculty or an officers mess, if they practiced vigorous, mutual criticism in public. I may say that I have tried it, and I have had it tried on me, and my conclusion is that the hard feelings it causes are out of all proportion to the public benefit it causes.*

To all of this, anybody who has written much about the news media would probably agree. But it does not, for one thing, entirely accord with the record of Walter Lippmann in his earlier days as an exuberant and penetrating commentator and philosopher, engaging in regular jousts with his colleagues, freely criticizing the performance of rival newspapers and newsmen, and writing enduring studies of the working of a free press in our society. And still less does it answer the question raised by Lippmann in the same column: "How the press itself, since it is a primary institution of a free country, is to be reported, reviewed, explained, and criticized?"

The older and presumably wiser Lippmann would rely on some mechanism for bringing to bear upon the press the criticism of outside, private citizens, leading figures in other fields — but excluding, as almost every thoughtful newspaperperson would, any form of oversight by the government. And Lippmann, on balance, may be right. It may be that the answer lies with some variation of the national news council which is now getting into operation in this country, something on the order of Britain's Press Council, to answer the question described, again by Lippmann, as that of "who watches the watchman, who inspects the inspector, who polices the policeman?"

But somehow, as the 1960s with all their turbulence gave way to the 1970s, it seemed to the editors of the *Post* that something urgent needed to be done—something other than the laborious creation of some private, nongovernmental instrumentality. For one thing, neither the machinery nor the tradition for it was there. What was there, however, after Vietnam and the rioting in the cities and the problems of student upheaval and drugs and pollution and all the rest, was a crisis of public confidence in the news media and an administration in Washington prepared to exploit it and to pervert the very meaning of a free press for its own political profit. We had the visible evidence of Vice President Agnew and the invisible activities, subsequently exposed, of a team of White House aides actively engaged in writing phony letters to the editor, tapping the telephones of newsmen, intimidating television network executives and the owners of affiliated stations, and otherwise seeking to discredit the media by way of devaluing or somehow making unbelievable anything that was reported in newspapers or on television which did not serve the interests of the administration. We were being robbed of our one essential asset, without which no reporter or newscaster can operate, which is public confidence, or to use the more fashionable phrase, "credibility."

In 1969 the media task force of the National Commission on the Causes and Prevention of Violence had concluded that "a crisis of confidence exists today between the American people and the news media." At about the same time, the Associated Press Managing Editors Association reported that American newspapers "have a credibility gap of substantial proportions."

The way to deal with this problem, it seemed to us, was to begin by talking about it, by acknowledging its existence, and by conceding that some part of it, at the very least, was a consequence of our own frailty and fallibility. It seemed a time to stop taking for granted public acceptance of the critical importance to democratic government of a freely functioning press, to stop counting on an automatic public commitment to the sanctity of the First Amendment. It was a time to begin informing the public, as we would in the case of any other institution under challenge, about what we were up to and what we were up against in going about our business of gathering and disseminating the news.

With all this in mind, we created in January, 1969 a category of editorials entitled F.Y.I., a piece of shorthand familiar to all of us in the newspaper business as a means of identifying something we are passing along in a casual, informative way. The objective was twofold: to make available a rubric under which we could, as graciously as possible, admit to being mistaken once in a while; under which we could examine not only ourselves but the news media as a whole with an eye both to praise and censure, but above all with an eye to making ourselves not necessarily lovable or even admirable but understandable.

We began with a short satirical piece attempting to explain a self-serving leak from the Justice Department — a leak which carried no attribution beyond the phrase "it was learned." Our second effort was directed towards a misquotation which we had used as the headline on an editorial and which turned out to be a gross distortion of testimony before a congressional committee — a distortion which had been compounded in *Time* magazine, the *Wall Street Journal,* on the Huntley-Brinkley show, and twice in the *New York Times.* We moved on to take the *Los Angeles Times* and *Life* magazine to task for pre-trial publicity in a murder case and to take our own news coverage of a murder case to task for the same reason.

Over the intervening years we hailed the creation of an English-language edition of *Le Monde,* paid tribute to *Life* magazine's expose reporting, engaged in a protracted debate with CBS over editing techniques employed in a documentary entitled "The Selling of the Pentagon" — and came to the rescue of Vice President Ford.

<hr>

In 1970 the news department of the *Washington Post* took a giant step in roughly the same direction — towards self-criticism of the press, by the press — with the establishment of an ombudsman to monitor the performance of the *Post* on a daily basis and write regular critiques of it for the benefit of editors and reporters; to deal with complaints from readers; and to contribute on a regular basis to an editorial page feature entitled "The News Business," which also served as a vehicle for commentary by other staff members and by outsiders on matters having to do with the workings and the performance not only of the *Post* but of the rest of the news media.

This book is one result. It is a compilation of F.Y.I. editorials, News Business columns, and internal "oversight" memos* by two of the *Post*'s ombudsmen, Richard Harwood and Charles Seib. Given the sheer volume of writing from which these selections were drawn, this book is, in one sense, unique, in that it reflects quite probably the largest collection of commentary by any newspaper about the newspaper business ever published over so relatively brief a period of time. It is also, in its way, a primer of a sort on journalism, both of the print and electronic variety, for there is virtually no corner of either trade that is not explored either in the ombudsmen's memos or the signed columns or the editorials.

By broad category, it deals with the problem of defining and handling "facts"; with the pitfalls in dealing with cliches and stereotypes; with problems of taste whether in connection with photographs or the written word; with backgrounders and anonymous sources; with discrimination in the newsroom and technology in the composing room; with the economics of journalism — and with the legal aspects of it as well.

---

*These memos, retyped for publication, remain unedited, except for the removal of names in two cases. They were written to the attention of the executive and managing editors.

The bulk of the signed pieces represents the work of Harwood and his successors in the difficult and often hazardous role of ombudsman— Ben H. Bagdikian, whose tour was the briefest of the four in part because he devoted much of it to a memorable series of articles on the wholly unrelated subject of prison reform; Robert C. Maynard, who would have served out his eighteen-month sentence had he not been persuaded to take a job on the editorial page; and the present title-holder, Charles B. Seib.

But there also are contributions from Executive Editor Benjamin C. Bradlee and Philip Foisie, the assistant managing editor for foreign news and one of the earliest proponents of ombudsmanship at the *Post;* from news staff writers Haynes Johnson, Jules Witcover, Bill Greider, Steve Isaacs and Bernard Nossiter; from Meg Greenfield, the deputy editorial page editor, as well as from editorial writer Colman McCarthy, columnists David Broder and Kenneth Crawford, and Supreme Court Justice Potter Stewart. When you add to this list not only the present members of the editorial page staff of the *Post* but such past members as Ward Just and Roger Wilkins, it does not seem overly immodest to state that so rich a concentration of talent and expertise has rarely been brought to bear within the covers of one book upon the inner working of the news business, which makes this volume in another sense unique.

<hr/>

But it is only fair to add, by way of putting the whole subject into a broader perspective, that neither the concept of ombudsmanship nor of the press writing about the press is, strictly speaking, unique. Lippmann's work is but one historical case in point. Another is a brief chapter in the extraordinary career of Arthur Krock. Long before he rose to pre-eminence in his field as the Washington correspondent of the *New York Times,* Krock served as assistant to the publisher of the *New York World* with the general assignment of providing a daily critique of that newspaper's performance in relation to the rest of the New York press, and with a specific instruction "to ride herd" on Herbert Bayard Swope, then managing editor of the *World.* The repercussions from this last role are recounted in Krock's *Memoirs;* it was Swope's habit, Krock recalls, to telephone him "every once in a while" and tell him to "keep your goddam hands off my department."

By Krock's account, his "presence in that particular job was also distasteful" to Lippmann, who was editor of the *World's* editorial page, and to at least two other important executives over whom he had been assigned a supervisory role. Krock's experience perhaps may sound not entirely unfamiliar to latter day ombudsmen, although the conduct of that office at the *Post* has not been either as controversial or as unrewarding as some outside accounts have made it sound, in part perhaps because its tenure has been kept relatively brief by mutual agreement among all concerned.

After Krock, as far as can be determined by the most superficial scholarship, ombudsmanship languished through the years until the idea was revived in 1967 when John Herchenroeder was given that title at the *Louisville Courier-Journal* by Executive Editor Norman Isaacs, who had been prompted by a suggestion made in a *New York Times* Sunday magazine article by A. H. Raskin, the assistant editorial page editor of the *Times*. Raskin, in turn, had apparently been inspired by a piece by Ben Bagdikian in the March 1967 *Esquire*. All this is by way of saying that criticism of the press, by the press, is an idea that may die hard—but that also has not exactly caught fire.

So what does this history tell us? That it is too hard? That the news business is better off covering everything but the news business?

The answer, it seems to me, is that it is obviously hard—perhaps too hard to sustain as a regular thing—but that the concept of self-criticism is no less sound on this account and that the practice of it is no less needed in direct proportion to the amount of disfavor and distrust the press, for whatever valid or invalid reasons, may be encountering at a given time. For when the press is out of favor, people get to talking about doing something about it, and inevitably they get to talking about the government doing something about it; at about that time, it seems to me, the press is well advised to start thinking in very serious ways of doing something of its own in the way of policing and examining and criticizing itself.

In *Liberty and the News*, published in 1920, Lippmann predicted that "on some form or other the next generation will attempt to bring the publishing business under greater social control. There is everywhere an increasingly angry disillusionment about the press, a growing sense of being baffled and mislead; and wise publishers will not poo-poo these omens."

Lippmann accompanied this rather extraordinarily prescient warning with some sound advice. Publishers, he said, "might well note the history of prohibition where a failure to work out a program of temperance brought about an undiscriminating taboo . . . If publishers . . . themselves do not face the facts and attempt to deal with them, some day Congress, in a fit of temper, egged on by an outraged public opinion, will operate on the press with an ax."

If that counsel was appropriate to the 1920s, the evidence of our senses commends it more than ever in the 1970s.

Getting at the Facts

A Question of What the Facts Will Support

By Richard Harwood

Newspapers make mistakes every day. Some of them are typographical errors—"house" comes out "mouse," "time" comes out "tame." Some of them are factual errors—wrong names, wrong addresses, wrong ages. Some are garbled quotations resulting from the fact that most reporters can't write in shorthand and don't use tape recorders.

Mistakes of that kind seem to be inevitable, given the pace of this business and the speed with which newspapers are produced. They ordinarily cause little harm and, where it seems necessary, can be rectified a day or so later through the printing of corrections.

The mistakes that are more difficult to fix are those that arise out of our selection and definition of the news. Often we are unaware of error until much time has passed and much damage has been done.

In retrospect, it seems obvious that the destructive phenomenon called "McCarthyism"—the search in the 1950s for witches, scapegoats and traitors—was a product of this kind of error. Joseph McCarthy, an obscure and mediocre senator from Wisconsin, was transformed into the Grand Inquisitor by publicity. And there was no way later for the newspapers of America to repair that damage, to say on the morning after: "We regret the error."

What they could have done was to take a serious look at themselves to discover the limitations and weaknesses of the news business and its practitioners, to recognize and remember what a journalist is and what he is not.

Harry Ashmore, once a newspaper editor and more recently a resident philosopher at the Center for the Study of Democratic Institutions, has written something on this subject:

"It might be useful to establish at least what a journalist is not. He is not a scientist, social or otherwise. The pressures of time and space rarely permit him to begin his examination of phenomena with a hypothesis; the data he collects are transient and fragmentary; the conclusions with which he ends his endeavor are tentative. His mission is to present the facts as they are available, but he rarely has reason to confuse their sum with the truth. He is not an artist. He has no claim to poetic license, and it is fatal to his enterprise if he attempts to employ his imagination to construct a larger view than the facts at hand will support."

Newspapers get into trouble—as in the McCarthy episode—when they ignore these beatitudes, especially the last one that says it's a no-no "to construct a larger view than the facts at hand will support." But the tendency to make big pictures out of small facts is even now so common-place that it often appears to be a beatitude in itself.

Back on the comics page November 17, 1970, the *Washington Post* carried a column by Jack Anderson under a headline that read: "Most of Governors' Offices Bugged." The column reported that all governors have "hot-line" phones that enable them and federal civil defense authorities to communicate in times of national crisis, that "most" of these phones are "bugged," and that the alleged culprit may be either the CIA or the FBI. The column seemed to be based on information supplied by Gov. Marvin Mandel of Maryland.

It caused something of a stir in the newsrooms of the *Post* and the *Baltimore Sun* and led to lengthy stories, some of them on page one. As it turned out, no evidence came to light that any governor's phone was "bugged," Mandel's included. It also turned out that all the phones in question had been installed by the American Telephone & Telegraph Co. and its subsidiaries, rather than the federal government; that six of them had been wired improperly by AT&T installers and that it was theoretic-ally possible to "tap" these phones at some point between a governor's office and a basement terminal box. That was all.

On that evidence one can only conclude that the Anderson column made much out of little or nothing, that it then became the subject of a great volume of "news," that the implication that the federal government was eavesdropping on "most American governors" (or on any of them) was false, and that the newspapers in this case constructed "a larger view than the facts at hand" would support.

The same thing seems to have happened recently in newspaper treat-ment of the "Besson Report." This was a report commissioned by the Pentagon early in 1969 and completed in June, 1970, by a committee of eight generals, admirals and colonels, headed by a retired lieutenant gen-eral, Frank S. Besson Jr. It dealt with a single question: What did the mili-tary learn from the Vietnam war about the problems of supplying troops in the field?

The committeemen apparently learned a great deal. Their report ran to three basic volumes, plus many appendices. It produced 265 recommenda-tions on things to be done the next time around. What it didn't produce, at first, was any stir in the Pentagon, where it was read by various officials as a rather dull and technical logistics treatise.

The Besson committee's main finding was that they and their fellow logisticians had done a remarkable job in Vietnam:

". . . The logistic effort often seemed to lag behind the demands for facilities, personnel, equipment and money. It was not until the end of 1968 that the logistic structure in terms of organization, personnel and facilities was fully adequate for the tasks at hand. A notable aspect of this situation was the almost unbelievably high satisfaction of the demands of the combat units. The military commander in Vietnam, the General Accounting Office, and Congress all have attested that, *with relatively minor and temporary exceptions* (italics added), U.S. forces committed to conflict have never been better supplied than those in S.E. Asia. . . .

". . . This report, like any analysis leading to recommendations or improvements, may tend to obscure a creditable performance by accentuating difficulties and inefficiency. In following the ensuing portion of this summary assessment, the truly remarkable logistic achievements of the Vietnam era should not be forgotten." Many pages later the point is made again: "The American fighting man has been better supplied and equipped than ever before in history."

Late in October (1970) a free-lance writer came across the report and described it in a column as a document highly critical of the Pentagon's civilian managers. A few days later the report came to the attention of *Army Times,* a weekly newspaper published by a civilian company. A long story followed under the headline: "LBJ & Co. Blamed for Botching War."

The Pentagon pressroom was set in action by the *Army Times* report. Reporters clamored for copies of the supposedly sensational document, flipped hurriedly through the volumes and raced to their typewriters. The Associated Press man verified the quotes used in the *Army Times* story but had no time to read through the report. His story made the television news that night and appeared in the *Washington Post* on the morning of November 6 under the headline: "Military Hits LBJ on Viet War."

The *Army Times* story best summarized — in its own language — the indictment:

"In the opinion of a top-level military review board, the Johnson administration made wrong decisions on Vietnam by planning for only a short war, by not calling the reserves, by not using any of the previously prepared contingency plans and by following the British example of fighting counter-insurgency in Malaya."

The *Post,* in a follow-up story on November 7, explored the Besson committee's finding that there had been a bomb shortage in Vietnam in April, 1966, and pointedly — and correctly — noted that former Secretary of Defense Robert McNamara had denied that at the time any bomb shortage existed. The story was headlined: "Military War Study Faults Mc-Namara."

The material on which all these stories was based was not invented. A careful reading of all three volumes turns up several critical references to the "political and economic constraints" under which the war was fought — the "constraint," for example, against bombing Hanoi and Haiphong. There are several critical references to the government's failure to call up the reserves, several references to the tight reins on logistics held by Mc-Namara and other civilians, several references to "contingency plans" that were never followed. There was also a lengthy discussion of the April, 1966, bomb shortage.

What the report did *not* say was that either Lyndon Johnson or Robert McNamara or anyone else had "botched" the war, that Johnson had used "faulty war strategy" or that McNamara was at "fault." Nor did it say, as a story in the *Post* claimed it said, that "the civilians who insisted on running the Vietnam war . . . never addressed it as a real war. As a result there was neither enough men nor material to do the job right. . . ."

It said, in fact, that "with relatively minor and temporary exceptions" the military machine had everything it needed in Vietnam, that the troops had been better supplied than troops in other American wars and that is really what the report was about — supplies.

Where did the literal "botching" allegations arise? They arose in the minds of reporters, some of whom had not even read through the dreary volumes and some of whom, as Ashmore put it, had constructed a somewhat larger view of the report than the facts at hand would support. That, at any rate, is my judgment of it. It is not the judgment of some poeple in the *Post* newsroom. What McNamara or Johnson think of it, no one knows; apparently no one asked them.

What does General Besson think? He is now retired and no longer subject to Pentagon management. His views are perhaps not decisive, in this case, but at the minimum they are of interest:

"I have not seen a responsible story on the report. What I have seen has been sensational journalism — picking out a statement here and there and sensationalizing it. . . . The (political and economic) constraints did not result in any major logistical problems, except some excesses at some times and some increased costs. But these costs were insignificant compared to the total costs of that war. . . . There were no serious differences between us and OSD (the Secretary of Defense). We would have spent more money faster in some areas but by and large OSD was right — in hindsight — in not following the contingency plans because those contingencies never materialized. . . .

"I felt, during this war, that I had less authority in the Pentagon in many ways than I had as a junior officer in World War II. But I always knew and told my people what McNamara had told me: 'Anything you really need, we have the money to buy.'"

4

What about the bomb shortage of April, 1966?

"Well," says Besson, "that whole business of the bombing is hairy because nobody ever knew how effective it was. Anyway, there was nothing OSD could have done about the bomb shortage. . . . When they started using B-52s for conventional bombing—something nobody had ever counted on—their demand for bombs got to be insatiable."

So much for the Besson report. It is now a footnote in journalistic history that the generals began blaming the civilians for "botching" the war and it is very difficult to erase footnotes of that kind. All we can do is flag them.

—November 30, 1970

Bugs

The Washington Post

Interoffice Memo

TO: Bradlee, et al.   November 18, 1970

FROM: Harwood

    Were we not conned by the Jack Anderson "bugging" expose? Our P. 1 head on November 17 says: "Mandel's 'Hot Line' Bugged, He Believes." The story goes on to suggest that the Feds (a) made these phone installations and that (b) if there is any bugging going on it is by the "FBI...(or) CIA."

    On November 18, on B-1, we report the denouement: (a) there is "no evidence" that the phone was "bugged" by anybody and (b) it was installed by AT&T, not by the Feds. So where does this leave us? It sort of leaves us with a hoax, I think.

More Bugs

𝔗𝔥𝔢 𝔚𝔞𝔰𝔥𝔦𝔫𝔤𝔱𝔬𝔫 ℜ𝔬𝔰𝔱

Interoffice Memo

TO: Bradlee, et al.   November 20, 1970

FROM: Harwood

The "bugs" story is back on A-1 today, which is a pretty good recovery from B-1 on Wednesday. My Wednesday epistle raised the intriguing question of whether this whole schmeer is something of a hoax or, at the minimum, rather misleading. It still looks that way.

The Anderson column and our stories implied or raised the possibility that the civil defense phones of various governors had been "bugged" deliberately and--presumably--this heinous crime was somehow or other related to the Feds. Facts:

(a) There is still no evidence that any of these phones were "bugged."

(b) There is no evidence that any of these phones were installed by the Feds; they were installed by AT&T.

(c) Even Mandel's antibugging expert is now saying that whatever happened with these crossed wires was evidently "unintentional."

One can make the case that this is a funny story, that AT&T is a big bungler, that there are echoes of Strangelove or 1984 in all of this. But we've been playing it straight and heavy and all over P. 1 and I'm still of the opinion that what we have been subliminally projecting to our readers is basically a hoax.

His Number's Up

The Washington Post

Interoffice Memo

Messrs. Bradlee/Simons: 8/12/75

Consider the case of poor Mr. Thorp. On Saturday he invested $18 in the Triple Exacta at Rosecroft. His number, he says, was 9-7-6. Saturday evening he bought the first edition of the Post and checked the race results. The winning Triple Exacta number was 9-5-8, so he tore up his tickets.

The next morning he looked at the Rosecroft results in his home-delivered Post and found that 9-7-6--his number--was listed as the winner, paying $767.40. But he had thrown away his tickets.

He's right. For at least part of the first edition Sunday we apparently ran Friday's results at Rosecroft rather than Saturday's.

Thorp says he called here Sunday and got someone in sports who laughed uproariously at his story, which he didn't exactly appreciate. I didn't laugh, but I told him that, sorry as we are, there's nothing we can do about it. He doesn't like that answer and asks that I refer his case to the responsible editors in the hope that they will come up with a better one. Which I hereby do.

Charlie Seib

FYI: Sins of Commission and Omission

It is with mixed emotions (chiefly envy and chagrin) that we call your attention to an article by Edward Jay Epstein in the February 13, 1971, issue of *The New Yorker* — envy because it is a work of debunking we wish we had undertaken ourselves, and chagrin because, For Your Information, we are among those newspapers whose careless perpetuation of an untrue statement Mr. Epstein has rightly seen fit to criticize.

The statement in question was apparently made in December of 1969 by Charles R. Garry, counsel for the Black Panther Party. In a week which saw struggles between police and Panthers in Chicago and Los Angeles, Mr. Garry was reported to have claimed that the two Panthers who had died in the Chicago gunfire — Fred Hampton and Mark Clark — were the "twenty-seventh and twenty-eighth Panthers" to have been "murdered by the police." The assertion (with a more neutral formulation, such as "killed by" or "died in clashes with") was picked up by the press and by a number of public figures in their comments. Attribution to Mr. Garry — or anyone else — tended to vanish. Thus, it soon became part of the "factual" background of stories and expressions of opinion concerning the Panthers and the police that "twenty-eight" Panthers had died as a result of armed conflict with the police. Mr. Epstein demonstrates this assertion to have been extravagantly untrue.

The *Washington Post*'s role in reinforcing this misconception was twofold, involving first a sin of commission and then a sin of omission. On the first count we did in fact fail to provide any attribution or qualifying "reportedly" or similar conditioner in a news story of December 9, 1969. Three days before, on the 6th of December, we had reported:

> Jay A. Miller, executive director of the ACLU in Illinois, said it is "absolutely imperative" that the facts be explored promptly (concerning the Chicago deaths) and that the public be given a complete report. . . . He said 28 Panthers have died in police shootings since January, 1968.

The next day, on the 7th, we reported:

> Twenty-eight Panthers have died in police shootings since January, 1968, according to Charles Garry, San Francisco attorney and general counsel for the Panthers.

On the 9th, in a story put together from news dispatches and added on to another such story dealing with the Los Angeles raid that had just occurred, direct attribution was dropped. Thus:

> Jay Miller, Illinois director of the American Civil Liberties Union, asked for an inquiry into a whole range of reported Panther slayings. A total of 28 Panthers have died in clashes with police since Jan. 1, 1968.

The source — or one of them anyway — was lurking right up there a sentence away — but the statement, inexcusably, was asserted as bald fact.

So far as our inkstained plunge into the clips has been able to indicate (and so far as Mr. Epstein charged), that was the one occasion on which the *Post* presented the allegation as fact, rather than as someone's version of the fact. With attribution, however, the figure darts in and out of subsequent material in the *Post,* and that brings us to our sin of omission, which seems to us, at the very least, to be as grave: in the weeks and months that followed, albeit with attribution, we reprinted this charge without ever subjecting it to scrutiny, without trying to ascertain that it was true, without — in short — doing what Mr. Epstein, to his great credit, now has done.

You will have wondered at what point, summoning our endless resources of self-pity and understanding of the difficulties of our trade and sensitivity to even slightly unfair criticism of our performance, we would choose to sob a little on our own behalf. The answer is, Now. So as not to be too embarrassing about it, we will run through the case for the defense quickly.

We note first the fact that we deal each day with a new torrent of conflicting and/or suspect assertions (the front page on the day of this writing, for example, presents a Calley version, a Stans version, a Udall version, and a presidential version of various facts and events under challenge). And in this connection we note that, by Mr. Epstein's own account, some six to eight months were required to produce his attempt to straighten out the faulty record and that even with time, checking and rechecking, his article is not wholly free of misimpressions as to who said what when.

Again, we suspect that Mr. Epstein is somewhat too dismissive in his attitude toward police-Panther encounters that have not ended in Panther deaths or any deaths, but which nonetheless have occurred and make an important part of the background that caused so much anxiety over the Chicago and Los Angeles encounters and their meaning and effect. Borrowing a page from Vice President Spiro Agnew's book we go on to observe that many of the quotations from the *Post* were cited in a way that made them sound more culpable than they were. Finally, we would invoke the case with which a busy, pressured deskman could have produced that unattributed quotation in an amalgam of dispatches on December 9.

Having thus functioned as counsel for the prosecution and the defense in our own case, we might as well complete the process by weighing in as jury. The verdict takes no time to reach. It is that the press of business, a slip of the hand, and the difficulty of getting to the bottom of a complicated assertion represent an insufficient defense on all counts. There is no adequate excuse for making this kind of error in the first place and none for failing to pursue the truth behind the phony "facts." In short, we find ourselves guilty and — with some reservations concerning Mr. Epstein's presentation of his case and his manner of quoting — we commend him for his effort to set the record straight.

— February 19, 1971

Can Newsmen Do Better on the Facts?

By Richard Harwood

On December 9, 1969, the *Washington Post* reported that 28 Black Panthers had "died in clashes with police since January 1, 1968." That statement, we learned much later, was incorrect.

On December 29, 1970, the *Washington Post* reported that Princess Margaret and Lord Snowden had agreed to a divorce and that "an announcement is expected soon." There has been no announcement and no divorce.

On January 25, 1971, we reported that 58 "conspirators" in the African nation of Guinea had been hanged. The story, we learned the next day, was untrue.

On July 21, 1971, we reported at length on "secret government documents" dealing with the war in Vietnam. These "documents," we learned the next day, were a hoax, perpetrated by *National Review* magazine.

On August 13 (a Friday, naturally), we reported that Tony Boyle, president of the United Mine Workers, was "under indictment in connection with contributions to his 1968 campaign for the union presidency." That statement was incorrect.

Six days later, in a news business column, I wrote that the *Post* earned profits of $9 million in 1970. That statement was incorrect.

Errors of this sort do not occur every day. But they occur often enough to reflect on our competence. At the least, they call into question our methodology; at the worst, they erode our credibility.

The problem begins with the information we receive—several hundred thousand words a day. It represents, Walter Lippmann once said, "an incredible medley of fact, propaganda, rumor, suspicion, clues, hopes and fears. . . ." Our daily task is to select from this mass of information—and misinformation—those things that seem to us to be "important" and "true" and to get them into print within a period of a few hours. The process is fallible every step of the way.

Who, for example, are the people who gather and supply us with this torrent of words? In many cases we don't know. They may be employees of other companies that are in the business of selling information to newspapers—the Associated Press, United Press International, Reuters and so on. They may be "stringers"—correspondents scattered around the country or around the world who sell us (on someone's recommendation) stories from time to time. In some cases our only dealings with them are through long distance communication. Are they all competent and reliable? Are they free of conflict of interest? Sometimes we don't know.

So we are compelled by the nature of the business to rely on a news-gathering apparatus over which we have only partial control. But if we controlled it completely, if we had battalions of correspondents spread throughout the world, serious problems would remain. The newsgatherer, whatever his competence, is always vulnerable to misinformation. If the government tells him that Presidential Assistant Henry Kissinger missed a dinner party in Pakistan because he was ill, his tendency is to take that information as fact (although, as it turned out, the fact was that Kissinger was flying to Peking to arrange a meeting). If Charles Garry, a lawyer for various Black Panthers, states that 28 Panthers have died in gunfights with policemen, there is a tendency to accept the number as "fact." If the *National Review* publishes "documents" of the Vietnam war that have the ring of authenticity, there is a tendency, as one news executive later explained, to "take these things on faith."

We are lied to and misinformed often enough in this business to develop a profound skepticism—if not cynicism—toward the "news" and "information" with which we deal. But some "facts" are more susceptible to proof than others and no matter how skeptical the reporter or editor might be, he remains vulnerable to misinformation. It took a very long time for reporters to examine thoroughly the government's assurances that there was a light at the end of the tunnel in Vietnam. On a much more limited scale, it took a trained scholar several months to examine—and disprove— Charles Garry's claim that 28 Black Panthers had been killed by policemen. But time is a tyrant in our business; the presses must roll if you're going to get your paper at breakfast time. Thus, when a Reuters correspondent in Africa cables a bulletin late at night about hangings in Guinea the metabolism of the newspaper gets it into print.

We have another problem. The deluge of fact, propaganda, rumor, suspicion and clues pouring into newsrooms and into the public consciousness has led newspapers to assume a function of analysis and interpretation, to deliver to its customers not only the "news" but explanations of what it means. This is probably an essential and inevitable function in an age marked, in Alvin Toffler's phrase, by "information overload." But sometimes it compounds the problem of misinformation. The most obvious example is an editorial or analysis based on an untruth. One could have written (and some did) of the Garry statement: "The killing of 28 Black Panthers suggests a nationwide effort by policemen to wipe out black militants." One could have written of the rumored divorce by Princess Margaret: "This is another symptom of the decline of the monarchy in Britain."

The emergence of this journalistic form also has led writers, on occasion, to take very broad liberties with the "facts." Karl Meyer, formerly of the *Post* staff, wrote a spoof some years ago on this tendency: "The feeling in this city is that the President has given a new twist to the tired formulas of foreign policy by his bold proposal to exchange the state of Alaska for the East German People's Republic. But despite the predictable outcry that has followed the President's carefully worded statement, the move is neither so ruinous as opponents contend nor as inspired a master-stroke as the administration's publicists insist. . . . To an objective observer, the controversy over the President's proposals clearly provides another melancholy example of how the methods of diplomacy lag behind the needs of the atomic age."

In one form or another, a great deal of that kind of mushy and subjective "information" gets into newspapers these days. Nicholas Von Hoffman recently wrote a column about the foolishness and hyperbole found in many commercials sponsored by car dealers. In the course of that essay, he tossed out—in a foolish and hyperbolic fashion—the "information" that "as a class, automobile dealers fall below even doctors, lawyers and plumbers in public disrepute." That is no verifiable statement of "fact." It is one man's opinion. Yet it got into the newspaper as "information." Another writer a few months ago wrote in the *Post* that "there was a time when people obediently took orders: young men all went dutifully off to war and women followed what Paris said they had to wear." That is not "information," it is not "fact" and it is not even "history." It is fiction, yet it ran in a "news" story.

Nat Hentoff, the press critic of the *Village Voice* in New York, commented recently on the "document" hoax pulled off by the *National Review*. "I wonder," he wrote, "how many of you are aware of how little checking goes on anywhere in journalism. I've written for a wide diversity of magazines and newspapers and only two of them fully check out the facts in a writer's piece."

The process here is not that sloppy, but the checking system is nevertheless flawed. There is too little time. Writers and editors are too harried and hurried. The newsgathering apparatus is too remote and dispersed for centralized control.

Given all that, however, newspapers can do better. They can improve their information facilities—their libraries, for example. They can do far more in the way of training writers and editors and in developing their expertise. They can rid themselves, to some extent, of the deadline mentality that sometimes forces them into print prematurely. They can develop new checking and verification techniques. And if they don't take steps to deal with the problem of misinformation they are going to have to live with their own credibility gap.

—August 22, 1971

Word for the Day

The Washington Post

Interoffice Memo

TO: Bradlee, et al.   January 15, 1971

FROM: Harwood

"Julius W. Hobson...has fought the establishment in Washington for 10 years..."

Webster's: establishment; n.; 1-something that
has been established.

Merriam-Webster: an organized force for carrying on public or private business.

Ergo: Mr. Hobson has fought "the Establishment"? Or "The Establishment"? Or those villains
listed in Mrs. Shaw's Green Book? Or Anita Allen
and her cohorts on the Washington Board of Education?
Or, or, thee? Or me? If it's me, I prefer uppercase.

Taking Wallace Out of Context

By Charles B. Seib

Did George Wallace get a fair shake recently in the *Post*'s coverage of his views on world affairs? Several readers think he didn't. I agree.

In early March [1975], Wallace was interviewed in Alabama by a group of foreign journalists. What he said received no publicity at the time, but two months later a *Post* reporter obtained a transcript of the interview. And on May 8 the *Post* published a front page story headlined: "Wallace Raps World War II Alliance/Preferred Japan." This story became the basis for much of the coverage of the interview in other publications and on the air.

The *Post* story began:

Alabama Gov. George C. Wallace told a group of foreign journalists he wishes the United States had been allied with Japan during World War II instead of with Russia and China.

"I think we were fighting the wrong people, maybe, in World War II," said Wallace in one of the rare statements of any length he has made on foreign policy issues. "In fact," he told a Japanese journalist, "I wish we had been on the same side in World War II." The story then went on to other things Wallace said in the interview and did not return to the World War II alliance until near the end, about 25 paragraphs later.

My trouble with the story begins with that second paragraph. Any reasonable person would assume the quoted sentences were spoken consecutively. The "In fact" beginning the second sentence clearly made it a further development of the first. Together, they made a strong, declarative statement. But that is not the way it was.

The first quoted sentence came from Wallace's final comment of the interview. It appears on page 49 of the transcript. The second quoted sentence, beginning "In fact," came from page one of the transcript. Both sentences are out of context in the *Post* story.

The context of the first quoted sentence I will come to in a moment. The second is taken from an informal remark Wallace made to a Japanese correspondent before the interview began. He was talking about Alabama's coal sales to Japan and said: "We're glad to do business with you. In fact, I wish we'd been on the same side in World War II. Instead of being on the same side (words missing here) China and Russia."

Putting those widely separated sentences together, and in reverse order, was improper quote-juggling, in my opinion. Interestingly, the second quote was not put there by the reporter but by an editor who felt that something more was needed to support the statement in the first paragraph of the story. It could be argued—as that editor does—that the quote-juggling did no harm, since Wallace unquestionably made the statements and they were not contradictory. Nevertheless, he certainly didn't make them in that form.

But now let's look at the context of that first sentence—the one from the last page of the transcript. To do that it is necessary to quote the last two pages of the interview:

"About foreign policy—I want to tell you something. I do not believe in Nazi-ism—just like maybe you don't believe in Wallace-ism. But that was not the German people. The German people were mistreated after World War I. The Versailles Treaty that was imposed on them by France and Britain and the United States—and, mainly, France and Britain—was a treaty that brought Hitler to power. And if it hadn't been Hitler, his name would have been Jones—it would have been Schmidt—it'd have been somebody else because—ah, ah, it was only—it was only sure that nationalistic feeling of the German people would be aroused from the mistreatment they got.

"And so our foreign policy over the years made a mistake in allowing that to happen. We ought to have (words missing) after World War I like we did after World War II—magnanimous—(words missing) West German people that are friendly people, that are friendly people because they are great people. And the Japanese people in my judgment, were provoked to a certain extent by people, by interests in this country that helped to bring about Pearl Harbor. And what I'm saying is that our true foreign policy in those years ought to have been cultivating—the friendship of the Japanese and of the Germans instead of being antagonistic. So that today we have a good buffer in the East against the Soviet expansion plans, and the Chinese expansion plans, which might stabilize and be good in the final analysis for the Soviet Union and the United States in that—and Japan—in that we might come near having peace—than one country beginning to get maybe so superior in, say, nuclear strength.

"*I think we were fighting the wrong people, maybe, in World War II,*" and I say that with all due regard to the Soviet, ah, person here. What I'm saying is—we fought on your side, but I wish the Soviet Union, or government rather, had been contained somewhat. And I do think we helped build up enemies in Western Europe, and in Germany, and in Japan, that we ought to have been 50 years ago friendly to. And then there wouldn't have been any Hitler, and there wouldn't have been any Jewish tirade." (The words that became the first quoted sentence in the *Post* story are italicized.)

Now, no one would defend that rambling, almost unintelligible discourse as a sophisticated or cogent discussion of the events leading up to World War II. But it supplies Wallace's own justification for the flat statements stressed in the *Post* story and it deserved to be represented in the opening paragraphs of that story.

The material quoted above was covered near the end of the two-column-long story—too late, in my opinion. Also, in the last edition that day the story included two final paragraphs on a telephone interview with Wallace in which he expanded on his condemnation of the Versailles Treaty, saying it permitted Hitler, "the most despicable unjust criminal in the history of the world," to rise to power by using Jews as scapegoats for Germany's economic problems.

To sum up, I feel that the *Post*'s story achieved impact at the expense of accuracy. I feel that the failure to present Wallace's startling statements about World War II in context gave the story a tilt—a subtle tilt, perhaps, but an important one in a report on the views of a man who aspires to the White House.

The story left the way open, in my opinion, for the less than careful reader and the reader who didn't read the story to the end to assume that Wallace wishes that when World War II began we had chosen to side with Hitler and Tojo.

The reporter who wrote the story and the editors who handled it disagree strongly with that opinion. While they concede that tying the two quotes together may have been unwise, they feel that the story conveyed in a fair and effective way what Wallace really thinks about World War II: that the United States should have been fighting the Communist nations instead of being allied with them. They do not feel that Wallace's justification for his view that we were fighting the "wrong people"— mismanagement of American foreign policy between the wars—demanded mention high up in the story.

Wallace did not protest the *Post* story; in fact his press aide told a *Post* reporter the governor was not upset by it. Wallace did, however, call a news conference the day of the story to say that the media had quoted him out of context and to again relate his remarks about the "wrong people" to the mistakes he said were made after World War I. He made similar comments in a speech here the next day. They were covered by the *Post* in a brief mention at the end of a story on page C-3.

Ironically, in reporting the Montgomery news conference United Press International pushed the *Post*'s tilt into a decided lean. It said, incorrectly, that the *Post* quoted Wallace as saying in March: "I think we were fighting the wrong people, maybe, in World War II. Our true foreign policy in those years ought to have been cultivating the friendships of the Japanese and Germans instead of being antagonistic."

Thus by its own rearrangement of quotes, UPI has Wallace saying this country should have cultivated Germany during World War II. Similarly, a few days later, a *Post* columnist ridiculed Wallace for saying that Hitler was despicable but the United States was unnecessarily antagonistic to Germany, again distorting the time frame.

One doesn't have to be clairvoyant to predict that in the politics-charged months ahead Wallace is going to be quoted as saying that rather than fighting Hitler and Tojo we should have been on their side. And all the protests and corrective statements are not going to change that.

—June 5, 1975

Senator Goldwater and a Serious Gaffe

By Robert C. Maynard

Once again, by coincidence, Sen. Barry Goldwater is the person at the center of a celebrated gaffe in the handling of the news. A short time ago, the subject was Goldwater and Watergate. E. Howard Hunt, this newspaper had reported one December day, engaged in a spying operation on the Arizona senator during his disastrous 1964 race for the presidency. The story was essentially corrected a day later by one that said Hunt's operation had been drastically overstated.

This time, Goldwater comes to our attention because he was badly misquoted on page one of the January 14 [1974] edition of the *Post*. Appearing on NBC's "Meet the Press" the day before, Goldwater had said Harry Truman "is probably the best President we have had in this century."

The *Washington Post*, alone among the media, had Goldwater handing that accolade to none other than Richard M. Nixon. Ordinarily any misquotation is a serious matter in the news business, but this one had political overtones of large dimensions, and the reason is Goldwater's unique standing with the American right from which Richard Nixon once drew so much of his strength.

It was wholly appropriate for the *Post* to correct the story next day in a prominent box on page one. Unfortunately for the business of journalism, a nagging question still remains as to whether the *Post* did all it could have done to attempt to counteract the error.

Public figures are fond of the truism, "the correction never catches up with the original story." In this case, there are reasons to credit that claim with a good deal of accuracy.

The timing of the Goldwater story is one of the reasons it is such a problem. It comes at the beginning of the most intense phase of the political battle over Mr. Nixon's fate. For that reason, the story was heavily played by many of the 225 clients of the *Los Angeles Times-Washington Post* News Service.

Furthermore, the correction the *Post* played so prominently on page one was not used by all the client newspapers. A random telephone survey found at least two newspapers that carried the original story but not the correction. They were the Lorain (Ohio) *Journal* and the Rock Island (Ill.) *Argus*. It is possible others of the *Post* news service clients also failed to correct the story.

Stories of that kind have a curious life of their own. They don't appear just once and die. They are filed in libraries under "Nixon," "Goldwater,"

"Presidency" and "Watergate" and sit there "waiting like time bombs for the unwary researcher of the future," as Elizabeth Peer so ably put it in *Newsweek*.

If that were the end of it, it would be troublesome enough, but such errors also seep into the stream of our political dialogue as columns, editorials and other forms of commentary.

Such a case involves the political columnist and associate editor of the *New York Times*, Tom Wicker. He picked up the error in the Monday *Post* and wrote his column on a theme that leaned heavily for support on the misquotation. People who don't read newspapers that use the *Los Angeles Times-Post* service might well read one of those that takes the *New York Times* service. There, too, one of Ms. Peer's time bombs is lurking and ticking.

Even though front-page corrections are rare, the question remains of whether the *Post* did enough to defuse those time bombs its mistake created.

Editors of the newspaper have since said they had hoped to correct the error by printing a story the next day that would acknowledge the mistake and then go on to explain why Goldwater considered Truman the greatest of the century's Presidents.

That plan went awry because Goldwater couldn't be reached to discuss the matter. Another idea, one the editors of the *Post* said they did not consider, would have been to publish a fairly full explanation of how the mistake occurred in the first place.

The box, prominent as it was, was rather cryptic as a way of communicating and it is possible that a front-page news story might have turned the trick and possibly attracted the attention of some of those editors who ignored the correction box the *Post* news service moved on its wires.

It wouldn't have taken all that much to have explained the origins of the mistake because they were fairly simple: human error.

On Sundays, the national news staff of the *Post* is often down to one or two reporters. A common assignment is to watch the news panel shows — "Face the Nation," "Issues and Answers" and "Meet the Press" — and take notes on what the guests say.

Ordinarily, the networks send messengers by courier to the major newsrooms in town with verbatim transcripts. On this particular Sunday afternoon, the reporter, Tim O'Brien, recorded the interview of Sen. Goldwater. It was one of three breaking news assignments for him that day.

Because the transcript did not come into the *Post* newsroom until about 5 p.m., O'Brien depended on his tape recorder and his own impression of what Goldwater said.

If O'Brien had the time and had checked the transcript it might have helped. According to NBC's transcript, this is what Goldwater said after he was asked if the standing of President Nixon in the polls did not make ruling the nation effectively a difficult task:

"I think the President can rule. I remember when Harry Truman sunk to about the same level of public opinion and credibility and today I think he is probably the best President we have had in this century. So I don't just take the fact that he has been down in the polls to mean that he can't lead. I think he can lead and I think he is leading."

O'Brien said the tape shows Goldwater pausing in such a way as to suggest to O'Brien that the Senator's reference to Truman was parenthetical. Goldwater's reference to "he" thus caused O'Brien to believe Goldwater went back to Nixon when he spoke of "the best President." O'Brien's misimpression was compounded by Goldwater's reference to credibility "today."

It was a mistake the *Post* could have explained the next day and perhaps done more to help expunge an error of serious political consequences, albeit very human error.

Edwin Newman of NBC News, who moderated "Meet the Press" that Sunday, said in simple terms what every journalist knows about such mistakes. "These things happen," he said. "They can happen to any of us." What we do about such mistakes when they happen is another matter.

—January 24, 1974

Pigeonholes and Prejudices

Putting People Into Pigeonholes

By Richard Harwood

One of our summer interns last year had an inspiration. He went up to a group of construction workers whom he had never met and asked a question: "Why do you beat up kids who protest the war?" The workers were stunned and angry and the conversation ended abruptly with no physical harm to the intern.

He later explained why he had asked those strangers such a question. He carried around in his head a stereotype labeled "hard hat." He had read in the newspapers that in some cities under some circumstances some construction workers had gotten into fights with some demonstrators. From that evidence, he had arrived at a "truth": the "truth" being that "hard hats" are all alike, that their attitudes and behavior are universal and predictable, that the label and the individual man are the same thing.

The novelist, James Michener, encountered the same phenomenon in his investigation of the tragedy at Kent State University (*Kent State, What Happened and Why,* Random House). Some townspeople in Kent, carrying around in their heads certain pictures of "hippies" and how they live, insisted to Michener that the two girls killed on the campus by National Guardsmen were "covered with lice," "on drugs," "pregnant," "ridden with syphilis," "tattooed from head to toe." None of these things was literally true, according to the coroner's report, but they were absolutely "true" in the minds of some townspeople because they seemed to fit a stereotype.

The habit of thinking in terms of stereotypes, of equating the labels we put on people with the people themselves, is a bad business. To be a "Jew" in Germany in the 1930s and 1940s was to be a "criminal." The women and children killed at Mylai were not "people," Lieut. William Calley said, they were "the enemy." A policeman, the Black Panther newspaper tiresomely reminds us, is not a "person" but a "pig."

People in the news business are supposed to be conscious of these problems, to be aware of stereotypes and of what they can do to people's minds. We no longer use words like Sambo and Aunt Jemima to categorize black men and women. We no longer depict American Indians as potbellied souvenir hucksters saying, "How" and "Ugh." We no longer portray Mexican-Americans as peasants in Pancho Villa hats sleeping under a cactus plant. At the *Post* we have even agreed, recently, to no longer insist that the words "Red" or "Communist" should always precede the word China when we are talking about China.

Nevertheless, the mass media are still full of stereotypes, labels, cliches and code words that confuse or mislead more than they inform. We still write about "hippies" and "hard hats" as if they were scientifically delineated species of mankind. We still talk about "suburbia" and "ghettos" as if these geographical concepts had assembly-line characteristics. We still discourse on the "middle class," the "military-industrial complex," "the poor" and the "Eastern establishment" as if, like bottles of milk, they are homogenous entities. We still hang on our politicians empty labels such as "liberal," "conservative," "hawk" and "dove" as if we — and the audience out there — had some clear idea of what information these labels are intended to convey.

These habits often lead us into nothing more serious than silliness, as in the recent case of a writer for the *New York Times* who observed that President Nixon is reverting to "the conservative themes of his 1968 campaign: a strong defense of free enterprise to the Chamber (of Commerce), a tough stance against the legalization of marijuana. . . ."

Logic suggests that if it is "conservative" to defend "free enterprise" it is "liberal" to attack it — perhaps at the annual stockholders meeting of the New York Times Company. If it is "conservative" to oppose the legal sale of pot, it is presumably "liberal" to advocate it. By those litmus tests, it may be difficult for the *Times* to find a "liberal" presidential candidate next year.

The country and the communications process can survive that sort of thing but there are times, as a British journal has noted, when "news can poison." It can poison our minds, our attitudes toward others, our perceptions of the world in which we live. The British study, carried out at the University of Leicester, found that the effect of the media in Britain on racial attitudes was to "perpetuate negative perceptions of colored people and to define the situation as one of intergroup conflict." Another effect was to create "the expectation of violence," especially among people with little firsthand knowledge of the situation.

One suspects that the same thing may be true in the United States, that in our preoccupations in the media with "white racism" on the one hand and "black militancy" on the other, we may have heightened or at least helped perpetuate "negative perceptions" and the "expectation of violence" in this country.

Robert Coles, a Harvard psychiatrist, has written in *Life* magazine that "some of us who are ever so clever at noticing inconsistencies in others never seem to remark upon our own confusions and mixed feelings. And all the while, I fear, we sell one another short. We categorize people, call them names like 'culturally disadvantaged' or 'white racists,' names that say something all right, but not enough—because those declared 'culturally disadvantaged' so often are at the same time shrewd, sensitive and in possession of their own culture, their own way of giving order to this world's complexities, just as those called 'white racists' have other sides to themselves, can be generous and decent, can take note of and be responsive to the black man's situation."

The label is not the animal and we in the news business ought to know that by now and know, too, that the labels and stereotypes we deal in—wittingly or not—are often more disturbing and confusing to the audience out there than the people and conditions we hang them on. We ought to know, also, that stereotypes are created not only by the repetition of a word—"hippie" or "hard hat"—but by the selection of the facts we choose to emphasize. If we decide that the only "newsworthy" facts about black people are facts about crime, public welfare and revolutionary rhetoric, we create a stereotype and deny the diversity of 20 million people. If all we report about the bodies littering the landscape in Vietnam is that they are "the enemy," we are left at war with bloodless phantoms, and it is unnecessary to think about phantoms.

Newspapers can do better than that. They can use language with more precision. They can develop better definitions of "news." They can recognize diversity. They can stop representing random—and often bizarre—opinions as The Voice of The People. Above all, they can ignore the labels and stereotypes that are hung on people and things and seek out the reality of the human condition.

"Good language alone," Stuart Chase has written, "will not save mankind. But seeing the things behind the names will help us to understand the structure of the world we live in. Good language will help us to communicate with one another about the realities of our environment, where we now speak darkly, in alien tongues."

—March 18, 1971

Words

The Washington Post

Interoffice Memo

TO: Bradlee, et al.   November 10, 1970

FROM: Harwood

　　The editors of the Manchester Guardian once said
their function is to "respect the news, the English
language and the reader." That means, I would guess,
that gee-whiz journalism is a no-no. Our piece on
A-13 today reports a "major fight" erupting inside
"the nation's largest consumer organization,"
involving a "militant" who has "the support of
scores of low-budget grass-roots consumers," and who
has "ruffled the feathers" of "the CFA power structure." Lined up on one side are the "large affiliates" and the "big cooperatives" against the "grass-
roots affiliates."

　　It is perfectly obvious from the story that the
CFA president is at odds with the CFA board of
directors over a government appointment. But why do
we bring all the actors onto the stage wearing these
stereotyped garments: "grass roots" versus "power
structure," "big" versus "little." What is a "grass-
roots consumer," anyway? From the story, you are a
"grass-roots consumer" if you are in the Massachusetts Consumer Association and you are not a "grass-
roots consumer" if you belong to Consumers Union,
even if you live in Massachusetts, I suppose.

　　Assuming that there are two classes of consum-
ers--"grass roots" and "non-grass roots"--this story
offers no evidence to support the claim in paragraph 2 that "scores of low-budget consumer groups"
are at the barricades. One man is quoted in support
of that claim.

(more)

People disagree all the time, even at The
Washington Post, and sometimes, perhaps, that can
be formulated in terms of a "power structure"
putting down the "militant" good guys. But gee whiz,
do we have to use all these cliches? And that
wonderful quote: "The need is for consumer spokesmen
to avoid like the plague all the typical organizational politics, intrigue, bigotry, power blocs,
and domination of the little groups by the big
money boys." Erma Angevine is a "big money boy"?

We're All Mugwumps

The Washington Post

Interoffice Memo

TO: Bradlee, et al.   May 26, 1971

FROM: Harwood

My Don Quixote crusade against labels, stereotypes and dead language continues. We still dot our
news columns with the words "liberal" and "conservative." What do they mean?

For openers, I challenge the Powers That Be to
request in 20 words or less a definition of those
labels from any random selection of people in the
newsroom and I will lay 2-to-1 odds that there is no
more than 50 per cent agreement on what they mean.

Beyond that, consider the reader. Communication
is a two-way street. If you print this paper in
Swahili you won't have much communication with the
audience out there. And you don't communicate a
hell of a lot with some of these labels we use.

Muffin

Her name is Debra Mattingly and normally we might not even know that much because she is only 14 years old and it is the practice in the District of Columbia and in a lot of other places not to release the names of juveniles in many cases. But the crime of murder of which she is accused took place in Virginia where there are somewhat different rules. So now it's Muffin, which fits easily into headlines and catches the imagination and tugs a little harder at the heart. She has accounted for almost as much space in this and other newspapers—she and her friends and the crime of which they are accused—as a presidential State of the Union message or the death of General Eisenhower or one of the more important stages in the flight to the moon, which is not inconsiderable for a 14-year-old girl. There were several hundred homicides in this community in 1969: a fair number of them were committed by juveniles and most of them did not even make page one. As often as not, the awful family quarrels that end up with a knife in someone's ribs or a bullet in someone's brain are lost in the inside pages—even if it's partricide, which this is alleged to be (except that it really can't be because Mr. Mattingly was the adoptive father, as the phrase apparently goes).

So you have to wonder what sort of roulette wheel turned up Muffin's name and why it is Muffin twisting on the end of a pin under a public microscope while civilized people peer and wring their hands and strain for more details. It is easy to put it all down to a human appetite for the sordid and the sensational as old as civilization, only much more easily fulfilled these days in the age of McLuhan and of a medium which can bring the Tate case on the West Coast into East Coast living rooms and the Mattingly case on the East Coast into the West Coast living rooms. That is certainly part of it—the old instinct to dwell, not to say dote, on horror, and the new means of gratifying that instinct.

But that is not the whole of it. For that, you have to examine a state of mind which is no less distorted or exaggerated because of the fact that it is so much easier now to encourage and cater to. One supects that one big reason we have come to know Miss Mattingly so well that we call her Muffin is that she and her friends are *hippies—and we all know what that means.* A hippie is Charlie Manson; so a hippie is a murderer. That's the way the mind leaps. A hippie is a runaway from home, a flower-child—fondling knives. . . . The fact is we don't agree on precisely what a hippie is but we call people hippies anyway because it's a nice convenient category into which to lump what is wrong with society. . . . Even when you can't define them, you can still put them in a cage and examine them in a morbid way and that is what has happened to Muffin who had the bad luck to be caught out in the open as it were and come to our attention when another child in another case on a busy night in Northeast Washington might become only a statistic in the police records. . . .

And so this becomes another sign of what's wrong with our times, or so it is said, although it seems to us that kids with crewcuts were running away from home before long hair became the thing. They were blowing their minds on booze before they were blowing their minds on drugs. There were broken homes and sour marriages and abandoned children, mentally crippled, some homicidally so, and in need of psychiatric help before we got to know Muffin. Before Manson there were Loeb and Leopold.

Maybe it's bigger by far now than it ever was before and the crimes are more hideous and the sickness more desperate. But we suspect that District Inspector John J. Kinney was closer to the mark when he said that "violence among what is called the hippie community has not been a police problem," and when youth counselor Judy Seckler said that "violence is such a very, very small part of the culture here," and when a reporter for the *Washington Post* conceded in the newspaper that the term "hippie" today covers such a variety of personality types that it is losing any semblance of precise meaning.

There are psychopaths among the young and there always have been. There are also those who are genuinely disturbed for a whole lot of reasons that have to do with war and injustice and the quality of life and the demonstrable unwillingness of the government or of the politicians or of the "straight" people to do nearly enough about it all. It is natural enough to be mesmerized by Muffin. But down this road lies not just morbid curiosity — or hysteria — on a mass scale. Much more important, at the end of it there is the worst kind of self-delusion. The death of Mr. Mattingly, and the pathological brutality of it, tells us something. So does the tortured young life of Debra Mattingly. But they are not particulars from which to generalize. The danger is that in our morbid fascination we will come to think that they hold, in a neat and compact microcosm, the clue to almost everything that is wrong with our youth and our society.

—January 15, 1970

Happy (Hippy) New Year All You Hippies, Hippys, "Hippies" and Beatniks

The Washington Post
Interoffice Memo

TO: Bradlee, et al.   December 31, 1970

FROM: Harwood

The Washington Post library, that repository of all we know, contains several brown envelopes labeled "Beatniks." To find a story about a beatnik you go to the envelope labeled "Beatniks." To find a story about a hippie you go to the envelope labeled "Beatniks." Eureka! A beatnik is a hippie or vice versa. Or is it?

The first time the word "beatnik" appeared in The Post was in August, 1958 (the files tell us). A 3-column cutline informed our readers that 100 San Francisco beatniks were touring the downtown area to see how the squares lived.

We were apparently 10 years late in our discovery of the term which Jack Kerouac claims to have invented in 1948. The related term--"beat generation"--first appeared in the public press in 1952 in a New York Times Magazine article. We discovered it, as noted, in 1958.

Beatnik was a word implying "the feeling of having been used, of being raw. It involves a sort of nakedness of mind and ultimately of soul...it means being undramatically pushed up against the wall of oneself...complete nonconformity, a preoccupation with drugs and cool jazz, passive resistance and a noisy voice of dissent...wherever they have appeared...the police have immediately recognized in them a sworn enemy to be stamped out...through harassment and arrest...From the pulps to the pulpits the beats (in the late'50s) became a required subject to be viewed with alarm as a dangerous contagion on our national soul or lauded as courageous nonaffluents."

(more)

In many stories at that time and through the early '60s, they were variously described: "bohe- mians"; "angry Americans"; "nomads, bums or beat- niks"; people with "squalid, hemp-enlightened joys."

On March 26, 1967, we first encounter the word "hippie" in The Post. It is used lowercase, without quotes as a common noun for people who "have made marijuana and LSD a way of life and are often noted for their unbathed bodies, filthy clothes, crowded 'pads' which they share with dozens of others"; "a bunch of marijuana-smoking hippies, boys with hair to their shoulders and barefoot girls in funny glasses"; "flower children."

By 1968 the term had come to include the Mc- Carthy "kids," the Wallace hecklers, etc., and by 1969 had come to include the campus scene, the under- ground press, dirty movies, revolutionaries, etc.; and then Manson and Muffin and proponents of the "new culture."

Even Nick Von Hoffman is derisively referred to by his critics as a "middle-aged hippie."

Through it all we have blithely applied this alleged common noun to whomever the writer wished to apply it--without quotation marks, without any serious attempt to define what it is the word is in- tended to convey. The exception to that statement was Sandy Ungar's editorial page column which had no more effect than most of these well-intentioned efforts.

But lo and behold, The Post on December 30 re- veals for the first time a certain ambivalence--a story (with cutlines) in which hippie is rendered both "hippie" and hippie and a wire story in which the same thing occurs.

That wire story, by the way, is terribly re- vealing. Who is the "hippie" or hippie? A college girl who moved out of a dormitory, went to a psychiatrist and got into a quarrel with her father. Today, however, we're back at the same old stand-- hippie without quotes around it.

(more)

Suggestion: let the principal editors each
write a 25-word definition of "hippie" or hippie and
if they come up with a common definition, publish it
in the Style book for the greater benefit of us all.
If they don't, let them sit down and figure out
what the hell to do with that word.

Superlatives

The Washington Post

Interoffice Memo

Messrs. Bradlee/Simons   3/10/75

Here's a law to go next to Murphy's: As soon
as you print that something is the biggest,
smallest, oldest, youngest, richest, poorest or any
other-est, someone is certain to come up with something that is bigger, smaller, older, younger,
richer, poorer, etc.

This morning a reader called to say that we
were wrong in calling Greenwood's the oldest major
black-owned firm in the District in today's paper.
He cited these as examples of firms that were
older and as large or larger: Hagan's Management
Corp., John P. Stewart Funeral Home, Jarvis Funeral Home, McGuire Funeral Home.

He may be wrong, of course. In any case,
those words "one of the" are awfully handy unless
you've got the superlative absolutely pinned down.

Charlie Seib

30

Questions on Coverage and Judgments in Editing

Kissinger's 'Mideast Force' Remarks

By Charles B. Seib

As the old year ended, Henry Kissinger mentioned the unmentionable. He discussed, briefly and guardedly, the possibility of the use of force by this country in the world oil crisis. His remarks and the press treatment of them raise questions of interest to the news business and its customers.

The remarks were made in an interview with the editors of *Business Week* magazine. They were significant not only for what Kissinger said but for the fact that he said anything at all on the subject; in a *Newsweek* interview published a week earlier he had ducked it.

The *Business Week* interview occurred Dec. 23 [1974]. Kissinger went over the transcript on Christmas Day and approved the section on force without change. The entire interview was released to the general press for use on Jan. 3.

The comments on force took up about four inches of the 128-inch text carried in the *Post*. Here is how it went:

Q. One of the things we also hear from businessmen is that in the long run the only answer to the oil cartel is some sort of military action. Have you considered military action on oil?

A. Military action on oil prices?

Q. Yes.

A. A very dangerous course. We should have learned from Vietnam that it is easier to get into a war than to get out of it. I am not saying that there's no circumstance where we would not use force. But it is one thing to use it in the case of a dispute over price, it is another where there's some actual strangulation of the industrialized world.

Q. Do you worry about what the Soviets would do in the Middle East if there were any military action against the cartel?

A. I don't think this is a good thing to speculate about. Any President who would resort to military action in the Middle East without worrying what the Soviets would do would have to be reckless. The question is to what extent he would let himself be deterred by it. I want to make clear, however, that the use of force would be considered only in the gravest emergency.

The *Post*'s story on the interview was given the most prominent page

31

one position that Friday morning and was headlined: "Kissinger: 'Use of Force' an Oil Option." The story began:

"Secretary of State Henry A. Kissinger describes military action to bring lower oil prices in the Middle East as 'a very dangerous course,' but he leaves open the possible use of force to prevent 'strangulation of the industrialized world.'"

The story then summarized other aspects of the interview, quoted directly from the comments on force, discussed the significance of Kissinger's speaking out and concluded with more details on the rest of the interview.

As this paper's ombudsman and internal critic, I raised a question with its editors: In the handling of this story was the *Post* guilty of using what journalists sometimes call "the needle"—which is slang for the technique of extracting the last drop of impact and urgency—some might say sensationalism—from a story without stretching the facts beyond repair. It is a device widely deplored and frequently used.

I was bothered by two aspects of the *Post*'s handling of the story. I did not feel that Kissinger's words added up to a statement that the use of force—war, in other words—was an "oil option," except in the sense that war is always an option when survival is at stake. So I was unhappy about the headline. More specifically, it seemed to me that Kissinger chose his words with great care when he, in effect, limited the use of force to a situation in which there would be "some actual strangulation" of the industrialized nations. I felt the *Post* went one small step too far in saying that he left open the possibility of force to *prevent* such strangulation.

In my memo to the editors, I argued that the word "prevent" was inappropriate because it means taking action before an event occurs, as opposed to Kissinger's apparent requirement that there be "some actual" injury.

The *Post* was by no means alone in using the "prevent" approach. It showed up on television and in many other newspapers (some, of course, relying on the *Post* story, carried by the Washington Post-Los Angeles Times News Service). In a number of papers Kissinger's words were changed through careless editing, so the word "prevent" became part of a direct quotation from him. United Press International went a step further than the *Post*, it seemed to me, saying that Kissinger had said this country would consider using military force if the industrialized world were *faced with the threat* of some actual strangulation.

The reporter and the editors who were responsible for the *Post* story are satisfied that it was on target in both display and content. They stress the significance of Kissinger's decision to comment on the force question after having avoided it and, in retrospect, of President Ford's confirmation that Kissinger's views were also his. They say they spent a great deal of time framing the lead of the story and, in fact, leaned over backward to avoid going beyond Kissinger's words.

As for my argument that "prevent" didn't fit the facts, they consider that more a matter of semantics than of substance and not relevant to the main question: Did the story and its display properly reflect what Kissinger said and its importance? Their answer to that is yes. There is some agreement that the headline was less than satisfactory, but that is blamed on the impossibility of conveying anything but the simplest thought in three lines of about 10 letters each.

All very well, but I must take the last word to say that I think an old newspaper rule applies here: Stick to the man's own words when possible. It is especially applicable in this case, when the man's own words— "where there's some actual strangulation . . ."—were clear and carefully chosen (although one could wish that Kissinger had been asked to define strangulation).

There the discussion must rest. For what it's worth, a Kissinger aide says the Secretary felt some of the news stories on the interview, including the *Post*'s, went too far. On the other hand, there is some feeling that Kissinger, an experienced Washington hand, knew how his words would be handled in the press and was not at all dismayed by the reaction caused around the world.

So what does it all add up to? Did the press, doing what comes naturally, escalate an already touchy situation? Was its need to turn shades of gray into black and white used to bring about a desired effect?

I don't know the answers. I do know that in a world of infinite complexity and infinite peril the tools we have devised to inform the public sometimes seem very crude for the job at hand.

—January 16, 1975

The Face of the Age

The Washington Post

Interoffice Memo

TO: Bradlee, et al.   March 8, 1971

FROM: Harwood

    One of the serious and persistent weaknesses of this newspaper is the one-dimensional report, the tendency to deal with the phenomena of our time through the eyes of a single beholder. It is as if we were to seek the whole reality of the Thirties from the movie tales of Bonnie and Clyde. That tendency often produces fascinating visions of the world in which we live. But often, too, they are private, distorted visions that give us no real clutch on reality and make us vulnerable to the charges of superficiality and bias that float around our ears.

    ITEM: The State of Maryland has sanctioned capital punishment since 1694. In 1971 we set out in a series of articles to tell our readers something about that law and its effects. And what is our technique? We tell the story through the eyes of the men on death row who, understandably, have little appetite for the gas chamber. For "balance" we throw into the last piece a quotation from a hanging judge, plus the views of a young penologist who is critical of capital punishment.

    The powerful thrust of the piece, however, is undiluted: it is the view from death row. It is an interesting view but it is one-dimensional. What are the views of victims and their families? What is the view of society at large as represented, perhaps, by the ordinary panel of jurors who sit in judgment on these cases? Without that dimension how do we possibly explain the survival of the Maryland capital punishment law for 277 years? Without that dimension we end up with little more than a special pleading, a Bonnie and Clyde vision of reality.

(more)

ITEM: Our long Sunday takeout on Catholic radicals tells us that they are a tiny fragment of the 47 million Catholics in America but their activities "have sent shock waves throughout the church." We are given an 88-inch glimpse of the radicals through their own eyes and through the eyes of three non-radical sympathizers. We are not given a glimpse of the radical movement through the eyes of, say, Cardinal O'Boyle, or the Legion of Decency or the Knights of Columbus. And that is all the more surprising since the movement's significance is related to the "shock" it has caused other Catholics.

One suspects that the Berrigans and other radicals may be, like Abbie Hoffman and Jerry Rubin, little more than media figures; we have certainly done our part to make them household names. But one can't know that if the only view of the movement we get is the view of the radicals themselves. Could it be that they speak for the Catholic majority? Isn't that a significant question to ask about this phenomenon?

It is our failure to explore the Other Dimension that led, I think, to some of the hysterical coverage of the "radical movement" on campus and that has led to other journalistic excesses in recent years. One can cite, for example, our extensive reportage on the abortion question which has led some people--myself included--to assume that there is a mass movement in America to enact very liberal abortion laws. It came as something of a surprise to discover in Science magazine that every public opinion survey of the past 10 years shows that opposition to liberal abortion laws is far more widespread and deep-seated than, say, opposition to the war in Vietnam; and to discover that this opposition is strongest--hold on to your hat--among women under 30. You would never know that from reading The Washington Post.

If it is our function as a newspaper to be "trendy," to pick up, exploit and promote every fad that comes along, then the points made here are irrelevant. But if it is our function, in that great phrase of Rebecca West's, to "set the face of the age" as it is--not as we would like it to be--then we would do well to look at our performance more carefully.

FYI: Partisan Phrases

George Orwell, who was prophetic about many aspects of modern life, once warned against the careless use of words. In his essay, "Politics and the English Language," he argued that the imprecise use of words often could be associated with policies that also were poorly thought out.

Ever since President Ford deplored "forced busing" in his press conference last Wednesday, it has been evident that he had not thought very hard about the problem before speaking as he did. He later found it necessary to send a message to Boston in the hope of reversing the damage his words had done.

The President might have intended a different tone, but his use of the phrase "forced busing" gave his remarks a particular flavor, because that term has become a code word. It will frequently be heard from those who wish to convey their displeasure with school desegregation, ordered by the courts in conformance with a long history of previously upheld legal doctrine. It is, in other words, a partisan phrase. Forced busing in fact means court-ordered desegregation, including court-ordered busing which some people regard as having been "forced" on them and which others accept without protest or complaint.

It is a good rule of journalism—although not necessarily of politics—to avoid the unattributed use of partisan phrases from one side or another of a political battle. Yet, more and more, journalists have fallen into the practice of tossing "forced busing" into their copy. Thus, the *Washington Post* the other day reported that South Boston residents always believed "that forced busing would never really happen."

Well, For Your Information, we thought we would note that there is a difference in tone and emphasis between "court-ordered desegregation" and "forced busing." Political figures may use the latter to their own ends, and often to their peril, but journalists do best when they stay as far as possible from the unattributed partisan language of those they cover.

—October 19, 1974

Comic Violence

The Washington Post

Interoffice Memo

Messrs. Bradlee/Simons: 1/2/75

We of the print press sometimes shake our
heads virtuously over the excesses of shoot-'em-up
television. At least we don't have anything like
back-to-back crime shows, featuring rape, sadism,
murder and guns, guns, guns.

The fact is, we do have, and are responsible
for, our own little ghettos of fictional violence:
the comic pages.

A reader reminds us of that by sending in six
clippings from one day's diet of Post comics. All
six--ranging from Broomhilda to Dick Tracy--show
handguns.

Comics, of course, have provided newspaper
readers with vicarious violence since the BAM,
WHAM, AAUUGH days. And I'm not suggesting that
reforming them is a high priority matter.

But we shouldn't forget that they are there.
And, by the way, that some of them are inching
into subjects and attitudes that wouldn't have
been thought of a couple of years ago. Who knows,
maybe in a few years more we can run the bootleg
Popeye and Olive Oil comics we old guys used to
pass around during recess.

                                        Charlie Seib

The Story the Eastern Liberal Press "Suppressed"

By Richard Harwood

The people, one suspects, may be getting a little bored with what the Eastern Liberal Press (ELP) has or has not done lately. Our sins and pseudo-sins have been aired ad nauseum from coast to coast since Vice President Spiro Agnew started the fad a couple of years ago. The reader deserves a respite from all that but a recent assault on ELP is too fascinating to ignore.

It began on August 5, 1971, when an Illinois congressman, Philip Crane, complained that ELP—specifically, the *New York Times,* the *Washington Post* and the *Washington Star*—had suppressed or ignored one of the great news events of our time. This event had occurred the previous night in the House of Representatives when either 82 or 86 or 100 or 106 congressmen had arisen one after one to warn the Republic that it was in military peril vis-a-vis the Soviet Union.

The story, as Crane noted, was not reported in the *Post,* or by the television, or by the wire services. Within a matter of days, ELP was on the griddle again.

The *Sacramento Union* on August 6 published a story about the "106 congressmen . . . rising one after another on both sides of the aisle, speaking and augmenting their arguments with lengthy defense dissertations. . . ." Crane's charge against ELP was quoted and a teaser headline on the story asked: "'Times, Post, Where Are You?'"

On August 20, Walter Trohan wrote a column in the *Chicago Tribune* about the "vital news story ignored by editors." He noted that "one by one the 86 (sic) House members rose to develop a theme vital to the security and the very existence of the country."

At about this time, News Perspective International, a Washington operation that keeps a suspicious eye on ELP and its sinfulness, fired off a newsletter under the title "The Media's Iron Curtain." A subsequent newsletter from NPI referred to "the enormity of the national news media's censorship of such an important story."

Another perennial ELP critic and monitor, Accuracy in Media, took direct action. AIM's one-man staff, Abraham Kalish, called the *Post* to demand an explanation of the "blackout" on the warnings of "nearly 100 congressmen."

Tactics magazine weighed in with this: "In print and on the air, this almost unprecedented action by elected delegates of the American people was boycotted—suppressed. . . . Yet the subject concerned the very survival of the nation physically. Its suppression, therefore, was incalculably more serious than anything yet perpetrated by our wayward channels of communication."

There was more of the same in various newspapers and columns that reflect, one could say, a more conservative view of men and events than ELP. So another "news management" issue was born and it is safe to say that we will hear more about it as time goes by. That's fair enough. All of us have to write about something, even on dull days, and if the *Post* provides the fodder on *really* dull days so be it.

In the interest of historical accuracy (and self-righteousness), however, let us examine the Iron Curtain that was drawn by ELP over the proceedings in the House on August 4. It was a long and tiring day. Passage of the draft extension bill coupled with a military pay raise and an appropriation for the emergency employment act had taken hours and it was well after suppertime when Congressman Crane and his colleagues assembled to raise the alarm over "the peril to our national security."

Kalish of AIM was not in the gallery. Nor was William Gill, the publisher of News Perspective International. Trohan of the *Tribune* was there but he left after a few minutes because it was late and he was tired. Ray McHugh, the correspondent for the *Sacramento Union* was there, but he, too, departed early—so early, in fact, that he heard none of the speakers who followed Crane to the floor. The *Post's* man in the House was not there at all; he was writing about military pay and the draft extension.

The most conspicuous absentees, however, were the 86 or 100 or 106 congressmen who were supposed to be on the floor deploring the decline in America's military might. Kalish doesn't know how many ever showed up. Nor does Trohan. Nor does McHugh, although McHugh estimates that maybe 10 eventually made it to the floor. The chief congressional correspondent for United Press International puts the number at "only five or six." Mississippi Rep. G. V. (Sonny) Montgomery, one of the organizers of the talkathon, figures that a dozen or so members may have taken the floor but he wasn't one of them.

Nevertheless, the *Congressional Record* came out the next day, loaded with 90 pages of oratory from (by actual count) 82 congressmen. It is impossible to tell from the *Record* how many of these speeches were actually given and how many were simply handed to the House clerk for printing in the *Record*. The *Record* is always produced in that way and is not subject to the Truth in Packaging law.

It's too bad, because it led McHugh to confuse fiction with fact when he wrote about 106 congressmen "rising one after another on both sides of the aisle." (Where the figure 106 came from is as much a mystery as the other figures that have been tossed around—86 and "nearly 100.") Everyone else who wrote about this nonevent—AIM, NPI, Trohan, etc.—was similarly confused about all those dedicated lawmakers orating late into the night. It just didn't happen.

No matter, Kalish now says, the important thing is what they would have said if they had hung around and what the *Congressional Record* of

August 4 claims that they said. Perhaps. But if you read that *Record* you make some interesting discoveries.

The first is that congressmen, like a lot of college theme writers, are notorious plagiarists and cribbers. The 90 pages of dire warnings consist, in substantial measure, of old newspaper stories, old columns by Joseph Alsop, old speeches by the late Rep. Mendel Rivers and Conservative Sen. James Buckley, old reprints from the American Security Council newsletter, old testimony from admirals, generals and Secretaries of Defense, as well as some lengthy quotations from the works of V. I. Lenin and others.

One of the major themes running through those 90 pages was the sorry state of the U.S. Navy and one of the major documentations of that theme came from the British publication, *Jane's Fighting Ships,* which each year evaluates all the navies of the world. It is indisputably true, as congressman after congressman (or their ghost-writers) pointed out in the *Record,* that *Jane's* had reported in July that "the situation for the U.S. Navy is serious" and that "by any standards the Soviet fleet now represents the super-navy." It is also indisputably true that ELP reported this gloomy prognosis in July, that we reported it (from *Jane's*) in 1967 and in 1968 and in 1969 and in 1970 and time after time (from sources other than *Jane's* — Adm. Elmo Zumwalt, for example) in 1971.

The same can be said for the other themes that run through the 90 pages in the *Record* of August 4 — the new "missile gap," the desires and needs of the Air Force, the stakes in the SALT talks, etc. It was pretty old stuff and while August 4 may not have been the liveliest news day in history, it was lively enough that we didn't have to quote congressmen quoting old stories from the *Post* in order to fill up the news hole. Oddly enough, Trohan and his paper, the *Chicago Tribune,* evidently felt the same way. The *Tribune* carried nothing on the matter. Trohan himself didn't write about it until two weeks later and even then his column didn't deal with the substance of all those alleged speeches. He wrote, instead, about the strange "blackout" imposed on this event by the media, specifically "the two newspapers regarded as the most important in New York (the *Times*?) and Washington (the *Post*?)."

Gill and NPI are still up in arms over this episode and over ELP's performance through the whole thing. Gill wrote to me about it the other day and said: "I am not only puzzled, but deeply troubled by your statement that after reading the statements of congressmen in the *Congressional Record* of August 4 you are 'more convinced than ever' that this story was 'absolutely not newsworthy'. . . ."

Alas, the statement is out and must become part of the record of this ELP episode: "It wasn't newsworthy."

— September 13, 1971

Take It From Here . . .

The Washington Post

Interoffice Memo

Messrs. Bradlee/Simons: 6/11/75

A reader (a retired news executive) complains
that the Post vastly overplayed its lead story Sun-
day--the one on the evacuation-day bombing of South
Vietnam. He noted "the degree of substantiation--
or lack of it."

I, too, am troubled by the play and the story
itself. What we have are unidentified "authoritative sources" making a very grave charge and two
identified responsible officials issuing categorical denials. The charge is given in the headline
and the first four paragraphs of the story. The
categorical denials are carried parenthetically in
the fifth through ninth paragraphs. There's something off balance about that.

My second-guess is that the story should have
been rewritten, making the denials part of the lead
or at least a second "but" paragraph. And then the
question of play should have been considered in the
light of the denials.

A final thought: Having given our readers
this sensational report, presented as the most
important news in the paper Sunday, are we just
going to drop it there? Surely we should be going
all out to verify it or knock it down. Considering
the mass of detail in the LA Times story, that
shouldn't be too hard. As of now, we've got a
large outstanding debt to our readers. Or did I
miss something?

                                          Charlie Seib

(more)

Was the Bombing Story True?

By Charles B. Seib

Two of the country's leading newspapers told their readers on Sunday, June 8 [1975], that the biggest news of the day was a report of theretofore undisclosed heavy bombong raids in South Vietnam while Americans were being evacuated at the end of April.

That story was published as the leading page one item in the *Washington Post* and the *Los Angeles Times* and was distributed to papers that subscribe to the Times-Post news service. It raises significant questions about the press view of the credibility of government officials, the responsibilities of newspapers to their readers and, finally, the credibility of the press itself.

The story was datelined Hong Kong and was written by George McArthur, a *Los Angeles Times* reporter. It quoted unnamed "authoritative sources" as saying that American planes conducted heavy raids the day of the Saigon evacuation. The purpose: to show Hanoi the United States meant business.

The raids, the story said, were of such magnitude and "sensitivity" that they almost certainly were cleared by President Ford. They were conducted, it continued, despite congressional strictures against military action. A source, unidentified but with access to "official after-action reports," was quoted as saying that "it was a very heavy commitment."

By coincidence both papers gave the story a major headline and the best position on page one, the day before having been a dull news day. "U.S. Bombing in Viet Exit is Reported," read the *Post*'s headline. "Heavy Raids at War's End Reported," read the *Times*', with a subheadline reading: "Bombings, Denied by the White House, Seen as Effort to Protect Evacuation."

Yes, the story was denied by the White House, and the Pentagon as well, before publication. Ron Nessen, the President's press secretary, denied it to a *Times* reporter who called him. He also told the reporter that the National Security Council said the story "is absolutely not true." Assistant Defense Secretary Joseph Laitin told the *Times* reporter who called him that the story was not true, making it clear that he had checked with Defense Secretary James R. Schlesinger. Both acknowledged that U.S. planes had provided cover for the evacuation and that several bombs had been dropped to subdue anti-aircraft fire, as had been reported earlier. But they acknowledged nothing approaching the "heavy raids" alleged in the McArthur story.

Nessen and Laitin say their denials were flat and unequivocal. Nessen adds that he urged the *Times* to check the story again with its source in view of the flat White House denial.

As the story was published, the denials were reported parenthetically, starting at the fifth paragraph. They were not reflected in the rest of the story which was "hard"—that is, after quoting the "authoritative sources" the story treated the raids as fact.

So this was the picture: Sources who could not be identified made an extremely serious charge carrying inplications of defiance of Congress and an official cover-up. Two identified responsible government officials issued the strongest denials. But the denials were relegated to parenthetical inserts and the story was displayed with great emphasis. To the reader this could mean only one thing: His newspaper was saying, "We believe our sources. We don't believe the denials, but in the tradition of journalistic fairness we publish them (in parentheses)."

Los Angeles Times editors say that they are satisfied with the way they handled the story and displayed it, and that they are still convinced it is true. The source—apparently there was only one basic source, although "sources" are quoted—was "excellent," they say, a man who knew what he was talking about. One editor admits he was somewhat shaken by the firmness of the denials, but he says he was reassured when he detected a softening as they were reiterated. (Laitin and Nessen say there was no softening. They say they still deny the story categorically and that they have checked with all possible sources, from the President down. On Tuesday, Secretary Schlesinger told reporters that the raids "did not occur" and that the story was "invented out of whole cloth.")

The *Post*'s editors did not know the identity of McArthur's source when they decided to publish the story and they still don't. They were and are relying on McArthur's reputation as a responsible, accurate reporter and on the judgment of the editors of the *Times*.

Nessen and Laitin are frustrated and indignant as a result of their experience with the bombing story. They can't understand why the most categorical denials they could express failed to deter the *Post* and the *Times* from giving the story prominent display and were relegated to parenthetical inserts.

It isn't hard to contain one's sympathy for them. They must, after all, carry the sins of their bureaucratic forebears—Ron Ziegler, of "just a third-rate burglary" fame, in Nessen's case, and Arthur Sylvester, who made history as a Pentagon spokesman when he declared the government's right to lie to "save itself," in Laitin's.

But what about the readers of the *Post* and the *Times* and the other papers that carried the story? Where are they left? Having printed the story and the denials, the *Post* and *Times* turned to other things. Except for a three-paragraph item on page 14 of the June 10 *Post*, in which Nessen's denial was repeated, they have been silent on the subject. So has their news wire.

Questions cry for answers. Was the story wrong? If so, certainly a page one acknowledgement of that is called for. Were Nessen and Laitin lying—or lied to? Certainly an affirmative answer on either point would make an important story with post-Watergate implications. Did the raids occur but word of them never reached the President and the Secretary of Defense? That certainly would be a good story. But neither paper has published a follow-up on the story. Further, there is no evidence that their reporters are hard at work on one.

So at this writing the questions stand: Did we give Vietnam one final pasting? Is official Washington trying another massive cover-up? Did someone in the field pull a fast one on his superiors? Or, heaven forbid, did the *Post* and the *Los Angeles Times* bite on a sour one?

Maybe the history books will tell your children or their children. So far, it appears that the papers that raised those questions aren't going to tell you.

—June 16, 1975

Author's note: Finally, on July 25, 1975, in the *Los Angeles Times* and on the news wire, and the next day in the *Washington Post,* the story was retracted. The retraction conceded that exhaustive investigation had failed to support the bombing report and that the story never should have been published.

The Way We See It

The Washington Post
Interoffice Memo

TO: Bradlee, et al.   January 29, 1971

FROM: Harwood

    Thursday morning, Secretary Rogers spent three
and one-half hours before the Senate Foreign Relations Committee. The meeting was closed. When it was
over, Rogers met the press briefly. Several members
of the committee were also questioned. The stories
subsequently written carried these headlines:

Wash Evening Star: "Senators Fear Wider War"

N.Y. Times: "Rogers Assures Senators on Role in
            Cambodian War"

WashPost: "Rogers Fails to Reassure Hill on War"

Wash Daily News: "Rogers Muffles the Doves"

    Each of the papers carried substantially the
same account of Rogers' version of his testimony to
the committee. Each of the papers quoted the same
five members of the committee--Church, Fulbright,
Cooper, Aiken, and Muskie. The Post also carried a
quote from Symington. The Times also carried a quote
from Javits.

    The stories in the four newspapers were sub-
stantially the same. The said (a) Rogers "assured"
the committee that the administration had not and
would not violate the conditions of the Cooper-
Church amendment; (b) that members of the committee
accepted the "assurance" that the amendment had not
yet been violated so far as ground combat forces
were concerned; and (c) that some members of the committee remained fearful of what may happen in the
future.

                    (more)

Why the headline confusion? Because the headline writers were trying to convey the "impact"
rather than the content of Rogers' appearance. That
is always a very difficult feat and it often fails
to come off. If it is too dull and prosaic to say:
"Rogers Claims No Violation of Cooper-Church," if it
is more important to deal with the "reaction," then
we should be precise: "Rogers Fails to Reassure Four
Senators on War, They Say."

More Than Enough Said

The Washington Post

Interoffice Memo

Messrs. Bradlee/Simons: 6/11/75

Last Friday, a split page story began this
way:

"America is a nation whose young have turned
on the aged: where elderly women are raped
repeatedly, mugged at bus stops and victimized by
teen-agers who steal their Social Security checks
and leave them with the fear that they will starve
to death or live to be victimized again.

"This grim picture emerged yesterday..."

An in-house reader comments: "Bullshit.
It's this kind of hyperbole that gives the Post a
bad name. America? or a small urban part of it?
All the young? or a small minority? Cheap sensationalism and smear on youth that should have been
desk-blocked."

AMEN.

Charlie Seib.

No Place for Hyperbole

By Robert C. Maynard

It is axiomatic in these times that when episodes of extraordinary violence occur, public officials—no less so than ordinary citizens—are prone to hyperbole. In the midst of trauma, we are given to "seeing" more than is actually there. That truism is so well known to the legal profession, for example, that some of its practitioners consider eyewitness testimony to dramatic crimes or accidents to be among the least reliable of available evidence. This is so because "seeing" is far from an objective pursuit for most of us. What we "see" is merely an assemblage of impulses ordered largely by who we are. That this is especially so when some spontaneous instance of drama crosses our vision ought to be manifest to those with the special charge of conveying the images of large events to the public mind.

Thus, what the news media conveyed from the roof of the Howard Johnson Motor Hotel in New Orleans on Sunday, January 7, 1973, and Monday, the 8th, is especially instructive on this point. In the first hours of the awesome tragedy, we were told the arson and the killing were not the work of one lone deranged gunman, but the opening round in a nationwide war against the public order, therefore against any or all of us. That, simply put, is what the embattled New Orleans police "saw" and felt in the midst of a hail of gunfire at about the time many in New Orleans were on their way to Sunday services. How many gunmen they were battling was in question then and was to remain in question for days afterward. Even the number of the dead would in early reports total 11, only later to be scaled back to six. In the midst of the chaos, the police "saw" several bodies twice—or, at least that would become the explanation.

Then there was the question of the phantom sniper, the dramatic television "live" action of the search for him and finally the plaintive conclusion about the second sniper from a fatigued superintendent of police, Clarence B. Giarrusso: "I'm undecided. Right now we have evidence on both sides. . . . I wouldn't say yes and I wouldn't say no." Any number of news organizations on Sunday evening were reporting as many as three snipers, and reporting it as pretty hard fact.

But the fact in such chaotic situations is that the police almost always exaggerate. Who can forget Newark and Detroit in 1967, when the police were reporting the existence of snipers on rooftops everywhere? No such snipers ever were actually identified. More than that, it was frequently the case that police officers and national guardsmen were firing at each other, each reporting the other as a "sniper" position.

If the police overdramatize, and if the media—having no other reliable source at the time—pass it along to their consumers, that is regrettable, but understandable. We would all benefit, I think, from restraint in such matters as action reports from the scene of ongoing events, to say less until hard information is available. It is questionable, for example, whether CBS and NBC should have gone live with that rooftop drama. I say that not because it proved fruitless. I would have been more appalled at what might have been the case if indeed there had been a sniper. Would we have wanted all of the gory details live and in color? I suspect, in any event, edited film would have been more appropriate.

But I am more concerned by what the news media pass along to their consumers that is "seen" by persons either hundreds of miles away or only remotely connected to the event, even if on hand. I have particularly in mind the vision of the events in New Orleans as seen in the *Washington Post* by three political figures.

As though the facts of this tragedy—such hard facts as were known—were not mind-chilling enough, Sen. James O. Eastland of Mississippi felt called upon to add his own hyperbole, what he "saw" from a distance of more than 1,000 miles:

"The evidence is unmistakable that this is a war on policemen. We face a crisis in law enforcement unless we act immediately."

The *Washington Post* passed on that information to its readers without any evidence from Eastland, or any caveat. The newspaper did not state that Eastland offered evidence and did not state that we pursued him for evidence and received none. We either should have stated that he offered evidence, or stated that he did not offer evidence. Instead, we just dropped Eastland into the story underneath a similarly apocalyptic paragraph from the Louisiana attorney general, William J. Guste:

"I am convinced that there is an underground, national suicide group bent on creating terror in America." Evidence? Apparently if the tragedy is of sufficient dramatic impact, scary observations have their own inherent defense and need no support.

But I think such circumstances need another component to qualify for the scary conclusion without a shred of support. They must contain either the element of politics or race. It is doubtful if either Eastland or Guste would have been so quick with theories of conspiracy had not a black man —or men?—been involved. And not just a black man, but one who is alleged to have been overheard shouting "power to the people."

The most recent tragedy that is analogous to New Orleans occurred on August 1, 1966, in Austin, Tex., when Charles Joseph Whitman, a white Marine veteran, stationed himself in the tower of the University of Texas and gunned down 13 people in 80 minutes. He was eventually killed by the police.

A cursory examination of the record of that tragedy fails to turn up any mention from Sen. Eastland of the danger of a national conspiracy. The argument that it was black racism motivating Essex may be true, but no story has explained yet how it is that his very first victim on New Year's Eve was a black police cadet. The point is not whether he was or was not politically motivated. The fact is that at this early point hardly any of that is actually known. So, the national news media, when it repeats the hyperbole of the police, is perhaps to be understood, deadlines and hysteria being what they are in such circumstances. To add the hyperbole of Sen. Eastland, though, is to compound the crime, add to the hysteria but add nothing of substance to the news, which is supposed to be our business.

Hyperbole being what it is, it is not surprising that it takes many forms. In that same story, but a little further along than the Eastland embroidery, this paragraph is to be found:

"Mayor Landrieu called the nightmare of murder and arson 'perhaps the most tragic criminal act in the history of this city.'"

If mayors tend not to be historically sensitive, newspapers should either correct their lapses or withhold them from the public. At great cost, we maintain an elaborate library intended to serve as a check against the memories of politicians and reporters.

As it happens, a criminal act occurred in New Orleans on March 14, 1891, that Mayor Landrieu — if he had time to reflect — might agree qualifies as at least a rival to the events at the Howard Johnson Motor Hotel. In fact, racial overtones are what gives it added historical significance by way of comparison. The chief of police was killed that previous fall of 1890. A group identified as "Italian mafia" was accused, tried and acquitted, 19 in all, according to Richard Hofstadter and Michael Wallace in *American Violence: A Documented History.*

On that March 14, after 6,000 New Orleans citizens listened to stirring speeches by a number of persons, they were led to the jail by a lawyer named William Parkerson, who had told the crowd:

"When the law is powerless, the rights delegated by the people are relegated back to the people, and they are justified in doing that which the courts have failed to do." With that, Parkerson, according to Hofstadter and Wallace, "led fifty men to the jail and, as authorities stood by, they killed eleven of the Italians. Most were shot inside the jail, but some were dragged outside where the crowd lynched them."

It was once said by an eminent journalist that our business at best is "writing the first rough draft of history." The emphasis in that formulation is obviously on the word rough: in such a process, we are bound to be excessive when the circumstances are dramatic. But we have a responsibility that senators and mayors, police chiefs and attorneys general don't have. That is the responsibility that accompanies the beleaguered blessings of the First Amendment. It is to be ever so restrained and thoughtful about the implications in the expressions of those with partisan interests in the stories we cover. Hyperbole has no place in the news.

—January 13, 1973

Voyeurism and the Real Thing

The Washington Post

Interoffice Memo

TO: Bradlee, et al.   March 11, 1971

FROM: Harwood

On the 4th of July or thereabouts, the carnival would arrive. There would be a ferris wheel, a couple of tired old elephants and, almost always, the tent with the girl. If you were 10 or 11, you could go in for a dime and watch with the fascination of neopubescence as the girl in the tent stripped all the way down to the waist. Jeezus...Real Boobs! And when that was done, they stopped the show and said that for another dime you could stay for the second part and that in the second part she would show it all and I'm positive she did but they always ran us out because we weren't 12.

We had other outlets for our voyeurism as we got a little older and left the little country towns for the city. There were burlesque houses and stag movies and the calendars with Nekkid Wimmen and the Petty girls in Esquire and what strikes you now is how little any of that has changed. The burlesque houses are having a hard time but the barrooms try to keep alive the tradition with topless girls. Esquire doesn't have Petty or those great comic panels with the fat businessman in bed with the big-titted girl; but Playboy has a centerfold and the same panels. The stag movies have moved uptown from 7th to 14th street. The great old tabloid newspapers, like the Daily Mirror, with their crime-sex formulae are gone: "Tragedy in Love Nest in Queens"; "Gypsy Rose Lee: Are They Real?"; "Enraged Husband Slays Wife, Lover." But you can still find the National Inquirer ("Shame: I Loved My Son"), Screw, and the old nudie magazines.

So one has to say that the voyeur business is about where it has always been, except that now we'll pay $10 a seat to take our wives and children to "Hair" at the National Theatre where we will wait

(more)

50

till the last part when they show it all and think
back to those days in the tent when we didn't have
the extra dime or got run out because we weren't 12.
And if that is true, what is all this Yuk-Yuk voyeurism in the good old WashPost over REAL Boobs at
Archibald's nightspot and massage parlors in Fairfax?

The argument, of course, is that we have a New
Generation, New Patterns of Sexual and Social Behavior and that--as a serious, honest newspaper--we
are obliged to deal with these new phenomena in
American life.

Fair enough. Let's deal with whatever "new
phenomena" we can discover. Let's write about
communes and group sex and homosexuality and the
serial marriage and whatever varieties of behavior
seem significant. No one can object to that if these
matters are treated seriously and thoroughly and
thoughtfully. But what has that to do with massage
parlors and Real Boobs at Archibald's? I'm baffled at
the contention that the "sexual revolution," if such
there be, is represented by these ancient varieties
of voyeurism, by the Tee-Hee-I-Saw-Your-Underpants
kind of journalism.

The Supreme Court, it seemed to me, was always
rather sensible about obscenity and pornography.
Among the tests was the question of whether the material at hand was "utterly without redeeming social
value." If it had "redeeming social value" it could
not be barred or censored. There is, I think, "social
value" in reporting the significant developments of
our time, sexual or otherwise. But "Boom in Busts"?
You've lost me there.*

(*The specific defense of "Boom in Busts" was
that the story reported a first, that for the first
time the pasties came off in Washington, revealing
the nipples whole. It ain't so, as the story points
out. The lead says: "Go-go dancers with entirely bare
breasts...returned to Washington last week." And
later on we are told: "Archibald's new policy does
not mark the first time bare breasts have been see-
able in Washington. At burlesque houses in recent
years along 9th and 14th Streets NW, they have been
common.")

'Dirty Words'

By Charles B. Seib

Every newspaper editor agonizes occasionally over whether to print dirty words. And most have found themselves in the uncomfortable position of using such ridiculous euphemisms as "barnyard epithet" (*Time* magazine once called it "the pastoral expletive") or "vulgar word for sexual intercourse" or playing fill-in-the-blanks with the reader, as in "b------t." Or in the more forthright but also uncomfortable position of having decided to print in its full glory a word that is bound to set off a storm of reader protest.

As society's restraints on bad language have slackened, the decisions on whether to print have become more difficult. Words once safely beyond the pale, no matter what the circumstances, must now be considered, and the sensitivies of a perhaps dwindling segment of readers must be weighed against the abstraction we call the public interest.

The rule followed on the *Washington Post* and on many others is that taboo words—any child over the age of eight could assemble the list—are used only if necessary to the story. That is, they are printed if they convey to the reader an essential fact or element of mood, situation or personality that can be conveyed in no other way.

It is a sensible rule and a fairly simple one, but it isn't easy to apply. As the *Post*'s resident gadfly, I objected recently to the use of a vulgarism (registering about 3 on an offensiveness scale of 5) in a story from Saigon. I felt it was a casual expletive, such as occurs often in conversation these days, and not necessary to convey the sense or the temper of the quotation in which it appeared. The editors who printed it had decided the other way, of course, under the same general rule.

Usually these decisions—and the protests that publication sometimes generates—are taken in stride. Troublesome as they can be, they do not rank among the major crises of the news business. But occasionally there is a forceful reminder of just how strong the remaining strands of taboo still are.

Which brings me to the case of Charles Alexander, until recently the editor of the *Dayton* (Ohio) *Journal Herald* and now at liberty.

Recently Alexander made one of those decisions. He had in hand a sensational document—the verbatim statement to authorities of a Treasury agent who had shot and killed a colleague during a bitter quarrel over which of them would get a transfer. The agent's description of the climax of the quarrel, just before the shooting began, included that vulgar word for sexual intercourse.

Alexander printed the transcript across the top of page one of his newspaper, using the taboo word twice. The next day, after a confrontation with the paper's management, he offered his resignation. It was accepted. He explains that he was asked if he had approved the publication. "I said yes. They said it was indefensible. After that, resignation was the only proper thing to do."

There may have been other elements in that outcome, but the fact is that publication of a word known to every American, literate or illiterate, triggered the departure of a respected journalist from a respectable newspaper.

Before he left the *Journal Herald,* Alexander wrote and published a column in which he movingly made it clear—clearer than I could—that when editors consider taboo words, it isn't simply in terms of the cynical old newspaper question: "Well, shall we rattle their teacups?" So I will let him have the last words.

After recounting the circumstances in which the word was used, Alexander wrote:

"What the account of Carroll Gibson [the Treasury agent] tells us with a vividness that I would hope none of us or our children would forget is that killing in most cases is the final, but not the crucial act. The crux comes when the common love and respect we ought to have for each other dissolves into hate, and we turn the corner from passionate verbal combat or quarreling to mortal combat.

"Psychologists are fond of telling us how healthy it is to 'let it all hang out.' That's true only to a point. Then comes the moment of truth when we must decide whether we are men and women or animals of the jungle. Carroll Gibson's account is the story of two men who made the turn. Pure logic tells us that at some point there must be restraint or we will destroy ourselves—physically or mentally—in an irreversible act. The weapon can just as easily be an accelerator and steering wheel in the hand of an enraged driver as a gun.

"To me the telling of that message from an incident of real life, including in one instance the raw vulgarity used by a man blind with rage, is a lesson that every man, woman and child should perceive in all its dimensions. It is shocking—it surely should be.

"The complaints we received had nothing to do with introducing a word into the culture, much less into the language. The objection was to putting it into print. I did not approve its publication lightly. I would have preferred to avoid it. As a matter of practice, it is not done at all on this newspaper unless it is deemed unavoidable. But if it seems unavoidable, I question that the basic cause of decency is served by playing euphemistic games. 'You don't have to print the word because everyone knows what goes in there anyway,' I was told by several callers.

"If its use in print contaminates children—and I am amazed at the number of children under 12 who, according to parents, read the paper from cover to cover—I would hope that parents would have the depth to realize that the real lesson here is not so much that the word in question is never used—children know better—but that intemperate language is often a prelude to intemperate behavior and tragedy. Language is the verbal expression of man's condition, not the source of it. Language is amoral.

"To view the story as a mere verbal account is to miss its deeper significance. In an era in which homicide is on an alarming rise, most of it resulting from arguments between members of the same family, or between friends and acquaintances, we wonder why the admonition that 'thou shalt not kill is having so little impact. Is it because of vulgar language? Or might it be because we are so pre-occupied with the superficialities of life—the trappings—that we ponder only casually, if at all, the real meaning of the drama that goes on amid those trappings?

"Finally, those who say that one would never have seen such a word printed in full in a family newspaper five years ago are probably correct. It is not common now, although not unheard of. It is most uncommon in this newspaper. I think it will be unknown henceforth. I don't quarrel with that point of view. That is a proper editorial judgment and obviously the more inoffensive one.

"I am not a champion of dirty words. I am a champion of the press trying, as the opportunity presents itself, to give mankind a telling insight into its own frailty. Perhaps that comes from a sensitivity to my own. The essence of the news is the classic struggle of man to overcome his frailty and his search for order to aid in that struggle. I would hope we can view the implication openly."

—April 16, 1975

Watch Your Language

The Washington Post

Interoffice Memo

Messrs. Bradlee/Simons: 4/2/75

I don't see myself as the language censor here, but since a staffer asked me about it I'd like to comment on the use of the word "shit" in the Saigon story in yesterday's paper.

I'm ready to go as far as anyone in permitting obscene words or other language that might be offensive to some readers when necessary to convey a mood, situation or personality.

In this case, I would say that the use of the word does not contribute to the reader's understanding and that therefore it should have been dropped.

Charlie Seib

Through a Glass Darkly on HHH

By Meg Greenfield

Press coverage of Hubert Humphrey's 1968 presidential campaign struck one viewer as sufficiently shoddy and misfocused to merit parody in the Post's *own pages.*

CENTER CITY, Sept. 27 — A group of idealistic young people chanting "Shut up" and "Drop dead" was interrupted four times this afternoon by Vice President Humphrey. The interruptions were part of a speech which the youths charged had been "planned." Visibly upset by the disturbance, the young people then sawed down a grandstand on which a crowd estimated at 20,000 was sitting.

The episode was further evidence of the Vice President's continuing failure to identify himself with the aspirations of the young.

"This is just another example of how the system works," one of the six disillusioned youths told reporters. "They have no sense of the relevant. I was for Marcus Raskin before the convention, but now I'll probably vote for General Walker."

Mr. Humphrey's inability to capture the allegiance of this key group of voters could probably cost him the election.

Despite this latest in a serious of major setbacks, Mr. Humphrey and his aides stuck to the line that the day had been a success. They professed elation at the size of the crowd, pointing out that it had cheered his remarks loudly and repeatedly until it became distracted by the sawing youths below. In the opinion of several observers, however, the cheering, though loud and frequent, seemed forced.

There was also some dispute about the size of the turnout which city officials claimed was unprecedented. They did not add that the rally had been planned, probably intentionally, to coincide with the annual autumn white sale at Markowitz's Department Store only two and a half miles away. Newsmen traveling with the Vice President counted several Markowitz's shopping bags in the crowd, and also uncovered evidence that the 20,000-person estimate had been padded.

Mrs. Winifred Hoskins, a grandmother who was interviewed at the entrance of the stadium, said that if she was counted in the estimate she should not have been. Mrs. Hoskins said that she had been changing buses when she heard all the noise inside and thought she would go in to see what it was. Asked her opinion of the Vice President, Mrs. Hoskins said, "I think he's a crook like all the rest of them. He really has a nerve comin' here."

Police refused tonight to say whether Mrs. Hoskins and five other persons who admitted walking in from the bus stop had been counted in the crowd.

In an address lasting more than 55 minutes, the Vice President once again failed to attack President Johnson. He also did not excoriate the slow pace of negotiations in Paris or condemn the administration's conduct of the war. Mr. Humphrey was pointedly silent, in addition, on what he would do if the Chinese invaded Nepal. He did not explain his differences, if any, with the Johnson administration over the handling of Fidel Castro and the recognition of Communist China.

Other subjects conspicuously not mentioned by Mr. Humphrey included the 1965 action in the Dominican Republic, General de Gaulle, and Billie Sol Estes.

Defensive Humphrey aides later attempted without success to meet the newsmen's complaints on this score by pointing out that the subject of the Vice President's address had been a comprehensive program of reforms for federal welfare law. They declared that the program represented four months of work by an academic task force. Newsmen, however, remained unconvinced.

This growing alienation of the press represents another major failure of Mr. Humphrey's campaign to date. Many observers believe that he has only a slim chance of election unless he manages in the short time left to capture the imagination of youth, the reporters traveling with him, and similar major sectors of the population.

Mr. Humphrey's proposals on social welfare included 11 points.

—September 27, 1968

Editing in the Electronic Media: A Documentary Dispute

The letter and editorial that follow are part of what developed into a serialized dispute in the spring of 1971 over television editing techniques. In the beginning there was only the CBS-filmed documentary, "The Selling of the Pentagon," which dealt with the public relations apparatus of the Department of Defense and some highly questionable uses to which it had been put. Then there were, among others, Vice President Spiro Agnew, who weighed in with objections to various aspects of production; the Pentagon; a number of congressmen; the Washington Post; *CBS News president Richard S. Salant; NBC News president Reuven Frank; and Fred Friendly, the Edward R. Murrow Professor of Broadcast Journalism at Columbia University.*

While not the complete record of the debate, the letter from Richard Salant to the Washington Post, *which reiterates — and rebuts — the* Post's *initial arguments, and the* Post's *editorial reply presented here cover the central issues that were raised.*

CBS Comments

This letter is in response to your editorial of March 26, in which you start by calling the CBS News documentary, "The Selling of the Pentagon," a "highly valuable and informative exposition of a subject about which the American people should know more," and then proceed to examine in some detail the specific editing of that film and general practices of television news editing technique.

The editorial was obviously written by one who has long labored on the editorial page — and not on the news pages.

You conclude that in some measure (not specified) public confidence and credibility are undermined by our editing techniques "innocent or not."

The question of how a news or documentary broadcast is edited is at least as important as you obviously consider it. It is precisely as important as, and possibly no more complicated than, questions pertaining to editing in the print medium (newspapers and news magazines) — the process by which any journalist rejects or accepts, selects and omits, and almost always compresses material available to him. You do not question the right, indeed the professional obligation of your reporters to do this, nor of your editors to continue the process once the reporter has done his job, nor indeed, of your senior editors to impose their professional judgment upon this same piece of work when or if it comes to them.

But you question not only our right to do the same thing, but also the methods by which we edit, and even our motives ("innocent or not"). You do not, in other words, grant us the right to do precisely what you do — and must do if you are journalists as distinguished from transmission belts.

Why?

The key to why you feel this way is spelled out in your editorial: "People who work in the nonelectronic news business know how readily they themselves may distort an event or a remark . . . these dangers are of course multiplied in the production of a televised documentary."

You are saying that good reporting — fair reporting — is a difficult business, with many pitfalls along the way, that television reporting is a more difficult business with more pitfalls. Fair enough.

Then you go on to suggest, indeed recommend, that our rules should be different than your rules, that sound journalistic ethics and the First Amendment are somehow divisible between rights granted to journalists whose work comes out in ink and somewhat lesser rights for journalists whose work comes out electronically. You say we should go out of our way to "preserve intact and in sequence" the response of those we interview. We both "go out of our way" to be fair and accurate, but we both have limitations of space, and we both seek clarity. Except in verbatim transcripts, neither medium preserves intact or in sequence everything it presents. You say at the very least we should indicate that something in the interview has been dropped. If we asked you to do this, you would properly respond that readers know, without a blizzard of asterisks, that material in your paper is edited, that these are not the complete remarks. Our viewers know it, too. And so do those whom we cover.

But most astonishing of all, you propose that we should give the subject of the interview an opportunity to see and approve his revised remarks. Is that now the policy at the *Washington Post?* Of course not. You know and I know that this strikes at the very core of independent and free journalism. To grant a subject such a right of review is to remove the basic journalistic function of editing from the hands of the journalist and place it — in the case of the documentary in question — in the hands of the Pentagon. I almost wrote — "tell you what, we'll do it if you'll do it." Then I had a second thought: No, we won't do it even if you should do it.

We are all after the same thing: to be fair, to inform the public fairly and honestly. We do not suggest that we — or any journalistic organization — are free from errors, but nothing in the First Amendment suggests that we must be perfect, or that we are not human. And nothing suggests that if our responsibility is larger, our job tougher or our coverage broader there should be some new set of rules for our kind of journalism, as if to say the First Amendment is fine so long as it doesn't count for much. You don't seem to mind if our end of the dinghy sinks, so long as yours stays afloat.

Fairness is at the root of all this, and fairness can be and always will be debated.

But I submit that we are as careful about editing, as concerned with what is fair and proper and in balance, as rigorous in our internal screening and editorial control processes as any journalistic organization.

The job of ensuring that fairness, that balance and that sense of responsibility is difficult. It is the subject of our constant review and concern. It is not a question that can be solved by a single statement of policy or staff memorandum. It must be, and it is, the daily concern of our working reporters, editors and management.

We believe, as I have said publicly before, that "The Selling of the Pentagon" was edited fairly and honestly. Long after the useful and valuable debate on this broadcast has subsided and perhaps been forgotten we shall be editing other news broadcasts and other documentaries as fairly and as honestly as we know how, and in accordance with established journalistic practice—just as you shall be so editing.

RICHARD S. SALANT
President, CBS News
New York

The Post Comments

In time the U.N. may have to be called in to arbitrate the burgeoning dispute over the CBS documentary "The Selling of the Pentagon," but for now we would like, in a unilateral action, to respond to the complaint of Richard Salant of CBS News.

We think it is off the point. And we think this is so because Mr. Salant invests the term "editing" with functions and freedoms well beyond anything we regard as common or acceptable practice. Mr. Salant taxes us with unfairly recommending two sets of standards in these matters, one for the printed press and another for the electronic. But he reads us wrong. We were and are objecting to the fact that *specifically, in relation to question-and-answer sequences,* two sets of standards *already* exist—and that what he and others in television appear to regard as simple "editing" seems to us to take an excess of unacknowledged liberties with the direct quotations of the principals involved.

Before we go into these, a word might be of use about the editorial practices (and malpractices) common to us both. When a public official or anyone else issues a statement or responds to a series of questions in an interview, the printed media of course exercise an editorial judgment in deciding which part and how much of that material to quote or paraphrase or ignore. The analogy with TV's time limitations, for us, is the limit on space: deciding which of the half million words of news coming into this paper each day shall be among the 80,000 we have room to print. Thus, "Vice President Agnew said last night . . . Mr. Agnew also said . . ." and so on; it is a formulation basic to both the daily paper and the televised newscast.

That bad and misleading judgments can be made by this newspaper in both our presentation and selection of such news goes without saying — or at least it did until we started doing some public soul-searching about it in this newspaper a good while back. There is, for example, a distorting effect in failing to report that certain statements were not unsolicited assertions but responses to a reporter's question. But that we do not confuse the effort to remedy these defects with a waiving of our First Amendment rights or a yielding up of editorial prerogatives should also be obvious to readers of this newspaper — perhaps tediously so by now. What we have in mind, however, when we talk of the license taken by the electronic media in the name of "editing" is something quite different, something this newspaper does not approve and would not leap to defend if it were caught doing. It is the practice of printing highly rearranged material in a Q-and-A sequence as if it were verbatim text, without indicating to the reader that changes had been made and/or without giving the subject an opportunity to approve revisions in the original exchange.

It is, for instance, presenting as a direct six-sentence quotation from a colonel, a "statement" composed of a first sentence from page 55 of his prepared text, followed by a second sentence from page 36, followed by a third and fourth from page 48, and a fifth from page 73, and a sixth from page 88. That occurred in "The Selling of the Pentagon," and we do not see why Mr. Salant should find it difficult to grant that this type of procedure is (1) not "editing" in any conventional sense and (2) likely to undermine both the broadcast's credibility and public confidence in that credibility.

The point here is that "The Selling of the Pentagon" presented this statement as if it were one that had actually been made — verbatim — by the colonel: TV can and does simulate an impression of actuality in the way it conveys such rearranged material. Consider, again from the same documentary, a sequence with Daniel Z. Henkin, Assistant Secretary of Defense for Public Affairs. This is how viewers were *shown* Mr. Henkin answering a question:

Roger Mudd: What about your public displays of military equipment at state fairs and shopping centers? What purpose does that serve?
Mr. Henkin: Well, I think it serves the purpose of informing the public about their armed forces. I believe the American public has the right to request information about the armed forces, to have speakers come before them, to ask

questions, and to understand the need for our armed forces, why we ask for the funds that we do ask for, how we spend these funds, what are we doing about such problems as drugs — and we do have a drug problem in the armed forces; what are we doing about the racial problem — and we do have a racial problem. I think the public has a valid right to ask us these questions.

This, on the other hand, is how Mr. Henkin *actually* answered the question:

Mr. Henkin: Well, I think it serves the purpose of informing the public about their armed forces. It also has the ancillary benefit, I would hope, of stimulating interest in recruiting as we move or try to move to zero draft calls and increased reliance on volunteers for our armed forces. I think it is very important that the American youth have an opportunity to learn about the armed forces.

The answer Mr. Henkin was *shown* to be giving had been transposed from his answer to another question a couple of pages along in the transcribed interview, and one that came out of a sequence dealing not just with military displays but also with the availability of military speakers. At that point in the interview, Roger Mudd asked Mr. Henkin whether the sort of thing he was now talking about — drug problems and racial problems — was "the sort of information that gets passed at state fairs by sergeants who are standing next to rockets." To which Mr. Henkin replied:

Mr. Henkin: No, I didn't — wouldn't limit that to sergeants standing next to any kind of exhibits. I knew — I thought we were discussing speeches and all.

This is how the sequence was *shown* to have occurred, following on Mr. Henkin's transposed reply to the original question:

Mr. Mudd: Well, is that the sort of information about the drug problem you have and the racial problem you have and the budget problems you have — is that the sort of information that gets passed out at state fairs by sergeants who are standing next to rockets.

Mr. Henkin: No, I wouldn't limit that to sergeants standing next to any kind of exhibit. Now, there are those who contend that this is propaganda. I do not agree with this.

The part about discussing "speeches and all" had been omitted; the part about propaganda comes from a few lines above Mr. Henkin's actual answer and was in fact a reference to charges that the Pentagon was using talk of the "increasing Soviet threat" as propaganda to influence the size of the military budget.

Surely, something different from and less cosmic than a challenge to CBS's First Amendment rights is involved in the question of whether or not the subject of such a rearranged interview should not be given a chance to see and approve what he will be demonstrated to have said. And surely this "editing" practice must be conceded — with reason — to have damaging effects on public confidence in what is being shown to have happened — shown to have been said. We agree with Mr. Salant's premise that we are all in the same dinghy. That is why we are so concerned that neither end should sink.

— March 30, 1973

Focusing on Photos

When Do You Use a Particular Picture–and Why?

By Richard Harwood

On September 1, 1970, many American newspapers, including the *Washington Post,* published a "sensational" picture. It showed six members of the Black Panther Party in Philadelphia lined up against a wall, guarded by heavily armed policemen. The five men at the wall were in various states of undress: two of them were naked, two were in their underwear and the fifth was in the process of taking off his clothes. The sixth Panther in the picture was a fully clothed woman. They had all been arrested in a raid on a Panther headquarters. The men had been forced to undress as part of a weapons search.

In the large sense, the background to that raid is found in the years of conflict and hostility between policemen and the under-class—mainly black—in American cities. In the immediate sense, the background was the unprovoked murder of a police sergeant by a young black gunman two days before and the subsequent wounding of three other Philadelphia police officers. Tensions in the city were high. There were fears of new ghetto riots, of more killings, of more random attacks on policemen. There were reports of a large weapons cache at the Panther headquarters. And so there was a raid and it produced a "sensational" picture.

It was published in the *Washington Post,* five columns wide at the top of page one, and it produced in the days that followed a variety of positive and negative reactions among our readers. One man praised the "courageous editorial decision" to use the picture. Another said he wanted to cancel his subscription but couldn't because he had done that two months before.

A black soldier at Fort Belvoir, Va., wrote: ". . . This photo does a great disservice not only to your newspaper but also to Negro communities throughout the USA. . . . Did you stop to wonder what feelings such a picture would generate? I, myself, am thoroughly disgusted. . . . Sure, you may say that your paper had nothing to do with the arrests, but you

DARED to print such a demeaning photo of my race. I can't help but wonder did it help sell a few more hundred or so papers that day for you."

A white Virginian protested the "obviously inflammatory aspects of the front-page picture of nude blacks. . . . Maybe you intended to convey a brutal Philadelphia police squad 'forcefully' stripping in public mere inhabitants of a Black Panther Headquarters clubhouse. The entire incident in Philadelphia was surrounded by the assassination-type murder of a police officer, shoot-outs, wounded men, yet—you chose to lead-out and emphasize the story with a bizarre account of nude arrests. Where is your sense of priority?"

"If I were one of those men," a Maryland reader observed, "I think I'd sue you for invasion of privacy."

Another reader regarded the picture as a "shining example of what black people meant when they say the news media are unfair and biased in their reporting and treatment of black persons."

The published and unpublished letters on the subject were evenly divided: half were critical of the police for their treatment of the Panthers, half were critical of the *Post* for publishing the picture. They demonstrated the obvious truth that there is no monolithic audience out there. It is as diverse in its passions and opinions and notions of good taste as the country itself. The same can be said for the mass media. The television networks chose not to use the shots of the Panther strip-down. The *Post* and other newspapers chose otherwise.

In our case, the decision was made by the executive editor, Benjamin C. Bradlee, and was concurred by various editors and reporters, white and black. Bradlee's reasoning was this:

"We saw right away that it was a loaded picture, that it was potentially inflammatory, that it showed a cruel lack of dignity. I decided to think about it and I did. I concluded that this event had happened: it had happened in connection with a subject of critical importance that day—a potential riot in Philadelphia.

"A policeman had been killed. Others had been shot. So this picture had an immediacy to it. It told a vital part of the story. It would have been censorship not to use it."

The key phrase there has to be "subject of critical importance" because "censorship" of pictures on grounds of "poor taste" is commonplace with newspapers, the *Post* included. During the May 9, 1970, antiwar demonstrations in Washington, dozens of young people cavorted nude in the Reflecting Pool. Our photographers had a field day with that. But no pictures were printed in which genitals or bare breasts were clearly visible. When the actress, Jayne Mansfield, was killed in an automobile accident we chose not to print pictures showing her head impaled on a shard of windshield glass and her body lying several feet away on the roadside. There is, in short, a consistent disposition at the *Post* not to use "sensational" pictures of gore and nudity.

But that does not translate into an immutable or inflexible rule. What governs, in the end, is an editor's sense of historic or social significance.

Pictures of Robert Kennedy were printed after he was shot, which must have been painful to his family and friends. There were many protests to the *Post* over a picture that appeared during the Tet offensive of 1968. It showed the Saigon police chief firing a bullet into the head of a Vietcong prisoner. A picture out of Vietnam showing an American tank dragging the body of an enemy soldier produced a similar reaction. The picture of a Kent State student lying in a pool of blood after being shot by a National Guardsman was considered tasteless and inflammatory by many readers. In each case, a judgment was made that the significance of the event outweighed other considerations.

Some critics of the media believe that political motivations enter into judgments of this kind. The famous picture of Lyndon Johnson showing off his abdominal scar following an operation produced considerable criticism in that vein. Our aim, it was said, was to ridicule Johnson and demean the presidency. Unflattering pictures of President Nixon have caused the same reaction. The journalist and author, Theodore White, believes that the political bias of the television crews showed up clearly in the film they produced for the documentary on his book, *The Making of the President — 1968*. They came back, he has said, with flattering footage of their idols, Eugene McCarthy and Robert Kennedy, and with unflattering footage of Nixon and Hubert Humphrey.

It would be foolish and untrue for journalists to claim that they alone among men are without sin, that their standards of taste are necessarily and always the best standards or that they are as evenhanded as automatons in all their work. Journalism is no exact science. Mistakes are made, biases crop up and judgments are often wrong.

It is also undeniable, however, that events have a way of asserting their own significance and that pictures of those events sometimes come along that are too powerful to be ignored.

—September 15, 1970

'Impact' Photographs and Reader Sensibilities

By Charles B. Seib

"Why?" the reader asked. "Why do newspapers print horrible pictures like the one of that poor woman in Boston?"

All day the calls came in.

"My whole family, kids included, felt it was gross of the *Post* to print that picture." "Sickening." "Distressing." "Yellow journalism." "I never thought the *Post* would sink to that." And in a clipped British accent, "You have made my day rather distasteful."

The calls were prompted by publication in the *Post* of a sequence of three photographs taken at a Boston fire, the third being a midair picture of a fall that killed a young woman and injured a child. They occupied almost half of page one of the July 24 *Post*. They also were published by newspapers all across the country and undoubtedly will be ranked among the top news pictures of the year.

The protest calls to the *Post* numbered about 70. That's a tiny fraction of the readers of a paper with a circulation of more than 500,000. But it is the largest reaction to a published item that I have experienced in eight months as the *Post*'s ombudsman.

The calls came from men and women in about equal numbers. The callers—at least those I spoke with—were temperate; the tone was often hurt rather than angry. Some said they felt the *Post* had let them down, had sunk to pandering to the most morbid instincts of its readers.

In the *Post*'s newsroom, on the other hand, I found no doubts, no second thoughts about publication of the Boston pictures. When they were discussed the evening before publication, the question was not whether they should be printed but how they should be displayed. When I talked to editors Thursday they used words like "interesting" and "riveting" and "gripping" to describe them. The pictures told something about life in the ghetto, they said (although the neighborhood where the tragedy occurred is not a ghetto, I am told). They dramatized the need to check on the safety of fire escapes. They dramatically conveyed something that had happened, and that is the business we're in. They were news.

The picture that upset the readers—the third one—was superb technically. For "impact," that quality for which journalism constantly strives, it couldn't be beat. The falling woman and a little girl, limbs grotesquely outstretched, a potted plant accompanying them down—it was the stuff of which nightmares are made. It was also the stuff that sets an editor to thinking about how big a chunk of page one space he can devote to it.

Was publication of the picture a bow to the same taste for the morbidly sensational that makes gold mines of disaster movies? Most papers will not print the picture of a dead body except in the most unusual cir-

65

The Washington Post

FINAL

The Weather

THURSDAY, JULY 24, 1975

Lisbon Move to Left Seen

Council Said To Approve 3-Man Junta

Fire Escape Collapses

Egyptians Agree To Extension of U.N. Sinai Force

Direct Talks Demanded By Israel

ANWAR SADAT   YITZHAK RABIN

Voting Rights Bill Modified in Senate

JOHN L. STENNIS

Area's Confidence In Schools Wanes

WASHINGTON SURVEY

Family Income Up, Buying Power Down

Area Is Typical   11.6% in Poverty

Callaway: Reagan Has Lead in South

cumstances. Does the fact that the final picture was taken a milli-second before the young woman died make a difference? Most papers will not print a picture of a bare female breast. Is that a more inappropriate subject for public display than the picture of a human being's last agonized instant of life? If the picture of the falling woman and child was fit for publication, where then do you draw the line?

These are questions I won't attempt to answer because I don't know the answers. As a former editor who now monitors the paper as a reader, I find myself afflicted with an uncomfortable schizophrenia. When I saw the Boston pictures in the *Washington Star* July 23 I had a feeling of revulsion. I felt it again when I looked at page one of the *Post* the next day. Something inside me said that the third picture—or the display of it—was obscene in the true sense of the word. But later when one of the *Post*'s editors asked me whether, if I had been calling the shots, I would have used the picture, I had to admit that I probably would have.

As a reader, revulsion; as an editor, acceptance. Why the difference?

Just by chance, the day the pictures appeared I came across an article in which a young police reporter told how he was able to handle his daily diet of death and despair. "I've got this little shell around me," he said. Perhaps that's the answer; perhaps the "little shell" newspaper people build around their professional selves so they can do their job dispassionately has the unintended effect of insulating them from the feelings and sensitivities of their readers.

As I said, I don't know the answers to the questions the Boston pictures raised in my mind. Most newspaper people would agree that in a business of many subjective decisions, picture selection is the most subjective of all. But I do know that any editor who decided to print those pictures without giving at least a moment's thought to what purpose they served and what their effect was likely to be on the readers should ask another question: Have I become so preoccupied with manufacturing a product according to professional traditions and standards that I have forgotten about the consumer, the reader?

It is not too far-fetched to suggest that the Boston pictures and the reactions to them shed some light on the strained relations between the press and the public. Our professional "little shells" can diminish our awareness of the human and humane feelings of the reader in matters far beyond picture selection. Fairness to individuals and institutions, regard for personal privacy, compassion, an awareness of the true interests of the person trying to make it in today's perilous world—these are crucial to effective and responsible journalism. But they will be slighted unless we chop some windows in our "little shells."

—August 3, 1975

Taste, Fairness and News Value

By Robert C. Maynard

On an uncharacteristically warm and sunny afternoon in March, 1973, a prominent star of the National Basketball Association stopped at a playground on Manhattan's Lower East Side and watched some small fry playing basketball. He was soon in the game, showing the youngsters how it's done. It was a heartwarming scene, and a photographer recorded it for posterity.

Because it was the kind of photograph sports editors like for a slow day between seasons, United Press International bought the picture and it ran on the wires for several hours before UPI sent an advisory to editors. The belt the star was wearing, the advisory said, "may be considered by some to be offensive." Engraved on the belt, and plainly visible in the picture, were figures of couples making love.

Picture editors merely airbrushed the offensive figures out of the belt or waited for the revised and retouched photo UPI moved on its wires moments after its advisory. The embarrassing incident helps to illuminate the endless complexities involved in the business of choosing pictures for a daily newspaper.

In the case of the basketball player's belt, the solution was relatively easy. At other times, the choices are not as simple. They frequently involve the subtler questions of fairness to the subject of a photograph, taste and news value. And superimposed on all of those considerations is the question on which agreement is sometimes impossible: What, after all, is a good picture in newspaper terms?

It is fair to repeat about good pictures what a Supreme Court justice once said of obscenity; he couldn't define it, but he recognized it when he saw it.

Essentially, a news picture must do what a good story does. It must reveal its point with clarity, simplicity and sharpness. If it adds light and grace to a page, it has done more than its job. What troubles journalists is that a "good" picture in anyone else's terms might prove to be unacceptable for newspaper purposes.

The reason is that it might have failed the test of fairness, good taste or news value. Because all of these are to some degree subjective judgments, journalists may differ about a given photograph. Here is an example of the fairness aspect of the business of choosing pictures.

In the first edition of the *Washington Post* of July 25, 1973, a four-column picture of John Ehrlichman dominated the top half of page one. It was Ehrlichman's first day before the Ervin committee, the day he forcefully defended the right of the President to order burglaries in "na-

The photo on the left was not published.

tional security" cases. The photograph must have been taken during one of the most tense moments in the interrogation.

As a reflection of Ehrlichman's demeanor and the toughness of the man, it was a "good" picture. His lower lip is jutting forward and his face shows hard lines. His eyes are firm in their gaze and Ehrlichman's uncompromising toughness is dramatic in the picture. But it only ran as a four-column picture for one edition. After much discussion among the editors, it was decided that the picture was altogether too unflattering to the man, no matter how revealing of his mood at that moment. It was reduced in size and three other pictures, reflecting different moods and expressions, were added to make up the four-column display that appeared in the editions most readers see.

A rough tally of Ehrlichman photos for that day — those taken by the staff and those supplied by the wire service — shows that of 36 pictures available of Ehrlichman that day, 19 fell — in my judgment — into the category of being unflattering to a decided degree. I would count the picture that was cut from a four-column to a two-column among the 19. It is the only one of that category that was actually used — not because it was unflattering, but because it was so revealing of his demeanor.

Of the rest, 14 reflected Ehrlichman in such a manner as to be called fair by any reasonable standard. Of those, eight have been used in the *Washington Post*. The last three deserve to be called questionable by the fairness standard, but one — considered again to be revealing of his demeanor at the moment — was used.

One of the problems is that we are all not equally photogenic, despite our other qualities, good or bad. Some handsome people look terrible on film and many people who are not striking in person photograph remarkably well. Trying to be fair in such circumstances presents its difficulties and disagreements, and the experience with Ehrlichman in the paper of July 25 reflects those problems.

Taste is an even more difficult problem than fairness. If it's a belt on an athlete that shows a copulation scene, the decision for most editors is easy —just retouch the picture. But suppose it's a grisly disaster?

In the *Washington Post* of August 1, 1973, a major story was an air crash in Boston that claimed 88 lives. The inside picture, with the continuation of the story, showed remnants of the aircraft, the firefighters and the shoeless feet and legs of one of the victims. It was hardly a pretty picture; air disaster photos never are.

Nonetheless, I'd have thought the picture within the reasonable bounds of taste. So did the editors of the paper. Gerald Rexrode, an Arlington, Va., reader, brought us up short with a letter in which he called it a "horrible, ghoulish picture" because it showed a portion of the body of one of the victims. Had it shown the victim's face I'd be more inclined to agree with Mr. Rexrode.

As with the photos of the war in Vietnam, the air tragedy photo brings home to the reader a sense of the dimensions of a tragic event.

Taste is probably the most significant area of disagreement about pictures. At that same airport about 10 years ago, a seat and its passenger remained intact after a crash. The seat was floating upright in Boston Harbor with the dead passenger still strapped in. Editors still argue over whether that picture was sufficiently in good taste to have been used. Mr. Rexrode asked of this more recent air tragedy picture how an editor would have felt about using it if one of his own loved ones had been in the accident. The argument over taste will be with us always, no matter how the question is posed. It must be addressed afresh each time. Agree with them or castigate them in a given instance, editors earn their bread making such decisions.

News value is easier to judge than fairness or taste because the picture must first meet the test of relevancy. But there is another element in news value that is important. And that is freshness of approach. A picture might be of something of which we have all seen 100 photos. It might be a person, a monument or a building, done in such a way as to arrest the eye and tell us something new about the subject.

Steve Northup, who once was a photographer for the *Washington Post* and is now working for *Time,* pointed out recently that the Greek word from which we have inherited the word photograph can be taken literally to mean "writing with light." Necessarily, the picture writes with shadows, too. It is this interplay of literal and imagined light and shadow that gives photography its enduring mystery and promises to assure us that we will never agree fully on any of the questions photography poses for those of us who practice and consume journalism.

—August 9, 1973

70

Covering a War

The War Reporter's Mission

By Richard Harwood

In the grand and grim years of our history, we have had all manner of little inquests into what went wrong. Who "lost" China? What happened at Pearl Harbor? Who promoted Peress?

These were scapegoating games in which official inquisitors sought to assign blame to the "striped-pants crowd" at State, late-sleeping admirals, and other long-forgotten functionaries.

The game is being revived with the war in Vietnam, but this time the cast of characters is different. Up to this point it is largely a journalistic exercise that finds the great men of our trade blaming one another—or themselves—for the course of this adventure.

Thus, Fred Friendly, the former president of CBS News, has written in the *Columbia Journalism Review:* "Those of us who were in key editorial positions at the time (1964-1965) can blame it all on the President, or his advisers—Robert McNamara, Dean Rusk, McGeorge Bundy, Maxwell Taylor—but we cannot forever paint over the stain left by our own ineffectiveness."

Thus, Joseph Alsop has said: "If we win the war the press and allied media will look inconceivably foolish, and if we lose it the press will just as certainly be blamed."

The first reaction to rhetoric of this sort is, "Good grief, Charlie Brown. How pompous can we get?" Do Mr. Friendly and Mr. Alsop *really* believe that they and their colleagues start, stop, win or lose wars? We are, perhaps, Very Important People but no one has ever established *that* kind of cause-and-effect relationship, despite the myth that William Randolph Hearst engineered the Spanish-American war single-handedly.

Pomposity aside, this retrospective debate has raised intriguing questions about the news business. One of them was formulated by Dean Rusk toward the end of his term as Secretary of State. During a discussion of the war with reporters, Rusk asked one reporter, "Whose side are you on?"

To that question, there has been a mixed response within this business. S.L.A. Marshall, distinguished military columnist and retired Army general, has said that a journalist in a war zone is obliged to be "an American first, a correspondent second." And some of them have behaved that way, going so far in some cases as to pop off a few rounds at the enemy. Some writers for the radical underground journals have, of course, gone the opposite route and advocate victory for the other side.

The dominant view of the people covering this war, however, was probably best expressed by Richard Dudman of the *St. Louis Post-Dispatch,* in response to criticism from General Marshall. "I have come to believe," he said, "that a news correspondent must try to be a detached observer, a neutral who can report what he can learn about the aims and actions on both sides without the burden of thinking in terms of 'we' and 'they.' "

That is the most difficult position a correspondent can take because it requires him to suppress his passions and prejudices and notions of loyalty in the pursuit of truth. And it is the only defensible position for a journalist whether he is dealing with wars or other human affairs. The reasons for that judgment are simple. A newspaper in this country is sold with an implied warranty, the warranty being that the news it prints is true. That warranty is not always honored in the product because journalists are not immune to ignorance, incompetence and other frailties.

But the warranty remains as a standard for the trade; it is the basis for whatever credibility the media enjoy. This means that even in a war the reporter has an absolute duty to his craft to seek the discipline of detachment and neutrality. If he sees himself as an agent of the American policies, he ceases to be a journalist and becomes instead a propagandist. Thus, Rusk's question — "Whose side are you on?" — might be appropriate in the Soviet Union or in North Vietnam where the press is an instrument of government. It is not appropriate in a free society.

Some people in our business argue that "detachment" and "neutrality" may be harmful to the "national interest." But defining the "national interest" is not the task of the reporter; it is not his mission to prove that this or any war is or is not in the "national interest." His mission is merely to provide the country with facts on which the country can make its own judgment as to where its interests lie and/or how they are being served.

On that point, J. R. Wiggins, the editor of the *Washington Post* who retired a couple of years ago, is fond of a quotation from Rebecca West:

"It is the presentation of the facts that matter, the facts that put together are the face of the age. . . . For if people do not have the face of the age set clearly before them they begin to imagine it; and fantasy, if not disciplined by the intellect and kept in faith with reality by the instinct of art, dwells among the wishes and fears of childhood, and so sees life either as simply answering any prayer or as endlessly emitting nightmare monsters from a womb-like cave."

This is the first of our wars in this century in which there was no censorship from the battlefield. It may be, as Kenneth Crawford claimed in a column in this newspaper, the first war in which "American media, measured by weight of viewership, readership and influence, has been kinder to the nation's enemies than to its friendlies." It may be, as Peter Arnett concluded after eight years as a correspondent in Vietnam, the first war in which we all learned that "the American Army, like all other armies, was composed of the good, the bad, the beautiful, the ugly, the cruel, the brutal, the kindly, the gentle, the strong, the weak." But who can say that facts of this kind, knowledge of this kind, and even the lack of censorship have been inconsistent with the "national interest"?

As the war has dragged on, popular support for it has declined, and that has been true in every American war, World War II excepted. War is a nasty business, whether it is fought in Europe or Indochina or the Middle East or Africa or here at home; no civilized society has much taste for it. And since this one — in the absence of censorship and with the presence of television — has become a living room war, it is remarkable that public tolerance has remained so high. Hazel Erskine published in *Public Opinion Quarterly* in 1970 an analysis of American attitudes toward the wars of the 20th century, based on various polls. "In spite of the current antiwar furor," she concluded, "dissent against Vietnam (58 per cent) has not yet reached the peaks of dissatisfaction attained by either World War I or the Korean War — at least in numbers."

That finding was not satisfying to those who would have us (as if we could) "stop" the war, nor to those who would have us "get on the team" and lead the cheering for the boys over there. It was, I think, a kind of vindication of the dangerous and honest work the grunts of journalism have done, by and large, in Vietnam.

— March 9, 1971

FYI: Protection of Press Credentials

Just as we were about to wax indignant about the news that two U.S. government agents, as well as two Vietnamese agents, were infiltrated into the Saigon press corps, the U.S. Command in Vietnam came through with as handsome an apology as anyone could possibly ask. Its statement acknowledged that press credentials had indeed been issued to the agents through "an erroneous assumption of authority" and that the officer principally responsible had been reprimanded, relieved of his duties and transferred to a new job.

"The U.S. Mission and MACV (Military Assistance Command for Vietnam)," the statement said, "recognize that the Saigon press corps considered that this incident directly impacted upon the integrity and personal standing of the press corps and each individual correspondent. The policies and procedures for accreditation are designed to protect the interests of the press corps as well as the U.S. government. Therefore the unauthorized accreditation was as much deplored by MACV and the U.S. Mission as it was by the press corps. Violations of policy of this type will not be tolerated."

When reporters in Vietnam discovered that press credentials had been given to security agents, they rather naturally assumed that the government was trying to spy on their activities. The common assumption was that behind the ruse lay an effort to discover the sources of news leaks and of unofficial information. Since the protection of confidential sources is a cardinal obligation of newsgathering, the intrusion was understandably resented. Reporters do, indeed, at times obtain news in unorthodox ways. It is an essential part of their responsibility to do so. And while the Army has every right, of course, to ride herd on its own personnel and endeavor to keep them from talking out of turn, there would be something very ugly about employing spies disguised as newsmen for this purpose.

It appears, however, that something quite different lay behind the infiltration. The Army, it can be said, was not spying on reporters. It was engaged in a counter-intelligence undertaking for which the press corps afforded a convenient cover. But this constitutes — as the military authorities themselves ultimately recognized — a still more offensive and dangerous incursion on the freedom of the press.

Disguising intelligence operatives as tourists, as businessmen, as diplomats is, of course, common practice; they are not likely to accomplish very much if they announce themselves frankly as spies. But to disguise them as newsmen is to imperil another kind of newsgathering even more vital to the welfare and safety of a free people. For if newsmen are generally suspected of being spies or government agents, they will be rendered incapable of doing their job. We think, therefore, that the press has something more than a selfish interest in being jealous of its integrity and in resisting every attempt to use it as a cover for clandestine purposes. It is reassuring to find an understanding of this at the top levels of the military.

Press credentials can be of value only in the degree to which they are trusted as being precisely what they purport to be. And so the safeguarding of them from subterfuge is an essential element of press freedom. Police authorities, or governmental authorities of any kind, poison the wellsprings of news and do an incalculable injury to freedom of the press if they impersonate reporters for the pursuit of their official business, no matter what its importance.

—February 11, 1970

Just the Facts

The Washington Post
Interoffice Memo

TO: Bradlee, et al.   January 26, 1971

FROM: Harwood

Following the events of last spring, a couple of our summer interns examined our Cambodian coverage--foreign and domestic. They concluded that it was one-sided and unfair.

We are now entering into a new debate over American involvement in Cambodia and it is in our interest as well as the public's to give the customer one crack at the naked facts, as Russ Wiggins so well put it some years ago.

What we--and most congressmen--presently know about the involvement comes, in large part, from the wire service men on the scene, as well as our own people. How precise and well qualified the wiremen are would be known better to Phil Foisie or John Anderson than to me.

I would like to recite an example of recent wire service reportage from Cambodia as an indication of some of the problems of precision that may be involved:

On Friday, January 22, the AMs carried fragmentary stories and the PMs fuller stories from the wires on the airport attack at Phnom Penh. The PM report said the attack had "wrecked" the Cambodians' "tiny air force." Newsmen were "barred" from the scene, but Cambodian briefers said six choppers were destroyed and two were damaged. From other sources, the wires reported destruction of "several MIG5s and French Fouga Magistere jets" as well as converted US T-28s. The following day's lead from the wires was that "95 per cent" of the Cambodian air force had been destroyed.

(more)

Our original wire story--AM for January 22--
said "several" planes were destroyed and "several
took off" undamaged. Peter Jay filed for January 23,
reporting that no one really knows how many planes
were lost but they included transports, "some
elderly T-28 fighters and some Soviet-made MIGs that
were unusable anyway because of a shortage of parts."
At least four choppers, Jay reported, were also lost.

The Times on Saturday and again on Monday
listed the number of planes lost at 10. So did the
Baltimore Sun.

On Sunday, we had two stories--one from Jay, who
mentioned again the airport attack, referred to four
lost choppers, but used no other numbers on plane
losses. Our second story was written here, was a long
takeout on "illusions" about Cambodia, and stated:

"...a squad of Communist sappers...destroyed
most of the small Cambodian air force early Friday
morning.

"'It wasn't much of an air force anyhow,' U.S.
officials said afterward.

"It was, however, the only air force Cambodia
had."

The statement that "most of the small Cambodian
air force" had been destroyed evidently was based
on early wire stories, since Jay had never filed a
statement of that kind. The statement is interesting
for another reason: it does not give any numbers on
the size of that "small" air force and gives no
numbers in support of the claim that "most" of it
was zapped.

There is a lot of impact in saying that a
country's air force has been "wiped out" in one fell
swoop by 10 sappers who carried out--as our Sunday
story said--a "brilliantly executed" maneuver. There
is a lot of impact there, but what does it mean and
on what is it based? Did the Cambodian air force
consist of 10 planes--the only number listed in any
of the stories I've seen--or something more?

(more)

One way to have answered that question for our readers would be to check the handy military reference book issued annually by the Institute for Strategic Analysis in London. For 1970-71, it listed 64 planes in the Cambodian air force.

Another way would be to check with "informed" sources in the government who would have put out these numbers:

There were 75 Cambodian aircraft at the airport that night of which roughly half were destroyed. The losses included 10 MIGs, which were unusable for lack of parts or pilots, five T-28s, 10 C-47s and 12 choppers. A half-dozen T-28s were undamaged, along with 12 choppers, 10 C-47s and 10 miscellaneous aircraft.

It is difficult to cover a war. It is difficult to sift chaff from wheat in the wires. But to the extent possible--especially in emotional situations such as this one--it is essential to use the naked facts if at all possible and to use them with precision.

Did Newspapers Muff the Job of Informing on Vietnam?

By Richard Harwood

Susan Welch, a political scientist at the University of Illinois, produced a document in 1970 that ought to be an appendix to the Pentagon Papers. It was a study of how three American newspapers prepared themselves and, to some extent, the American people for the military intervention in Vietnam. These newspapers were the *Washington Post,* the *New York Times* and the *San Francisco Chronicle.*

During the 1950s, the study demonstrates, these newspapers — along with the government — helped set in concrete in the American mind the "issues" in Indochina. They ensured, Ms. Welch wrote, "that the reading public would view the war as a struggle between Communism and the Free World, vital to the preservation of all of Southeast Asia, and perhaps all of Asia; that Ho Chi Minh and the Viet Minh were merely agents of Moscow and Peking whose primary means of gaining support was through terror and force (although occasional reference was made to his nationalistic appeal); and of a gallant ally, France, fighting alongside the United States to preserve 'liberty and justice for all.'" They also ensured, her analysis shows, that the public would see Indochina as "an area vital to our interests, that it was under challenge in a clear case of Communist aggression which had to be stopped, and that if the people of Indochina knew the facts they would naturally support the West in any struggle with the Communists."

Finally, these newspapers propagated the view that the "only way out of the crisis which could result in a satisfactory solution for the West was a military victory over the forces of Ho Chi Minh. . . . While there was some sentiment expressed against sending United States troops to Indochina, the major criticism which was directed against the administration was not for suggesting this, but rather for not being firm in pursuing a consistent policy." (The Welch study was entitled "The Press and Foreign Policy: The Definition of the Situation," and was delivered in September, 1970, at the American Political Science Association convention in Los Angeles.)

The *Times* and the *Washington Post* continued into the 1960s to accept the basic assumptions of the previous decade insofar as Indochina was concerned. In the case of the *Post,* it was only after a change in editors in late 1968 that doubts about those assumptions began to be expressed and to be replaced by a new set of assumptions that have become the prevailing wisdom of the 1970s: the assumptions that intervention was a mistake and that Indochina is not vital to U.S. interests.

It has become almost a childish game these days for journalists and politicians to dig back into the record in search of statements to prove that someone was a "hawk" or a "dove" at some point in time. Frequently the purpose of the game is to gain a debating point, to discredit an opponent or to destroy an argument. Scapegoating and masochism are also involved as in Daniel Ellsberg's famous declaration: "I am a war criminal."

There is none of this, however, in the Welch study. It is a serious effort to examine the processes by which issues are defined and policies are made in a democracy. Newspapers play a role in those processes as middlemen between government and the governed. The manner in which we play that role was the subject of the exercise by Ms. Welch. She concluded that we didn't play it well.

There was, to begin with, great ignorance about Indochina on the part of the press, Congress and the public. The academic community was only slightly better informed and most of *its* experts were working for the government.

The *Washington Post* was a case in point. All through the 1950s, while editorial positions were being staked out and attitudes were being formed, the *Post* had no correspondent in Vietnam or hardly anywhere else for that matter. So we became heavily dependent on the administration for whatever information and assumptions we acquired. Like the *Times,* we parroted those assumptions and, in effect, helped paint the administration into a corner by making it, in the words of Ms. Welch, "a prisoner of its own rhetoric."

We had no contrary wisdom to offer, no alternatives to put forward, little dissent to publicize. Lacking our own staff of correspondents, having no other institutional expertise to draw on, there was no way for the *Post* to subject the assumptions about Vietnam to the "demands of reality." We were unable, for example, to test the assumption that Ho Chi Minh was "a tool of the 'worldwide Communist conspiracy.'" That is the sort of thing one took on faith, especially since it fit the postwar assumptions of the *Post* and the *Times* relative to the Cold War and "collective security." Our ignorance about Ho was further compounded as the years went on by the closed society policies of North Vietnam; correspondents were not allowed into Hanoi.

There were, in the 1950s, a few protesting voices. The *Chicago Tribune,* the Welch study shows, opposed U.S. involvement in Vietnam every step of the way. If this country wished to fight Communism, the *Tribune* maintained, let it fight it at home, not in the jungles of Asia. But that kind of thinking in the 1950s was dismissed as "isolationism"; it had no credibility among "internationalists" any more than the dissenting views of John Stennis, Wayne Morse or Ernest Gruening had credibility later on.

The John Birch Society was bitterly opposed in the 1960s to intervention in Vietnam: "In the long run you are going to see the fact that we are at war used increasingly, and ever more brazenly, to enable the Communists in government, in the press, in the pulpit and in every other division of our national life, to label all criticism of their captive administration as treasonous. You will see that administration begin to establish controls over the lives and actions of the American people which will make the regimentation we have had so far look like a study in free enterprise; and begin suppressing all opposition by the usual Communist police-state methods." That was not a credible viewpoint at the time, although the same rhetoric, substituting "fascist" for "Communist," is popular today on the left.

The point is that alternative viewpoints about Vietnam — persuasive viewpoints — were not being developed in any effective way by nongovernment institutions in the 1950s and were not being developed by the press itself. By the time American reporters began discovering Vietnam in the early 1960s, editorial positions were pretty well fixed and governmental policies had a momentum of their own.

There was another failing by the press. Newspapers did not examine the American potential for protracted war or systematically examine the reasoning behind the thesis that this country should not get bogged down in a land war in Asia. The Korean experience provided clear evidence of the low tolerance level in this country for "no-win" wars. Nevertheless, the American government during the 1950s was making military commitments all around the world, commitments that were reaffirmed by the Kennedy administration. The press could have explored through public opinion studies the governmental assumption that the country was prepared to make good on those commitments. But that was not done.

Newspapers function, as the Welch study indicates, as middlemen in a continuing dialogue between government and the governed, and when the dialogue is limited to a single point of view or single set of assumptions it has no more utility than an echo chamber. A polarized dialogue — right versus wrong — is not all that useful either, because the rhetoric too often obscures the realities.

What newspapers must do is to provide a forum for intellectual diversity of a range greater than A to B. They must also recognize, as Ben Bagdikian has put it, that they are not merely in the "printing" business; they are in the "information" business. This means that they need to develop the capabilities to acquire and process a far greater range of information than has been the case in the past. And they must have people with the skills to analyze and explain it. All this would cost money. It would alter many of the ancient routines of the trade. It would require new skills in the newsroom. But it would also provide newspapers — and the country — with alternatives to the echo-chamber trap that caught us up in the 1950s and to the dialogue of polarization that followed.

— July 27, 1971

FYI: Fun and Games?

It is not easy to convey indignation when what you are also feeling, deep down, is chagrin—the result is likely to be a strangled cry. Be that as it may, some response is indicated to the disclosure yesterday [July 22, 1971] that the "Buckley Papers," which we wrote about on page one of this newspaper a day earlier, were a fraud. To recall the first story: "High-ranking U.S. military officials twice recommended a 'demonstration' drop of atomic weapons in Indochina in late 1964 and early 1965, according to documents published yesterday by the conservative magazine *National Review*. . . ." The account went on in a serious and straightforward way to describe these alleged government documents, which had been presented by the *National Review* as "The Secret Papers They Didn't Publish"—as authentic additions, in other words, to the so-called Pentagon Papers which were published by the *New York Times,* this newspaper and others, and became the subject of a brief contretemps in the courts when the government attempted to suppress them.

So now we are told that the *National Review* papers were a parody, or a forgery, or whatever, and while this strikes us as a stunt well worthy of a college fun mag the fact remains that we were had, and in the worst sort of way, because the con-man in the case, Mr. William Buckley, is a colleague in a manner of speaking, being both a regular columnist and the editor of the *National Review.* We make this confession, strictly For Your Information, and by way of apologizing, in particular to those who may have read the first story and missed the second, and therefore may still be laboring under the impression that the original story was for real.

So much for our chagrin, which is not much relieved by the fact that a great many others were similarly taken in; the fact also is that some were not. As for indignation, it strikes us as not just sophomoric, but irresponsible to play games of this sort with an issue as deadly serious as the conduct of war policy and the manner of our tragic involvement in Vietnam. Mr. Buckley says he was only trying to point up the ease with which "forged documents would be widely accepted as genuine provided their content was inherently plausible."

Now this is a cute point for an ideologue to make on a television talk show, as was his further rhetorical question about the difference between publishing documents that have been "stolen" and publishing those that have been "forged." Leaving aside the question of theft, which has yet to be proved or even officially charged, at least insofar as the newspapers themselves are concerned, it seems to us that in our business there is, or ought to be, a rather considerable distinction to be made between documents or any other material that are authentic and those that are frauds.

Although the point could be argued, the *National Review* is widely considered to be a reliable purveyor of fact as well as of opinion of a particular stripe; thus the wire services and the Voice of America gave worldwide distribution to the Buckley Papers and to their suggestion that the United States had seriously considered the use of nuclear weapons for "demonstration" purposes in Vietnam; in these matters, the truth does not always catch up. And the truth, which is to say public understanding, is precisely what has been so tragically lacking from the start of our involvement in Vietnam. It is late in the day in this war for fun and games.

—July 23, 1971

Lessons From the Pentagon Papers

By Richard Harwood

The storm over publication of secret Pentagon papers contains lessons for all of us in the news business and for the country and the government as well.

The newspapers are learning from this episode and from the national loss of memory that has occurred since 1964 that their impact on public opinion in the United States is tragically limited. The substance and in some cases the precise details of virtually everything the *Washington Post* and the *New York Times* have printed from the Pentagon papers is ancient history. It was nearly all published while it was happening. And it was largely a futile enterprise; neither the public nor the congressional politicians were listening.

The government is learning something, too. It is learning that policy is poorly communicated and public opinion is poorly shaped by proxy. All through the early 1960s, government officials were anonymously "leaking" their fears and "options" for Vietnam through the press as a substitute for public candor and direct communication with the people. This produced considerable support for the government's zig-zag policies by most of the major newspapers, including the *Post* and the *Times*. But newspaper editorials are not necessarily the voice of the people, and newspapers, as is now evident, are inadequate instruments for public education.

What the public and politicians could learn from this experience is that if they sit there asleep in the back row while their destinies are being debated, they are in a poor position when the slumber ends to cry foul and search for scapegoats.

The facts of this particular case are that the *Post* and the *Times* and other large news organizations published thousands of stories, editorials and essays in 1964 describing the deteriorating military and political situation in Vietnam — just as it was described in the official memoranda and cables in the Pentagon papers. The various options and contingency plans being put before the President at that time were reported repeatedly and accurately — as they are now reported in the official papers.

The growing combat role of American forces was laid out in impressive detail on front pages all over the country — the first uses of napalm against suspected enemy villages, the commitment of U.S. helicopters and crewmen to the battlefields, the reconnaissance, bombing and strafing missions of U.S. aircraft in South Vietnam and Laos, the U.S. role in the training and transport of South Vietnamese raiding parties into North Vietnam, the participation of U.S. advisers and Special Forces teams in major battles, the use of U.S. troops in perimeter defense at military bases. The circumstances of the Tonkin Gulf incident, including the prior raids by

South Vietnamese forces against North Vietnamese territory, were reported accurately at the time. The possibilities of U.S. air raids on North Vietnam were reported and discussed in the press repeatedly far in advance of the event. U.S. casualty lists and the new funerals at Arlington National Cemetery received increasing prominence in the news as the war revved up in 1964.

"Today," one of our correspondents wrote in February, 1964, "there are 15,500 military personnel in South Vietnam; some 275 Americans have died, about 100 of them in combat, but there has been no outcry whatsoever at home for pulling out our troops. This attitude, one hopes, is an expression of maturing American opinion, of a willingness to face up to wars that are neither 'won' nor 'lost'; to accept the fact that the Korean War was the first of what probably will be a host of 'mean, frustrating and nerve-wracking wars,' the term Secretary of State Dean Rusk applied last April to the struggle in South Vietnam."

Following the Gulf of Tonkin incidents the *Times* editorialized: "United States determination to assure the independence of South Vietnam, if ever doubted before, cannot be doubted now by the Communists to the north or their allies."

A few days later the *Times* said: "The Americans went into Vietnam in 1954 to fill the vacuum left by the French and to contain the advance of communism in that part of Southeast Asia. The motives are exemplary and every American can be proud of them, but the crucial questions are: Can it be done? . . . Is this war necessary?"

These readings of "mature" and "united" American opinion toward the war were probably wrong. What the evidence from that time suggests is that despite the preoccupation of the newspapers and of the government with Vietnam, the public was both ill-informed and not greatly interested. The Gallup Poll in May, 1964, reported that 63 per cent of the American people had no opinion about the war or how it was going or what the United States should do. The reason for that, Gallup explained, was that this 63 per cent were paying no attention to developments in Southeast Asia; neither the newspapers nor the government had gotten their attention. Six months later, when the war fever in Washington and in the press was rising, the Council on Foreign Relations reported the results of another poll. One in four adult Americans, the council found, was not even aware that a war was going on in Southeast Asia.

What had they been told by the press? If they were readers of the *Washington Post,* they had been told in February that Secretary Rusk was saying that retaliation against North Vietnam was a future option in American policy, that "government sources" had made known plans for South Vietnamese guerrilla operations in North Vietnam, that contingency plans for a sea blockade and bombing attacks on the North had been drawn and that proposals for the commitment of U.S. troops were under study.

In March, *Post* readers were told that "preparations already are being made for the various kinds of direct action against North Vietnam that are considered most likely to get good results," that Secretary McNamara was leaving open "the option of direct military operations against North Vietnam," that napalm was being used on Vietnam villages, that U.S. naval forces were operating small patrol boats on Vietnam rivers. Various columnists—Joseph Alsop and Roscoe Drummond, among them—were writing approvingly of the possibilities of bringing "the war to the north."

In May and June and July the *Post* was full of gloomy accounts of the military and political situation in South Vietnam and there was widespread speculation in the paper that an "all-out war" might be in the offing. Secretary Rusk appeared at a background session of the Overseas Writers Club in Washington and spoke so belligerently that the European press said he had "delivered an ultimatum to Red China." Murrey Marder wrote in the *Post* that Rusk and the President were "signaling Communist China and Communist North Vietnam that they were running the risk of bringing the United States into a headon war." The war talk was so intense that Walter Lippmann chastised the administration for "making public declarations about our willingness and readiness to fight a great war in hypothetical and undefined circumstances . . . (the warning) should have been delivered privately through diplomatic channels."

On July 10, Arnold Beichman of the *Herald Tribune* reported the "specific details of a United States contingency plan" for bombing North Vietnam, a plan that contained a list of 400 North Vietnamese targets to be hit in retaliatory raids. Two weeks later, John Maffre of the *Post* published a detailed account of guerrilla raids into North Vietnam and reported that U.S. pilots were using "Vietcong rebels as 'live targets' in the course of training Vietnamese pilots."

In August, in addition to the extensive Tonkin Gulf coverage, there were detailed stories of the use of U.S. helicopter crews on combat missions in South Vietnam, on the Laos-Cambodia border operations by U.S. Special Forces teams, and on the CIA contract with "an American aviation company to airlift guerrillas and supplies behind enemy lines in North Vietnam and Communist-held sections of Laos."

Week after week similar stories were published and were given prominent space in the newspaper. But if the opinion polls at that time are valid, as one presumes, the public was simply not interested. Nor were most members of Congress.

There was assuredly no outcry and no demand for court injunctions from the administration against the "security breaches" involved in many of these newspaper reports. On the contrary, it is obvious in retrospect that various factions in the administration were deliberately and consciously "leaking" top secret plans and recommendations in order to build support for future U.S. actions. And it seems obvious, in retrospect, that both the administration and the newspapers were deluding themselves in assuming that "leaks" were an adequate substitute for the kind of public awakening and education that sometimes arises out of vigorous public debate by public officials. What may have been happening, as Douglass Cater has suggested in another context, is that the media were having more influence in making up minds *within* the government than in influencing the public whose support the administration was seeking.

People in the news business are now indicting themselves — wrongly — for not "telling the truth." Politicians, who ought to know better, are claiming that no one told them what was going on. And the administration charges, years after the fact, that security is breached by the recounting of ancient history. It is a strange spectacle.

— November 30, 1970

Peace Talks and Press Talks

By Jules Witcover

Ｐresident Nixon's press conference yesterday [January 31, 1973] marked the first step toward the fulfillment of a promise his press secretary, Ronald L. Ziegler, made on the last day of the first Nixon administration—that Mr. Nixon would have more press conferences in the second term than the 28 he had held in the first.

But yesterday's give-and-take, the first the press has had with the President in nearly four months, does not remove a serious concern for the future of the White House press conference raised by Ziegler when he discussed the matter on January 19.

"For the last year or so," Ziegler said by way of explaining the relatively low figure, "we have found ourselves in a situation in which a number of very sensitive negotiations were taking place."

The words were an echo of those uttered a few days earlier by the White House's director of communications and dispenser of glad tidings, Herbert G. Klein, in a breakfast meeting with reporters. Klein cited Vietnam and the Nixon trip to China as impediments to more sessions with the press.

The argument that such negotiations make press conferences too risky is not a new one in this administration. The President himself, in a post-election interview, said "it would not have been in the best interest of the country" to have held them during "delicate negotiations" last year.

But Klein's pointed reiteration of the defense inspired one of the beneficiaries of his glad tidings, Peter Lisagor of the *Chicago Daily News*, to remind Klein that "this administration did not invent negotiations."

The contention of Mr. Nixon and his two press aides that sensitive negotiations and an informed public must be mutually exclusive does not hold up under the test of presidential history.

Almost exactly 30 years ago, on January 9, 1943, Franklin D. Roosevelt held a two-hour press conference in his office and thoroughly discussed the new wartime budget he was about to send to Congress. Later that day, he secretly boarded a train to Miami and then a clipper plane that took him, by way of Trinidad, Brazil and Gambia, to the Casablanca Conference with Winston Churchill.

The circuitous route was an intricate security measure involving supersensitive negotiations on the very conduct of World War II, but that did not stop Roosevelt from meeting the press.

Harry S Truman similarly met the press in the most sensitive of times. On May 2, 1945, just six days before the German surrender that ended the war in Europe, Truman held a press conference in his White House office and fielded a number of delicate questions about the war and rumors of peace. When he couldn't answer, he simply said so. For example:

Q.—"Mr. President, have the negotiations which the State Department just told us about, being carried on by the Swedish government and the German government—have they broken down completely?"

A.—"I can't answer that."

But in the same session, on the extremely sensitive matter of the reported death of Hitler, this exchange took place:

Q.—"Mr. President, would you care to comment on the death of Adolph Hitler reported, or Mussolini?"

A.—"Well, of course, the two principal war criminals will not have to come to trial, and I am very happy they are out of the way."

Q.—"Well, does that mean, sir, that we know officially that Hitler is dead?"

A.—"Yes."

Q.—"Do we know how he died, Mr. President?"

A.—"No, we do not. . . . We have the best—on the best authority possible to obtain at this time that Hitler is dead. But how he died we are not —we are not familiar with the details as yet."

Q.—"Could you name the authority, Mr. President?"

A.—"I would rather not."

Even Mr. Nixon's old mentor, Dwight D. Eisenhower, met the press during periods of sensitive negotiation. In July, 1953, when President Syngman Rhee of South Korea was writing the book on armistice monkey-wrench-throwing that doubtless has been high on President Thieu's reading list, Eisenhower held three press conferences.

In the third, just four days before Rhee capitulated and the Korean armistice was announced, Eisenhower answered 10 questions on a wide range of foreign and domestic matters. When asked about points of misunderstanding in the Korean truce talks, he said:

"No, I can't pinpoint them for this reason: the whole arrangements to be made in the truce itself are still in executive session. They are confidential and secret, and I will not talk about anything that could be remotely interpreted as my violating that particular thing."

John F. Kennedy, just five days before the Bay of Pigs attack on April 17, 1961, and four days after it, held press conferences. In the first, he dissembled on Cuba, saying in response to a direct question, "there will not be, under any conditions, an intervention in Cuba by United States Armed Forces" and the government would "make sure that there are no Americans involved in any actions inside Cuba." In the second, he clammed up on Cuba, but in the two he answered a total of 46 questions on other subjects.

Lyndon B. Johnson, on the day before he sent U.S. Marines into the Dominican Republic on April 28, 1965, held a press conference in the East Room, said he deplored the fighting that had broken out there and expressed hope "that order can be promptly restored and that a peaceful settlement of the internal problems can be found."

Johnson then answered 14 questions—none on the Dominican crisis. It can be argued that in this instance, as in the Bay of Pigs, probing questioning at the press conferences not only would have done no harm to national security but might have obliged each President to think more about the public impact of his decision.

Even Richard Nixon, during the time White House officials later said he was engaged in secret, sensitive negotiations leading to his historic trip to Peking, held a press conference and answered a question on U.S.-China relations.

On June 1, 1971, in the East Room, he cited progress in the areas of trade and travel and quoted the old Chinese proverb that "a journey of a thousand miles begins with a single step." Six weeks later, Mr. Nixon announced that he would be taking the next step personally—obviously unimpeded by the fact he had held a press conference while the delicate negotiations arranging it were going on.

In his remarks to the press, at Camp David on November 27, 1972, Mr. Nixon took note of "the tendency . . . for an administration to run out of steam after the first four years, and then to coast, and usually coast downhill." His answer, he said, has been to shake up his team as it starts the second lap.

But if the President is worried about coasting, there may be no better insurance against that prospect than committing himself to frequent, even regular, hell-or-high-water press conferences. He has pledged "change that will work," and such a commitment would certainly be a change. Then it would be up to the press to make it work.

—February 1, 1973

Covering the White House and Watergate

Presidents and Pavlovian Journalism

By Richard Harwood

One of our news editors, Robert Webb, took out his ruler some time ago and used it to produce an interesting document. He found that in the 17 days preceding the November, 1970, elections, the front page of the *Washington Post* had a strong Republican flavor.

We printed in that period 30 page one stories about the GOP campaign, stories that took up 268 inches of front-page space. In the same period, we printed six front-page stories about the Democrats, stories that took up 35 inches of space. Along with the stories, we printed 15 front-page pictures of Republican campaigners (principally the President) that took up 306 inches of space and one picture of a Democrat that took up 10 inches of space: In sum, the Republicans got 12 times more space on our front page than the Democrats.

A graduate student in journalism may one day appropriate those numbers to prove something about the "one-party press" in America. If he does, he will be daft. The *Washington Post*, as our readers and the White House are well aware, is no organ of the Republican National Committee. But like most American newspapers, we are vulnerable to a syndrome that might be called Pavlovian journalism after the Russian who taught dogs to salivate when bells rang.

We salivated over the Republicans for one reason only—the President was out campaigning for them. No matter that he had very little to *say* that was significant or unpredictable at the whistlestops along the way. No matter that he *did* very little beyond waving at crowds. No matter that there was little or no evidence that what he said or did affected a single vote. The mere fact that he was out there was "important," we told ourselves, because Presidents are "important" men.

That kind of circular reasoning frequently affects our news judgments and results in statistical imbalances of the sort described in the Webb analysis. It says something about our sense of values and about our perspectives on the world.

We know, as everyone knows, that Presidents often say and do inconsequential things and that there is less substance to much of the presidential pageantry than meets the eye. But we have a tendency to overlook those things and to be mesmerized by presidential myths and stereotypes.

One explanation, Thomas Cronin of the Brookings Institution has suggested, is that there has grown up in this country a "textbook" conception of the presidency. It attributes to Presidents "omnipotent" and "moralistic-benevolent" dimensions that amount almost to a deification of the office and the men who occupy it. These myths, Cronin thinks, have been reinforced by the fact that Presidents now have nuclear weapons at their command. This has led people — wrongly — to "infer from a President's capacity to drop an A-bomb that he is similarly powerful in most other international or domestic policy areas."

People who work closely with Presidents quickly discover the limitations of the men and the job. Among White House staff members in the Kennedy-Johnson era, according to Cronin's findings, only 10 per cent thought a President has "very great impact" on policy matters. Twice as many thought he had "relatively limited impact." Official memoirs invariably reinforce the latter view.

Nevertheless, the news media tend to operate according to the "textbook" conception of the President. He commands space in the newspapers about as easily as he commands television and radio time. If he holds a news conference, anywhere from 150 to 300 journalists dutifully appear. If he travels anywhere, a planeload of news people follows him. He is treated, in short, as the pre-eminent American celebrity, which he is. What sets him apart in the news business from other celebrities is the weight we attach to his words and deeds.

There may be a bit of the "royal family" syndrome in this; witness the attention paid to the weddings of presidential daughters. There may be a bit of naivete in it, a sense of awe in the minds of journalists toward the office. After all, most Washington correspondents have little more *personal* contact with Presidents than the ordinary White House tourist. They deal with him from a distance, in most cases, and under formal circumstances such as a news conference or a ceremony. That is especially true now. Tete-a-tetes between Richard Nixon and individual journalists at the White House are virtually nonexistent. So he exists in their minds primarily as a symbol rather than as a familiar, flesh-and-blood human being. This creates mystery and helps create myths. Most editors are even further removed from the reality of the man and the office and their news judgments are affected by that fact.

The phenomenon of excessive deference to presidential "news" carries over to presidential candidates as elections draw nigh. Let a man declare for the presidency or become a prospect for the job and all of a sudden words that otherwise might never see print become very newsworthy.

Our practice, in short, is to apply different news standards to Presidents and to presidential candidates than we apply to ordinary mortals. Their platitudes become "pronouncements" and "declarations" and "policy statements." That is why the Republicans dominated our front page before the election and why a lot of obscure congressmen may become household words in the months ahead.

—June 14, 1971

The Problems With
Presidential Press Conferences

By Haynes Johnson

A s Al Smith used to say, in one of those obvious aphorisms so endear-
ing to politicians, the only cure for the ails of democracy is more
democracy. Today, many members of the Washington press corps would
apply that kind of reasoning to another subject. They think one solution
to the old problem of friction between the press and the President is self-
evident. Hold more presidential press conferences.

Meet more regularly. Restore the press conference to its former high
estate. Let it become, once again, the reporters' conference, not just a personal forum for the President. The President — and particularly this President — has permitted a worthy institution to deteriorate by increasingly
isolating himself from the press, and therefore the public.

Thus, the arguments. And if more evidence is needed to prove the
thesis, the reporters will point to the presidential press conference tonight
[December 10, 1970] as an example. Richard Nixon is meeting the press
for the first time since July. It will be only his fourth full-dress press conference this year, and only the 12th in the nearly two years of his presidency. It is an all-time low for a President. (Franklin Roosevelt met the
press twice a week, Harry Truman once every 10 days, and Dwight Eisenhower, John Kennedy and Lyndon Johnson held press briefings about
every two weeks.)

Deplorable condition, clearly. Well, here's a heretic's view. Press pride
notwithstanding, the public is missing little by the infrequent nature of
the conferences — at least, the kind of conferences we have seen in Washington of late.

Questions are often self-serving, or occasionally obsequious. There are
all too few sharp exchanges, or pointed follow-ups or relentless pursuits of
the sort that provide fresh insights into the President's thinking, or help
to explain his actions. Important topics are often ignored, or glossed over.
Under the eye of the television camera, the conferences have been transformed into nationwide theater. Style, not substance, wins acclaim and
builds reputations. Some of the questions are, in reality, speeches or personal points of view. The press, like other professions, is not without its
prima donnas.

So whatever else may be said about the failures of the press conferences,
part of the problem rests directly with the press itself.

Lest this article be misinterpreted as a rare and bold iconoclastic exercise, these kinds of criticisms are not original here. They have been expressed frequently — and by members of the press themselves. Hedrick

Smith of the *New York Times,* writing in the *Atlantic,* gave a detailed analysis of the President's press conference at the time of the Cambodian and Kent State crises. He found that conference "as real-life as a minuet, as illuminating as a multiplication table," and concluded: "President Nixon held the assembled reporters at bay as easily as Cassius Clay dabbling with a clutch of welterweights."

Alan L. Otten, in a *Wall Street Journal* column, pointed out another problem. Seldom does a reporter even try to ask a second question to clarify a subject he opened, Otten said. Then, turning to television, he commented that: "TV tends to inhibit tough, aggressive questioning. Most reporters are loath to appear loathsome to a nationwide audience, and so serve up puff-balls—would the President please 'comment on' such and such a subject?—instead of asking the hard, searching questions they should be asking and so often used to ask."

Jules Witcover of the *Los Angeles Times* [now of the *Washington Post*], in a thoughtful article for the *Columbia Journalism Review,* wrote of the unsubtle "planting" of questions by the administration, giving the President "even greater advantage than he ordinarily had." And just this week, a number of Washington correspondents met to explore ways to sharpen their professional performances at tonight's conference. They discussed such suggestions as limiting the number of questions asked, insuring follow-up questions, and letting senior correspondents select the kind of questions to be asked.

However those questions are resolved (and they themselves raise serious questions in turn about execution, individual independence, news management in reverse), there is no doubt about the main criticism. The press conference is in trouble. It is, as presently constituted and carried out, a terminal case. Rather than illuminating the workings of the government, it is all too often an exercise in tedium and pomposity.

The President's last conference, held in Los Angeles in July, probably fixed a new low. Some kind of record for long-windedness was set when a reporter asked:

"Mr. President, in regard to your anti-inflation policy and unemployment, especially among blacks, some statistics last June: the unemployment rate was 4.7 and among blacks it was 8.7. Locally here in the Los Angeles area, there are no specifics since no agency will speak out, but the limited concentrated survey by the Federal Bureau of Labor Statistics last year in South-Central and East Los Angeles brought it at 16.2 for blacks. Representative Augustus Hawkins has viewed the area and said that conditions are worse than in 1965 prior to Watts. . . ."

The reporter wandered on for another 70 words or so before finally asking, "The question is, will you continue your present anti-inflationary policy despite such warnings of rising employment rebellion?"

And the conference concluded on this tough note: "Mr. President, this press conference in Los Angeles is sort of a climax to the series of activities that you have described as bringing the government to the people—such as your recent meetings in Louisville, Fargo, Salt Lake City, and your work at the Western White House in San Clemente. What benefits do you see to you and to the country from such activity?"

When last seen, that softball had cleared the Coliseum and was heading out into the Pacific.

Those are not isolated examples. When the President returned from his first trip to Europe in 1969, he was asked:

"Mr. President, mindful of your ground rule against revealing contents of your conversations with leaders, I ask you this question: Did the atmosphere of mutual trust generated in your long conversations with Gen. de Gaulle give you any fresh indication, any fresh hope, that France might be helpful in the future of NATO, and/or France could be helpful in settling the war in Vietnam, either directly or indirectly?"

And Mr. Nixon, like his predecessors, has had to deal with the editorial-in-the-guise-of-a-question. Sarah McClendon, who represents a group of Texas papers, asked him this some time ago: "Mr. President, would you please tell us when you are going to make some real, honest-to-goodness changes in personnel in these bureaucrats who have been in power through many generations, who are still wasting the taxpayer's money and making errors on the war and policy and are unqualified to high jobs?"

The individual questions, whether sharp or otherwise, are not the real problem. Since the televised news conference has become the established format, several trends have developed. The conferences are attended by such large numbers of correspondents that they become unmanageable. An arbitrary 30-minute deadline further restricts the conference.

Suggestions for improvement are many: cutting back the number of correspondents permitted to attend, limiting the conferences to only a few major topics, or meeting longer in less formal surroundings. Those are all worthy ideas—but, good as they are, they are basically beside the point. The quality of the conferences will rise only when the nature of the question improves.

The old days, as ever, may look better in retrospect, and they do provide some notable examples of journalistic performance. One of the classic examples was the questioning of Dwight Eisenhower at a news conference during his first term of office.

The President met the press at a time when his Attorney General, Herbert Brownell, had asserted that Harry Dexter White was a Communist spy, leaving the strong implication that President Truman had knowingly appointed such a person to high office. The questions dealt almost exclusively with that issue. They resulted in a full airing of a major issue.

Reporters today understandably are concerned about their lack of access to the President and are frustrated by their inability to gain more insight into his thoughts and actions. But, in fairness, the problem (and its solution) is not only with the President. It lies also with the press.

—December 10, 1970

Questioning the President

By Charles B. Seib

The President and the press have met twice in the wake of his surprise shakeup of his official family. The contrast between the two encounters, both viewed by television audiences, raises serious questions about the way presidential news conferences are now conducted.

The first meeting was in the traditional format—a free-for-all in the East Room of the White House, with reporters clamoring for the President's attention and the usual hopscotching from subject to subject.

To borrow from the vocabulary of the Nixon oval office, the President stonewalled. The changes—which saw the firing of Defense Secretary James Schlesinger and CIA Director William Colby and a slight clipping of the wings of Henry Kissinger—were made, he said, simply to get "my guys" onto his national security team. As for Nelson Rockefeller's withdrawal that day from consideration for the second spot on the 1976 ticket, that was Rockefeller's decision and there was nothing more to be said about it.

Some of the press's questioning was aggressive, and frequent use was made of the follow-up question, an innovation started early in the Ford administration. In the old days, a reporter was limited to a single question, no matter how inadequate the answer might be. Under the follow-up rule, he or she can ask a second question.

When it was introduced, the follow-up was hailed as the greatest journalistic advance since the typewriter. It was supposed to bring a modicum of order to the helter-skelter of the news conference and discourage the President from ducking a question because he knew the next one would probably wheel off in another direction. But in the post-shakeup conference, the follow-up proved no match for the President's determination to stick to his "my guys" story line. The questioning was fragmented and the stone wall was not breached.

On Sunday, November 9, the second encounter occurred. The President was questioned by four journalists on an hour-long "Meet the Press" program. The session was extremely productive. After first maintaining that his earlier explanation of the shakeup was "the simple truth," Mr. Ford disclosed that there had been a "growing tension," presumably between Schlesinger and Kissinger, and that he wasn't comfortable with tension. Hence the housecleaning. He also responded informatively on a wide range of other subjects, ranging from a possible future in the administration for Richard Nixon (he saw none) to the possibility of giving advance notice of his vice presidential selection (he thought it might be done).

A comparison between the two sessions is unavoidable. The first was chaotic, although not as chaotic as those of the last days of the Nixon administration. It may have raised some questions in the public mind about the President's early promises of openness and candor, but it produced little of substance for those trying to understand the firings and the Rockefeller decision.

The second, on the other hand, was more effective. The calm atmosphere, the ability to pursue a question to a responsive answer, the firm hand of the moderator all helped make it informative and useful.

This is not to say that the free-for-all should be abandoned. There is a unique democracy about it that would be lost if the press were required to interview the President by committee. Also, even the most unproductive press conference conveys information about the mood and attitudes of the President. But changes should be considered. There have been a number of proposals. It has been suggested that instead of shouting for the President's attention, the reporters should register in advance their desire to ask a question and that someone other than the President—perhaps a person from the press itself—should call on them. Another suggestion is that the conference be conducted on a subject-by-subject basis, with a referee, again possibly someone from the press, deciding when a subject has been adequately covered. Still another is that the White House regulars be allowed to question the President first, after which the conference would be thrown open to all accredited correspondents. And there have been others.

Academics and others outside the press come up with such proposals from time to time, but the White House press corps is reluctant to accept any restructuring. Perhaps the time has now come for the regulars themselves to consider changes. A good way to start would be a session with the tapes of the November 3 news conference and the November 9 "Meet the Press" program.

—November 15, 1975

FYI: The Press and the Press Secretary

In the waning days of the Eisenhower administration, a television producer devoted a long program to what was then an unusual subject: White House correspondents, their lives and thoughts. You can measure how far we have come in relations between Presidents and the press merely by savoring for a second the title of the program, "The White House Boswells." Any notion today that the White House press corps is composed of adoring biographers of a President is will-o'-the-wisp. Not only has the relationship of press to President changed substantially, but so has the concomitant relationship between press and press secretary. Once there was a certain civility that governed these relationships. But time, Vietnam, Watergate and myriad modern phenomena appear to have wiped that civility away, possibly for a very long time.

Where once the atmosphere was adversary, it is now frequently acrimonious, hostile for the sake of hostility and mean-spirited for no reason that any of the participants can lucidly and persuasively articulate. We take this topic up—For Your Information, and as a part of our occasional effort to enlighten you about the workings of our business—because both sides appear to believe they are acting in your interests as reader, viewer, citizen, voter. And we have a document that—without exactly solving anything—offers an illuminating case study of the problem.

The document is a study, conducted over an 8-month period by the National Press Club, the second it has conducted in a little less than three years on the quality of the relationship between White House and press. Simply to say the document is at times unfriendly to the White House will not be as persuasive as this sample excerpt: "Press Secretary Ron Nessen, who has consistently had grave problems with foreign affairs, plunged to his nadir on the recent China trip by what many White House reporters believe was the most inept performance in modern times in handling the press relations of a president's mission overseas." To add emphasis, Mr. Nessen was advised to improve on his "disastrous nonperformance." Mr. Ford, although credited with improving relations with the press over what they were under Richard Nixon, is nonetheless chided for lapses of candor.

Disturbingly, at no point does the report provide for a direct White House rebuttal, either from Mr. Nessen or from the President. There is a passage from a Nessen speech but that is not at all the same thing as giving Mr. Nessen an opportunity to explain, for example, what factors—such as the cooperation he had from the President or other officials—may have contributed to his problems in China. But that is not the most serious flaw in this report. The flaw that strikes the reader immediately is that the White House press corps seems in this report to assume a few things that good reporters have no right to assume. One of these is that press secretaries are merely an adjunct to good reporting. In the main, press secretaries, wherever they are found, are dedicated to the business of promoting, or at the very least, protecting, the image of those who pay their wages. They are not, by and large, to be mistaken for dutiful, or even reliable purveyors of news, on the record or off.

At one point in the Press Club report, there is this astonishing statement: ". . . a press secretary must probe within the White House to learn what is going on and we are not persuaded that Nessen has done all he could in that regard." Well, for our part, you could make that statement read: ". . . a White House reporter must probe within the White House to learn, etc." Somewhere along the line, the idea seems to have taken hold, in some reporters' minds, that the press office is a service for them, like transportation or hotel accommodations, to be complained about when found lacking as one would lodge a protest with the assistant night manager.

Somewhere between Vietnam and Watergate, that is to say between the Kennedy administration and the Nixon administration, the press office bureaucracy grew by leaps and bounds. People began expecting things of that operation that they could probably have done very well without—reams of statistics on demand, background on this and that, access at times to remote figures in the administration, and the like. There was a time when reporters routinely found those things on their own. They didn't travel in herds, but worked the phones or made connections and developed sources who gave them information not available in open briefings or in clean mimeographed form.

Much is responsible for the creation of the herd. Television, for one. When the networks put a story on the air, the individual newspaper reporter is under great pressure from the home office to duplicate it, or explain why not. The group effort has meant homogenized news and less of the individual reporting that is based on a long afternoon trudging around from source to source. As a result, to quote one White House reporter, "The (daily press) briefings have taken on a life of their own. They have become the source for daily stories that don't reflect what's going on. They have become a dueling exercise . . ."

Needless to say, a dueling exercise sometimes draws responses that help the reader understand the recession, detente or Angola. But that has never been enough; perhaps the next time the National Press Club sets out to study a local problem in the press, it might want to examine the current state of old fashioned reportorial enterprise.

—January 3, 1976

The Goat Feeding at the LBJ Ranch

By Richard Harwood

SAN ANTONIO, Tex. — Norman Mailer, having nothing better to do a few years ago, consigned himself to the training camps of Sonny Liston and Floyd Patterson. He was fascinated by the publicity buildup before the Big Fight, although there was nothing complicated about the techniques.

Each day (or several times a day) public relations artists hired by the fighters tossed out odd bits of fiction and trivia for the consumption of insatiable sports writers from around the world. Mailer invented a phrase for the ritual. He called it "Feeding the Goat" and concluded that the mass media, like other varieties of goats, would devour almost anything thrown their way.

The Goat is now in Texas for the New Year, drawn by the irresistible presence of the President and by the prospect of heavy holiday feasting. The diet can be rich, as it was at yesterday's press conference, when the President himself was dishing it out. But this is the exception; as a rule, most days produce more famine than feast.

It is not for the lack of professional Goat Feeders. The President's publicity staff is here en masse, attended by secretaries, messengers and mimeograph machines. Nor is it for any lack of effort on their part. A regular Feeding is conducted each day at 10:30 a.m. by the White House press secretary, George Christian, or one of his earnest assistants. At that hour, writers, cameramen and broadcasters assemble in the Feeding Room at the El Tropicano Motel and hungrily wait for the ritual to begin.

We are invariably let down. Instead of raw meat and rich sweets, the fare is dry little scraps brought in from the presidential ranch 70 miles away.

Such things as: "The President today received a report that vocational rehabilitation is good for the handicapped."

Or: "The President today signed a bill to equalize pay, allowances and other perquisites for certain members of the Government Medical Corps."

Or: "The President today talked with John Doe, a 30-year-old member of his staff, who was educated at Harvard and the Sorbonne and was highly regarded by his previous employer."

Or: "The President was giving thought today to a variety of problems, among them international developments, the budget, inflation, unemployment and health care. I am not at liberty to say what his thoughts may have been."

Goats can perhaps maintain life on a diet of this kind but it is not the stuff from which big reputations or big headlines are made. And so, the tendency is to demand from the Feeders a more adequate diet.

"Does the President intend to authorize American troops to invade Cambodia in pursuit of the Viet Cong?"

A hurt look crosses the face of Secretary Christian and he replies, in the manner of Mother Hubbard: "You know I can't get into those matters."

Another occasion finds the assistant press secretary, Tom Johnson, distributing tidbits about "high level" budget discussions at the ranch.

"Can you give us any figures?" one asks.

The reply is, "No."

"Well, can you at least tell us what this year's budget figure is going to be?"

"I'm very sorry," the assistant press secretary responds. "I've been trying to get some of those figures from Washington. We didn't bring any with us."

At that moment, one longs for Washington, where Goat Feeders can be found on any street corner, in any corridor of the bureaucracy, in any cranny of the Capitol. But here the press is at the mercy of Christian and his staff. It is not even possible to roam around the ranch, which is sealed off like a Balkan fortress. Our world is defined by the walls of the El Tropicano Feeding Room.

This raises, of course, the inevitable question: Whose interests are served by these ritualistic Feedings? The President's? The public's? Or the Goats'?

From the meager diet found in Texas this week, one might conclude that the ritual is purely for the convenience and needs of the media. But even that is not certain. One of the President's publicity agents approached a hollow-cheeked reporter one morning with a mild rebuke. "I hear," he said, "that yesterday you wrote that nothing much was happening at the ranch. Did you, by chance, miss the Feeding?"

—January 2, 1968

Portrait of a Press Rehearsal

By Robert C. Maynard

On October 10, 1972, the *Washington Post* reported that evidence had been uncovered linking the break-in at the Democratic National Committee's headquarters to an extensive campaign of political sabotage, conducted by officials of the White House and the Committee for the Re-election of the President. The story named Donald Segretti as one of the agents involved in the sabotage campaign and described dirty tricks perpetrated against various Democratic primary campaigns. Five days later the Post connected Dwight Chapin, then Mr. Nixon's appointments secretary, with Segretti.

Now, courtesy of memos provided by former White House counsel John W. Dean III, we are able to gain some insight into the manner in which members of President Nixon's staff decided in October to respond to those disclosures in the press. We also gain some idea of what they considered to be their obligation to inform the American people.

Chapin's response to the charges in the *Washington Post* came on October 13 in a terse statement of 80 words. It said that the *Post* story was based on "hearsay and is fundamentally inaccurate." He denied knowing E. Howard Hunt, admitted having known Segretti "since college days," but "I certainly have never discussed with him any phase of the grand jury proceedings in the Watergate case. Beyond that, I don't propose to have any further comment."

Aware that such a response was bound to be unsatisfactory to the press, officials at the White House set about preparing for the next meeting of the White House press secretary with reporters.

The scene is the Roosevelt Room of the White House on October 15, 1972. Those present were, according to Dean, John Ehrlichman, Ronald Ziegler, Patrick Buchanan, Richard Moore, Chapin, Dean and—by some fluke of history—Chapin's secretary. She took notes, which have become Witness Exhibit 22 accompanying Dean's testimony before the Ervin committee.

As Dean has told the committee, the purpose of the meeting was to prepare Ziegler to answer questions about the Segretti connection. Dean testified that many similar meetings had occurred in the White House, but it would take 200 more pages of testimony to describe them.

In just about 10 pages, we can get the idea of how those sessions were conducted. They were devil's advocate sessions in which Ziegler ran through the standard denial; then others present either supplemented his position or attempted to shoot the kinds of holes in it that they imagined the press would attempt to shoot.

"Now I can tell you," Ziegler says early in his rehearsal, "I have nothing more to say or add on this subject beyond what Dwight Chapin said in his statement. But I can tell you this. At no time has anyone in the White House or this administration condoned such activities as spying on individuals, surveillance of individuals, or sabotaging campaigns in an illegal way." He goes on to note that "the President has said before, and I will repeat again: He does not condone this type of activity."

We see again the studied manner in which the aura of the White House is used as a device to quiet questions. Ziegler again: "I am not going to inject the White House into these stories. I am not going to assume the responsibility from this podium and from the White House press room to answer every unfounded story based on hearsay or unidentified sources. . . ."

Ehrlichman offers some augmentation at various points and is especially adroit at wrapping the mantle of the White House around accused staff members. He would have Ziegler say: "Dwight Chapin is terribly offended at the treatment he got over the weekend. I approached him (on) the possibility of coming out here" to the press briefing. "He said he would never again speak to any member of the press and he would like your apologies. . . ."

Moore offers language to buttress that stance of reproach of the press for its behavior: "What is the right of anyone to expect an answer from this podium on a story based on sources you will not reveal. Good citizens are being vilified based on irresponsible, unidentified stories and stories which draw broad-sweeping conclusions."

Then they got down to the specifics of how to deal with Segretti's dirty tricks. It is not clear from the fragmentary transcript who is the author of this language:

"As a man who has worked in campaigns for X number of years and has seen many pranks and hoaxes, it occurred to me we should have our own Dick Tuck (as a political prankster) in this campaign. Gordon Strachan recalled that our old friend, Don Segretti, was coming out of the Army in September."

It continues in the same casual vein: "We called him and he expressed interest in the assignment of being counteragent. . . . On that basis, I said to him that perhaps I could get an okay for (him) to be supported and take off on (his) own on activities as long as they were legal."

As for the President's personal lawyer supplying the cash: "I referred him to Mr. (Herbert) Kalmbach, who did supply funds which would allow him to act on his own for a few months."

Segretti was to have been treated as a distant relative off on a lark: "The most I heard was a postcard or a clipping from a newspaper."

It gets sticky when those at the rehearsal contemplate involving Mr. Nixon, when someone in the room suggests that he issue a statement.

Ehrlichman didn't care too much for that idea: "Chapin is the White

House, and the separation—you bridge the separation when you get the President in it."

Dean suggests at several points that one tack to take is to assure the newsmen that "we are looking into (the charges) and we are going to have a response for you." Chapin, according to the transcript, suggests that Ziegler say, "I am not going to dignify desperation politics."

Occasionally, the devil's advocates cut through the transcript of the rehearsal with a piercing question: "Ron, that was a self-righteous, self-serving statement. Did Dwight Chapin, the President's appointments secretary, a man who meets with the President regularly, hire Segretti and instruct him to engage in sabotage?"

Ziegler: "Gentlemen, I have nothing to add to what Mr. Chapin has already said on this and that the story is fundamentally inaccurate and based on hearsay."

Devil's Advocate: "But Ron, why don't you just ask Dwight or why doesn't the President ask him. Did he or did he not hire Segretti?"

Ziegler: "Gentlemen, I have nothing to add to what Chapin has already said on the subject."

The following morning, Ziegler was questioned by the White House press corps. He was asked if the President was concerned about the allegations of Chapin's connections with Segretti. Ziegler responded that the President's concern "goes to the fact that stories are being run that are based on hearsay, innuendo, guilt by association and character assassination."

Surveillance, Ziegler added, was not "condoned by anyone in this administration, and are not directed by anyone in this administration." When pressed, Ziegler said: "Here again, I am not going to dignify with comment from the White House stories that are based on sources which do not reveal themselves and hearsay."

What the episode proves is that only a misleading fragment of the truth known to at least some of the men who participated in the Ziegler rehearsal was shared with the press and, thus, the American public.

—June 28, 1973

A Revealing Performance of the Press

By Kenneth Crawford

President Nixon's San Clemente press conference on August 22, 1973, has been analyzed, criticized, defended and commented upon in exhaustive detail. Why shouldn't the performance of the White House press corps, whose questions provoked the much-discussed answers, be evaluated too?

It was a revealing performance on both sides—perhaps more revealing of the state of mind of reporters who cover the White House than of the President who occupies it. He was for the most part repeating and elaborating what he had said before or what had been said before on his behalf. The reporters were being exposed to public view as they had not been for a long time.

What showed through some of the questioning, though not all of it or even most of it, was a degree of hostility unprecedented in the give and take between the working press and successive Presidents. Most of this can be attributed, no doubt, to the unprecedented character of the Watergate scandals. But not all of it.

The result must have seemed to the national television audience, or to a considerable part of it, a vivid dramatization of the 1972 Agnew thesis that the press is so biased against the President and his administration that it could not be fair to them if it tried, which it doesn't.

Such an impression would be unjust to the press as a whole but a few of its representatives at San Clemente asked for it. Their questions were fair enough in substance but the manner of their asking, in some cases, was less than civil. The First Amendment doesn't impose an obligation on the free press to be needlessly offensive in its dealings with elected officials.

There was, for example, the questioner who prefaced his inquiry with the comment that he respected the office of the presidency, the implication being that he did not respect the present holder of that office. This, however it was intended, appeared snide and gratuitous, not to say pompous. A reporter's attitude toward the presidency is not a matter of intense interest to the nation—not in prime time anyway.

Then there were questions as to whether the President didn't think he owed an apology to the American people for his covert bombing of Cambodia, whether he hadn't made a subtle attempt to bribe a federal judge by offering him the directorship of the FBI, whether he hadn't considered resigning, whether in 1970 he hadn't approved a plan to break laws against burglary, mail tampering, etc.

These were all legitimate areas of inquiry. But the way the questions were asked suggested that the object of the questioners was to display their own censorious opinions rather than to elicit information or explore the President's attitudes. It would seem that the reporter's function either has been changed by television or that it is misunderstood by some of the trade's current practitioners.

Nobody asked the questions: "Why don't you commit political hara-kiri in expiation of your obvious sins?" But the purport of the most brutally put questions was not very different from that. Even a President is entitled under our system to the presumption of innocence until proved guilty.

If the purpose of these questions was to humiliate a chief executive already humiliated by Watergate, the method was self-defeating. The effect was of a President beset by fierce enemies. The performance could not but have gained him sympathy.

The fact is that the press conference format has been useful to Presidents in the past and can be again. It casts the President as one against many; he is in a sense the underdog even when gently handled.

The harsher the questioning the better a President fares in press conferences. The irony of the San Clemente performance was that the press, or the most hostile part of it, played into its villain's hands. The rough questions couldn't have been better for Mr. Nixon had he written them himself. They were sympathy-getters of the most effective kind.

Most of the reporters at San Clemente were White House regulars — permanently assigned to cover the presidency. They are in a sense an elite corps, the White House being in these times a choice beat. It was not always so. Up to the Hoover administration it was a training ground for the young and inexperienced. Since Roosevelt it has been a hunting ground for seasoned journalists.

The regulars constitute a relatively small, self-contained group. The White House press room since the advent of the Nixon administration has not been a happy place. The camaraderie the press enjoyed with President Kennedy and his circle is no more. Information is hard to come by.

Frustrations have been taken out on the press secretary at daily briefings. These sessions have become downright ugly at times — on both sides. The querulous few seem to vie with each other to see who can be toughest. It is a situation in which the good opinion of one's peers is not commanded by moderation. Yet some of Washington's best and most judicious reporters are White House regulars.

The consensus among reporters is that bad blood between Nixon administration functionaries and the press derives from the President's penchant for secrecy and withdrawal, which filters down through his command. But on the other side of White House partitions the complaint is that the reporters are implacable — that nothing Mr. Nixon could do would win him much favor in the press room.

A return to something like normal civility in relations between the President, who, like it or not, apparently will be around until 1976, and the

White House press might be mutually beneficial. But it is not likely.

More restraint on the part of the press is needed, not to spare the President's feelings, but to spare the press a reputation for immoderate bias. Its standing with the public is probably not much better, if any better, than Mr. Nixon's, Watergate and all. The press has gained public confidence from the excellent job it has done on Watergate but not enough to coast on.

The President might shake off some of his feeling of persecution if the White House atmosphere were cooled off. And the press might still fulfill its obligations, retaining the watchdog's bite while curbing its Pavlovian bark.

—August 27, 1973

Mr. Ehrlichman's Interview, Case Study in the Contradictions of Watergate

By Robert C. Maynard

> *Sen. Montoya: Now, on July 21, you were quoted in an article in the* New York Times *as being in favor of releasing the tapes which are in controversy. Did you make that kind of statement?*
>
> *Mr. Ehrlichman: Well, I have had a lot of trouble with quotations in the* New York Times, *Senator, and that is one of them.*

As Watergate stories go, it was hardly earthshaking. Simply put, John Ehrlichman, whose defense posture and strategy have been intimately linked to President Nixon's, told a reporter something that journalists on two continents took to mean that he favored the release of the White House secret tape recordings. And he was quoted as saying it only a day before the Nixon administration said that the tapes would not be released.

Precisely what Ehrlichman said, and the circumstances under which he spoke, have become a matter of dispute. As with much else that has passed between the Nixon administration and the press, especially regarding Watergate, the media consumer has had to decide in each dispute in whom to have faith.

Sometimes, because of the clouded character of the material, the choice has been difficult. Deciding whether Colson-told-Dean-what-Ehrlichman-says-Haldeman-told-Clawson-Dean-told-him-about-what-Colson-said has left many a citizen limp with confusion.

For that reason, the exchange outside his house in Virginia between Ehrlichman and Gerald Seymour of Independent Television News of London about the presidential tapes is significant and interesting. What they said to each other about the tapes is on film. Moreover, the circumstances under which they said it can be corroborated to some extent by disinterested bystanders.

It would have been easy for readers of the *Washington Post* and the *New York Times* to have missed the story altogether. It appeared in paragraph 13 of the lead story of the *Washington Post* on July 21, 1973, a Saturday. The three-paragraph insert said:

"One major figure in the Watergate case, former Nixon aide John D. Ehrlichman, said yesterday he was 'delighted' to know the tapes had been made and he expected 'they will be sort of the ultimate evidence in this thing.'

"Ehrlichman, interviewed by the British Independent Television News, said the tapes 'certainly' should be produced for the committee.

"'I may have said some things about some people to the President that were very frank and candid and unvarnished,' he said, 'but as far as events or circumstances or my position in this whole controversy, I don't have a thing to worry about as far as those tapes are concerned.'"

After paragraph 18 of its main Watergate story, the *Times* added a "shirttail" story from London saying essentially what the *Post*'s story said.

The *Times* story, four paragraphs from the Associated Press, ended with this sentence:

"Asked if he thought the tapes should be released by the President, Mr. Ehrlichman said: 'Certainly.'"

It is to the use of that quoted word, "certainly," that Ehrlichman took exception. When it appeared on the AP wire from London, a reporter in Washington undertook to confirm the story with Ehrlichman.

The reporter, Barry Kalb of the *Washington Star-News,* reached Ehrlichman at home that Friday morning, July 20, and told him what the AP was moving on its wires from London.

Ehrlichman told Kalb his actual views had been misrepresented in the AP dispatch. "They were asking me if the tapes would clear up any question," Kalb recalls Ehrlichman telling him, "and I said 'certainly.'"

Kalb said he then phoned the local office of the AP and told a newsman he knows there that Ehrlichman denied the substance of the agency's report. On that basis, the AP man said, he called New York, told the agency headquarters that AP's story had been challenged by the source and suggested it be checked further.

For a little more than an hour, the AP withheld the story. New York notified London AP that the story was being challenged. London obtained a transcript of the interview, as aired on Independent Television—the private competitor of the government-owned BBC—and sent it to New York.

When New York AP received the transcript from London, the story was released, this time with some more from the interview quoted in an additional paragraph.

Seymour and officials of ITN insist that "not a scissors went in" to the portion of the interview ITN broadcast on the tapes controversy. The tape discussion was aired intact. Here is that portion of the interview, as it was broadcast and as it appears in the ITN transcript:

Seymour: The matter of the secret tapes in the Oval Office, did you know about those, Mr. Ehrlichman?
Ehrlichman: No, I didn't.
Seymour: They could perhaps vindicate you, couldn't they?
Ehrlichman: I would think they will be sort of the ultimate er, the ultimate evidence in this thing.
Seymour: You'd want those produced, would you?
Ehrlichman: Oh, certainly, certainly. I don't have, er, thinking back I may have said some things about some people to the President that were very frank and candid and unvarnished, but as far as events or circumstances or my position in this whole controversy, I don't have a thing to worry about as far as those tapes are concerned. I'm delighted they're there.

We will return to the question of how Seymour obtained this remarkable interview with Ehrlichman, what Ehrlichman said of those circumstances and what a witness says. First, Ehrlichman's answer to Sen. (Joseph M.) Montoya as to what he told the reporter, as it appears in the official transcript of the proceedings of the Ervin committee:

Ehrlichman: . . . this fellow said something to the effect, "Do you have anything to worry about if these tapes get out?"

And I said, "No I don't think I have anything to worry about. I didn't know I was being taped, but I don't think I said anything there that would, that I would be ashamed of."

And he said, "Well, then you think the President ought to release these?"

And I said, "Well, you know you have got to look at this from two standpoints. Certainly from my standpoint I have no problem, but he has a much larger picture to look at."

Well, the word "certainly" is what carried on the wire, and the rest of the sentence didn't get carried, and so I saw the wire story and it said, "Ehrlichman today in response to a question, 'Should the President release these tapes?' said, 'certainly.'"

Well what I said was, in effect, "Certainly I don't have anything to worry about but the President has got a lot more worries than I have about the country and the separation of powers and his relationship with the Congress and so on."

Now, having just said that sentence, I will bet you the *New York Times* tomorrow says, "Ehrlichman says the President has a lot more to worry about than he does."

A journalist in his thirties, Seymour does general assignment reporting for ITN. The week before he came to Washington, he'd been in the Bahamas for the independence story.

Stopping in Washington, he suggested to his colleague and friend Mike Brunson, the ITN correspondent here, that he might take a run at an interview with Ehrlichman.

As he recalled it in a telephone conversation from London a few days ago, Seymour set out from Washington in a taxicab for Great Falls, Va., late Wednesday afternoon, July 18, to find Ehrlichman's house.

Seymour had no intention of trying for a filmed interview that evening, he said, and so did not bring along a film crew.

"It was my idea that Ehrlichman might be willing to talk about life in his household since the whole disgrace of Watergate and the loss of power and so forth," Seymour said. "I arrived at the house at about 6 that evening and found a *Newsweek* photographer there."

Ed Streeky, a Washington free-lance photographer on assignment for *Newsweek,* remembers Wednesday the 18th vividly. "When I got out there, hoping to get some shots of Ehrlichman, there were some kids riding by his house on horseback," Streeky recalled. "They shouted at me, called me a snoop and threw eggs at me. They told me I had no right to be there, that it was a private road."

Seymour and Streeky, strangers until then, waited together for Ehrlichman's arrival, after Seymour rang the doorbell and was told by Mrs. Ehrlichman that her husband would be home around 7.

When Ehrlichman arrived, Seymour spoke with him and told him of his desire for a "soft" interview, one that would explore family life and circumstances, not the hard details of Watergate. Ehrlichman, to Seymour's delight and surprise, was readily agreeable. They made an appointment for 9 the following morning.

Streeky fired off a few frames as Seymour and Ehrlichman chatted that evening, but the light was fading. Since he knew he would be able to obtain better shots in the morning, he decided to wait.

At 8:30 the following morning, Seymour and a film crew set up a camera on a tripod outside the Ehrlichman home. At 10 minutes before 9, Seymour, anxious to get underway, rang the doorbell, only to be told by Mrs. Ehrlichman that her husband was still eating breakfast and would be out at 9.

"Right on the dot of 9," Seymour reported later, Ehrlichman emerged from his home. "He was in a most affable and friendly mood," Seymour recalled.

The microphone Seymour chose to use would later prove to be significant. Ehrlichman was wearing a bow tie that morning and Seymour clipped a small microphone on the front of his shirt. It is plainly visible in the film and in the photographs Streeky took as the interview proceeded.

They talked for 15 minutes, consuming more than 400 feet of color film, stopping once to change the film magazine, and then continuing on for a few more minutes. Ehrlichman talked about the effect of Watergate on his life, of having more time with his family, of their plans to leave Washington: "It's the most expensive city in the country, I guess."

The neighbors have been "just terrific" in their support and he said he thinks they believe his version of the Watergate story.

He doesn't think any member of Congress is "gunning" for him, Ehrlichman said, but he conceded that "I've broken a few hearts in Congress by saying that we can't build that dam, or he can't have that appointment. . ."

One week after that interview, on Thursday, July 26, in the morning session of the Watergate hearings, Sen. Montoya asked about the quotation in the *New York Times* and received Ehrlichman's response that "I have had a lot of trouble with quotations in the *New York Times* . . . and that is one of them."

Ehrlichman then went on to testify to Sen. Montoya and the rest of the Ervin committee as to the circumstances under which he gave the interview, before contradicting its substance as to the tapes.

"What happened," Ehrlichman said of the interview with Seymour, "was that I gave a television interview to a fellow; you know they come out and sit on my lawn and as I come out in the morning, it's pretty well unavoidable. . ."

He then went on to his version of the conversation, placing "certainly" in a context the film does not support. Nor does the film support the contention that Ehrlichman was taken by surprise and said just a few words on the run, words which were later misinterpreted by the press.

People stumbling over reporters on their front lawn in the morning don't stop and allow the pesty reporter to clip his own microphone onto their shirts.

More than that, when it was all over, Seymour asked Ehrlichman if he would get in his car and drive it slowly out of the driveway so that British viewers could see a major Watergate figure driving off to work.

Ehrlichman did indeed drive off somewhere, leaving Seymour behind to pack his gear and head home to London with something of a prize for his television station. It would be 24 hours before it went on the air, and at that, the ITN only used about one minute and seven seconds of the 15 minutes of film.

When it finally was broadcast, the story was playing beside such other developments as the hoaxing of Sen. Ervin by a caller making believe he was Secretary of the Treasury Shultz, the departure of Mr. Nixon from the hospital, and the first firm indications that the President would withhold the tapes Ehrlichman seemed to think on Thursday it would be all right to release.

Seymour talked about his experience with Watergate America after having returned to London from yet another assignment, this one in the Mideast.

After all that running around, Seymour said, he felt "a bit knackered," a British expression that means very weary, precisely the way many Americans have come to feel about the contradictions of Watergate.

—August 4, 1973

The Press: A Lack of Vigor

By Haynes Johnson

In these post-Watergate days of self-congratulations among members of the American press, it is popular to hear all the old journalistic chestnuts about rugged independence and the people's right to know and the special adversary role that must exist between journalists and public officials. Watergate, it is being said, was the American press' finest hour, a classic example of what freedom of the press is all about.

The Nixon administration, ironically, is lending credence to this impression of an all-powerful press performance. Vice President Agnew has warned his "good friends and old sparring mates in the nation's press" that their splendid Watergate role ("to their great credit") has now changed. In the weeks and months ahead, he says, the news media will be put to an acid test in deciding how to handle "those sensational leaked-source stories that might boost circulation but which could also malign the innocent and help to acquit the guilty."

A presidential propagandist, Pat Buchanan, has mounted a familiar administration counterattack. In his view, the liberal, elitist, Eastern press axis is up to its old conspiratorial tricks. It is carefully orchestrating a campaign designed to discredit the President and arrogantly "demand that he surrender a slice of his government to his ancient adversaries." Other administration aides have been busily promoting the wisdom of a *London Times* editorial that takes the American press to task for conducting a presidential "trial by newspaper allegation."

And while the White House is anxiously awaiting—and assiduously trying to discredit—the forthcoming testimony of John Dean, this private word is being passed from some people in the Executive Mansion: The polls are wrong, the President is still immensely popular, and the press will pay the penalty for its excesses in the Watergate coverage.

A Permissive Tabby-Cat

All this is heady material for the American press, particularly as the accuracy of so many controversial Watergate reports continues to be confirmed. The trouble with these accolades is that, with a few shining exceptions, they aren't deserved. Far from being the fiercely independent government interrogator of vaunted legend, by and large the press has been a permissive tabby-cat. Its record on Watergate, as media critic Ben Bagdikian has said, is hardly praiseworthy. The vast majority in the press, as he has noted, were only spectators at "the biggest political story of our time."

But the problem of the press goes beyond its specific handling of Watergate. Writing in the *Washington Post* recently, William Greider spoke of the mentality and attitudes of those implicated in the scandal. Watergate, he said, was crime-by-the-group. Well, it seems to me that when the definitive book on Watergate is written — the book that explores and explains all the national attitudes that contributed to the corruption — the American press must share in the collective guilt.

For the press, Watergate was only a symptom of a larger pattern of behavior, a pattern that permitted it to be used by government, a pattern that exalted and sanctified the presidency into an office that could do no wrong, a pattern that led many in the press to think of themselves either as important adjuncts of government policy-making or key components of a patriotic team.

In spite of its breast-beating stance of independence and unrelenting government criticism, for years the Washington press corps was a willing accomplice of government secrecy, official trial balloons and justifications for policy failures. It was, for the most part, a staunch supporter of government policies, especially in foreign affairs. (It is hard to realize now, but as late as August 8, 1967, Sen. J. William Fulbright was describing the *Washington Post,* the present *bete-noire* of the government, as "a newspaper which has obsequiously supported the administration's policy in Vietnam.")

Over the years, a cozy relationship developed between the working press and Washington officials. The press cooperated — indeed, often helped draft the rules — for mutually advantageous private meetings in which public officials were allowed to advance positions, many dubious, many purely political, under a cloak of anonymity. These background meetings, as they came to be known, were both the grist for the Washington press and the vehicle for Washington officials.

The officials quickly learned they could promote pet projects and policies anonymously, and pass on tidbits of gossip for which they would not be held accountable. Journalists came to like the informality and the close association with the cream of Washington officialdom. Out-of-town publishers and editors relished having their men in Washington set up meetings with major figures, including an occasional presidential session. Reporters could glory in the social relationships they were able to develop. It was heady wine to be able to call the eminent secretary or ambassador by his first name, and even more seductive to be referred to in turn on a first-name basis. (Even now, I hardly know a prominent journalist who doesn't say, with casual and familiar pride, "Henry" when referring to Henry Kissinger.)

Joining the Government

As a corollary to these kinds of relationships, the lines between press and government often became blurred. A generation ago, few who went into daily journalism thought of their work as a springboard to government service. A young reporter might have wanted to follow the example of an Ernest Hemingway and leave journalism to become a novelist; but he didn't look to the government for the fulfillment of his ambitions. In recent years, this has changed notably. Not only do journalists go into government, primarily as press or public relations aides, but often they consciously take that step in hopes it will lead to a more powerful role in the press.

Carl Rowan went from reporter to government official to columnist and commentator. John Chancellor followed a similar route and returned to network television in a higher position. James Haggerty was a reporter, press aide, and then a network executive. Robert Manning, editor of the *Atlantic,* and James Greenfield, foreign editor of the *New York Times,* had come to prominence as State Department officials. Herbert Klein has moved from newspaper work, to a Nixon press spokesman's role to an executive position in television. John Seigenthaler, publisher of the *Nashville Tennesseean,* and Edwin Guthman, national editor of the *Los Angeles Times,* had worked in Robert Kennedy's Justice Department.

Nor is lack of professional journalistic background any bar to climbing into journalism's elite for those who served as government press aides. Bill Moyers, Lyndon Johnson's press secretary, became publisher of *Newsday,* and is now a TV commentator. Tom Johnson, a press aide to LBJ, later became editor of the *Dallas Times-Herald.* William Safire, a New York PR man who helped stage Richard Nixon's 1959 "kitchen debate" with Nikita Khruschev in Moscow, went on to become a White House speech writer; he is now a columnist for the *New York Times.* Kevin Phillips worked for John Mitchell in the Justice Department; he, too, has become a syndicated columnist. Ken Clawson, a *Washington Post* reporter who joined the Nixon PR team in the White House, frankly said his move could turn out to be advantageous in later obtaining a more prominent position in journalism.

None of this is to suggest that the journalists who enter government service are somehow venal or merely men-on-the-make—or that they cannot perform again with independence, integrity, and a better understanding after they return to the profession. But it does indicate a departure from the generally rigid lines that had existed between press and government, and to some degree an inevitable erosion of the journalist's traditional adversary role when dealing with public officials.

A Pugnacious Tradition

Anyone who thinks the present state of the press in America is outrageously critical of everyone in government from the President on down should look at the earlier record. The modern American press comes out of a tradition of savage independence and caustic, often unfair, criticism characterized by a belief that no official is above rebuke or harsh examination.

As James Reston of the *Times* has written in spelling out the old creed:

"The United States had a press before it had a foreign policy. This is a large part of the trouble between its writers and its officials today. The American press was telling the country and the world where to get off before there was a State Department. The 18th century American pamphleteers not only helped write the Constitution but thought — with considerable justification — that they created the Union. They believed that government power was potentially if not inevitably wicked and had to be watched, especially when applied in secret and abroad, and they wrote the rules so that the press would be among the watchers. In their more amiable moods, they no doubt conceded that the press should serve the country, but they insisted that the best way to serve it was to criticize its every act and thought, and something of this pugnacious spirit has persisted until now."

Certainly that pugnacious spirit existed for a long time. Shortly after George Washington's farewell address, a Philadelphia paper, the *Aurora,* paid its respects to the first President by saying:

"If ever a nation was debauched by a man, the American nation has been debauched by Washington. If ever a nation has suffered from the improper influence of a man, the American nation has suffered from the influence of Washington. If ever a nation was deceived by a man, the American nation has been deceived by Washington. . . ."

Some 80 years later the *New York Sun* commonly referred to President Rutherford B. Hayes as "The Fraudulent President." The "fraud" was reiterated throughout the paper in scores of connections.

It is that kind of tradition to which Reston referred. But I think it fair to say that such pugnaciousness has not been a hallmark of the American press in recent years.

So pin no laurels on the press as a whole for Watergate. Salute a few, if you will, but remember that for large segments of the press the Watergate story was basically unexplored. In retrospect, it should have come as no surprise last fall, months after the break-in, that George Gallup would report only about half of the American people had heard or read about Watergate. Or that the President's popularity remained at such high levels for so long while the story was unfolding.

Finally, as the press began to pay more attention and the cumulative weight of the story took hold, those conditions changed. Now, Gallup says, 97 per cent of the people have heard or read about Watergate. As that general knowledge has increased, so has the President's popularity curve continued to plummet.

In the end, the press has done its job, but like so many others involved in Watergate, it has been a most reluctant hero.

—June 24, 1973

Not for Attribution

FYI: Background to the Backgrounder Game

In the article that follows we offer what might be called an anatomy of a background press conference with the President of the United States. The facts of this particular encounter between a select group of newsmen and Mr. Nixon are set forth by Richard Harwood, an assistant managing editor of the *Washington Post*. To his play-by-play account, we would like to add, For Your Information, a few thoughts of our own, a little background, you might say, to the backgrounder game, which is something newsmen and officials play together in hopes of some mutual gain but without any real regard for you.

No matter who wins—and in this particular case it is not clear whether it was the *Chicago Sun-Times* or USIA or, in some inscrutable way, the President—you lose.

You can see this in the ground rules. Whether what is said is "off the record" (which means essentially that the whole thing was a nonhappening) or "for background only" (which means that you can attribute the contents to some anonymous source such as High Officials), the point is that the central figure who is doing the talking is not obliged to take responsibility for what he says. The newspaper or the television station takes the responsibility if what is said proves wrong, or misleading, or embarrassing to the source; whatever happens you are stuck with it because under the rules there is no recourse.

In this case, it seems safe to say that President Nixon had *something* he wanted to put about, as it were, (but not take responsibility for) with regard to the crisis in Jordan. For all the doubt about what he did say, and even about the ground rules, it's clear he said something about possible American intentions to intervene in Jordan, and he said it for a particular effect. It was reported more explicitly than he wanted, perhaps. In any case, for reasons not clear, he changed his mind, or the situation in Jordan changed, or something we can only guess at happened, and the story was quashed.

So the reader winds up with a baffling string of assertions and denials and retractions, and the press winds up being used as an instrument of government policy; a few words from the President, *not for attribution,* can become an ominous warning to an adversary; if ignored, they do not oblige the President to follow through, because he never said it, really; *it was for background.*

It is an old game, born of compromise between the needs of press and government, and we bring the matter up, not with any real hope of ending the game, but with the thought of making it more intelligible, which is what we like to think our business is all about.

— September 20, 1970

Anatomy of a Backgrounder With the President

By Richard Harwood

On Thursday, September 17, 1970, at 10 a.m., President Nixon drove up to the handsome building on North Wabash Avenue that houses the *Chicago Sun-Times* and the *Chicago Daily News*. He stopped in the lobby to look at a plaque that said: "Our newspapers have one duty above and beyond all others: to find and portray the truth."

Then he took an elevator to the seventh floor where, in the corporation's boardroom, he drank tomato juice and coffee for nearly two hours while he expounded on the state of the world. His audience included all of the principal executives of the two newspapers, including Bailey Howard, the president of the parent corporation, Field Enterprises. Out of that meeting came an ambiguous report to the effect that the United States was "prepared to intervene" in the internal conflict in Jordan.

Whether the President made that statement is now in dispute. The context in which he may or may not have made it is in dispute. Whether it should or should not have been published under the "ground rules" of the meeting is in dispute. But it produced one of the most curious journalistic reactions on record and raised some very basic questions about the responsibilities and competence of Presidents and newspapermen.

Roy Fisher, the editor of the *Daily News,* was at the luncheon. He got the impression, he later said, that the President was going to talk on a "deep background" basis which, in the jargon of this business, seems to mean that whatever a public official says for "deep background" may be published but without attribution to anyone.

Any confusion over the "ground rules," however, presumably was cleared up at the outset, said Fisher, by the senior newspaper executive present, Bailey Howard, who told the President: ". . . We're going to handle this off-the-record today." That meant nothing Mr. Nixon might say would be published in any form: it would be a completely private discussion.

"The President smiled," Fisher recalled, "and said that would be satisfactory." Nearly two hours later, the meeting came to an end. The President went on to other meetings—including a late afternoon "backgrounder" with executives of the *Chicago Tribune* and *Chicago Today.*

The *Daily News* people went about the task of putting out two more editions that afternoon. Fisher left orders that nothing the President had said during the morning should be printed and those orders were followed. Fisher left his office at 4:45 p.m. and a little while later got a shock.

The first edition of the *Sun-Times*—a "morning" paper—hit the streets at 5:05 p.m. and it carried a banner headline:

120

U.S. ready to act
to save Jordan king

The story was written by David Murray, a *Sun-Times* reporter who had been at the luncheon, and it said, "The United States is prepared to intervene directly in the Jordanian civil war should Syria and Iraq enter the conflict and tip the military balance against the government forces loyal to King Hussein, the *Sun-Times* learned Thursday."

Learned from whom? The story didn't say but the source was obvious from other material in the *Sun-Times*. A story on page two described Mr. Nixon's visit to the newspapers and said he "discussed domestic and foreign policies, particularly the Middle East, and economic questions." Another story on page three also referred to the visit and a picture on the same page showed the President in the boardroom with his hosts.

Fisher of the *Daily News* was "astonished" at the *Sun-Times* story and "thought they had violated the rules." The editor of the *Sun-Times,* James Hoge, ordered the Murray story printed and insists that "we didn't violate any ground rules." The President, he said, was not speaking "off-the-record"; he was merely speaking on the basis of "no attribution."

So you have a basic conflict to begin with over a very simple and elementary fact. Was or was not the President speaking "off-the-record"? And it is not a conflict between two cub reporters. It is a conflict between the principal news executives of two major newspapers.

A second conflict has arisen over what the President did or did not say and over the context in which he said it. It is Fisher's recollection that the President outlined several hypothetical "options" for U.S. policy in the Middle East, that one of those hypothetical "options" was direct intervention by the U.S. but that the President "immediately characterized it as undesirable and knocked it down."

It is the recollection of people from the *Sun-Times* that the President did not outline several hypothetical options, that the only option he mentioned was intervention, and that he suggested that the papers might want to print the fact that intervention was under consideration. So you have another conflict over the basic facts of the meeting. The two newspapers cannot even agree on what the President said or how he said it.

Subsequent events on Thursday night did nothing to clarify the situation or to add to the credibility of either the press or the administration.

A couple of hours after the first edition of the *Sun-Times* appeared, Edward Weintal, a former *Newsweek* diplomatic correspondent now at the U.S. Information Agency, got a call from Chicago about the *Sun-Times* story. He notified the agency's director, Frank Shakespeare, and alerted the Voice of America to be prepared to broadcast the story around the world. Shakespeare evidently did some checking on his own because he appeared at a reception at about 8 p.m. and told a reporter for the *Washington Star* that the United States "might intervene" if "Iraq and Syria move" against the Jordanians. A reporter from the *Washington Post* was also at the reception but missed Shakespeare's remarks. Score one for the *Star*.

Before the night was out, Shakespeare was to "disassociate" himself from the statement he made at the reception. But before that happened USIA—at about 9 p.m.—had called the *Post* to find out how the *Sun-Times* story was being handled. That was the first news the *Post* had of the *Sun-Times* story. And there is an explanation for that. The wire services— the Associated Press and United Press International—routinely pick up through their regional bureaus major stories that appear in the daily news-papers. The *Sun-Times* story—"U.S. ready to act"—was promptly picked up by both the UPI and AP bureaus in Chicago. They notified their Wash-ington and New York offices and asked for instructions. At about the same time, however, *Sun-Times* news executives were calling the wire services in Chicago to "kill" the intervention story and to "plead" that it not be put out across the country to AP and UPI subscribers.

"They (the *Sun-Times*) said an 'incredible blunder' had been made," according to Marvin Arrowsmith, chief of the AP's Washington bureau. On the basis of these calls from the *Sun-Times*, both AP and UPI "killed" the story. And the *Sun-Times* killed it, too, in its later editions. As a sub-stitute, it inserted a generalized story about the Middle East, based on comments from the State Department and the Pentagon. The story was written in Chicago. But it carried a Washington dateline and the label: "Special to The Sun-Times." Nevertheless, the Voice of America put the story on the air and broadcast it to the world. The *Post* checked out the original *Sun-Times* story, concluded that the President had made a state-ment about "intervention," and decided to print it.

By that time, calls were coming in to the *Post* from the *Sun-Times* edi-tors who said they "no longer stand behind the story" and "disassociate (the *Sun-Times*) completely" from it.

What was that all about? Editor Hoge of the *Sun-Times* had this ex-planation: Before leaving Chicago at about 7:30 p.m. the President's staff had learned of the *Sun-Times* story. After they were airborne in the Presi-dent's plane, they placed calls to a *Sun-Times* executive who talked to the President's press secretary, Ronald Ziegler, and to the administration's communications director, Herbert Klein. The discussion, said Hoge, had to do with the ground rules of the morning meeting at the newspaper office. "It was a very low-key discussion," said Hoge. "At no time did anyone (from the White House) request that we kill the story."

Why was it killed then? Hoge's answer to that one is that it really wasn't killed, that the paper merely put together a more "lucid and logi-cal" explanation of what was going on in the Middle East.

The fact is, however, that the key language in the earlier story—"pre-pared to intervene directly in the Jordanian civil war"—does not appear in the later story. The further fact is that the *Sun-Times* took extraordinary steps to keep the story off the wires and to emphasize that it no longer "stood behind it."

There are two obvious points to be made about all this. The first is that newspapers are terribly fallible institutions that sometimes do their job so badly that they cannot even agree on the simplest facts. The second is that "background" sessions can be the worst possible forums for the propagation of foreign policy, especially in explosive situations such as prevail in the Mideast. Nobody's "credibility" was enhanced by the Chicago episode—not the credibility of the government and not the credibility of the press which is constantly taking public officials to task for doubletalk.

Did the President threaten to intervene in Jordan? Or did a major American newspaper distort and misrepresent what he said? When people who heard him in Chicago are unable to agree on such a simple fact as that, it makes you wonder what you *can* believe in the newspapers.

—September 20, 1970

A Conspiracy in Restraint of Truth

By Benjamin C. Bradlee

It's perfectly possible that the first background briefing was held by Adam to give his version of the embarrassing murder of Abel by Cain.

But in the memory of living authorities like Kenneth G. Crawford and Edward T. Folliard, the first backgrounder more likely was held on March 5, 1933 — the day the United States went off the gold standard.

Steve Early was FDR's press secretary, and early that day he broke up the White House press room card game to tell the "regulars" — less than a dozen of them in those days — the momentous news. Like the well-trained generalists that they were, the reporters rushed to their typewriters and started banging out leads:

"In a move that shook the economic capitals of the world, the United States today went off the gold standard."

And there they froze, unable to write another word. If any of them knew the country was in fact *on* the gold standard, none of them knew how to get off it, or what being on it or off it meant to equally ignorant editors and readers.

One by one the reporters sidled up to Early to confess the depths of their ignorance, and in one of the least illuminated critical moments of history Early called in an anonymous expert from the Treasury Department to give the boys the word "for background only."

Suddenly as authoritative as Keynes himself, the reporters returned confidently to their typewriters and finished the stories that were headlined all over the world on March 6, 1933.

Of course, the reporters had no way of knowing whether their stories were true. They knew only what an anonymous government official had spoonfed them as the truth. And of course, under the ground rules of this first backgrounder and the thousands that have followed, they were not permitted to identify their source. In mutual complicity, the press and the government had conspired to deny the public the whole truth.

It's all been downhill from there.

It's not enough to say that many of us have enjoyed the slide from time to time. To our discredit, we have, but after 25 years in journalism I have yet to meet a serious reporter who does not feel discomfort, if not guilt, over his role in this conspiracy.

My own personal experience with backgrounders began in the early '50s — on the other side of the fence, when I was the press attache in the United States Embassy in Paris. One of my duties was the janitorial chore of setting up background briefings for "high American officials" and the press.

My first doubts about the morality and honesty of what I was doing came with the telephone calls that inevitably preceded any international conference. "Who'll be doing the background briefing?" reporters would ask, a week before the events. "What time is Chip's briefing tonight?" they would ask (about Ambassador Charles E. Bohlen). It was perfectly obvious that the journalists—and foreign offices—of any country, friend or foe, knew who was briefing, when he was briefing and, by reading the stories that ensued, what he was saying. For a fledgling diplomat, that was fine: the U.S. was getting its story across in the way it desired. As an ex-journalist, soon to re-enter the field, I had the guilties: how come newspapermen were helping governments give the reader the short end of the stick?

Back in journalism, I began to learn some of the answers:

Background briefings are seductive. It's pretty heady wine for a journalist to turn to his friends (much less his editors) and say, casually: "Dulles, (Dean, Bill) told me last night that (Ike, Jack, Lyndon, Dick) is really sore at old Gromyko (Diefenbaker, Golda)."

The trappings of a well-staged background briefing—an honest-to-God "high government official," the exclusion of TV cameras and tape recorders, the red plush of the White House (Air Force One, Palais Rose) setting —plus the information that is dished out convince the reporter that he has his story and blind him to the fact that he has *their* story. (One of the greatest myths in the current controversy lies in the claim that the press is not the docile recipient of the party line, but the relentless prosecutor at background briefings, pulling information out of a reluctant briefer fact by fact. Former Presidential Press Secretary Bill D. Moyers once said, "Yeah. They pull it out of me until there's nothing more I want to tell them." Whether birth is by Caesarian section or natural delivery, the child of background briefings is government propaganda.)

Background briefings are convenient for the press. It is a cardinal if regrettable rule of journalism that a story dropped in the lap of a reporter is "better" than a story that must be dug from a dozen different mines. It is easier to write, easier to edit, easier to read and often easier to understand, even if it may be incomplete, misleading or even false. Normally querulous editors are easily mollified by the knowledge (which they often dine out on) that the high government official quoted in the story is in fact the President of the United States. The lazy reporter can file his backgrounder and be out on the golf course after lunch. The confused reporter can convince himself he has the truth by the tail at long last. And even the conscientious reporter knows that if he doesn't file the story fast, he will get scooped.

Background briefings are useful to the government. All governments are understandably and instinctively interested in giving out information of a quality and in a manner that reflects maximum credit on themselves. That, as the saying goes, is show biz. Only two barriers exist to prevent the government from so limiting the news about government.

First is the danger that other information may come into the public domain — information that does not reflect maximum credit on the government, information that clouds the whole question of credit, or information that actually reflects discredit.

Second is the little problem of accountability. A government official — high, low or jack-in-the-game — will generally say one thing if he is sure that his identity will be publicly unknown, and quite another thing if the public can call him on it if he is wrong or misleading. If you will, "senior Defense officials" will say one thing about Lamson 719, the South Vietnamese incursion into Laos with heavy U.S. logistic support, that Lt. Gen. John W. Vogt, Director, Joint Staff, JCS, would not say. Yet they were one and the same man.

The background briefing is the one mechanism by which the government can surmount both barriers. By its control of the briefing, it can withhold whatever information it wants to withhold, and by forbidding identification of the briefer, it prevents accountability.

This may be a legitimate aim of government, but it is a perversion of journalism. Government is a noble career. So is journalism. They are not the same.

Consider some unforgettable abuses:

• A Secretary of Agriculture (Orville Freeman) gives a briefing for background only. Why background only? His stenotypist is sick. And only one reporter walks out.

• Israeli Ambassador Izhak Rabin speaks to more than 100 members of the Overseas Writers "for background only," and blasts the Arabs from soup to cigars. There are 20 to 30 waiters present and a sprinkling of Washington diplomats. No journalist objects. It's cozy.

• President Kennedy calls the White House regulars to his Palm Beach winter White House for a little background chat about what a hell of a legislative record his administration had chalked up in its first year. Next day, the stories list these accomplishments — without attribution. (These year-end reviews are something of a tradition in Washington. For the first time in the memory of White House correspondents, the Nixon administration gave its year-ender for 1971 on the record.)

During his eight years in office, Secretary of State Dean Rusk regularly met with State Department correspondents at the end of the working day every Friday for a scotch on the rocks or two and a little "background only" conversation. Every Saturday morning, alert readers like you and me and the embassies of the Soviet Union, the People's Republic of China and Castro's Cuba could read the results: "The administration is worried that . . ."; "The government is known to feel . . ."; "High officials in the State Department think . . ."

• Background briefings by the White House officials are normally and regularly made available to any reporter accredited to the White House, specifically including the three correspondents of Tass, the Soviet news agency, now accredited to the White House.

• My own all-time "favorite" example of the abuses of background briefings involved a performance in the White House theater on the eve of President Johnson's speech at Johns Hopkins University, announcing for the first time that the U.S. was ready to engage in unconditional discussions with North Vietnam. On stage — literally — were McGeorge Bundy, Robert McNamara and George Ball. In front of them, perhaps 150 reporters, plus the ever-present TV crews, cameras silent. For 45 minutes they went through their dog and pony act — three "high government officials" secure in their anonymity and not accountable for their words, but hell-bent on spreading the new gospel. When it was all over, the reporters were herded out the door, but a straggler watched dumbfounded as the same three high government officials went on camera for the television audience to say virtually everything they had just told the reporters on "deep background." And no journalist objected.

In the name of common sense, who is kidding whom? When is the thoughtful professional in government and in the press, each properly concerned with his own credibility gap, going to stop it?

—January 22, 1972

A Barrel of Fun

The Washington Post

Interoffice Memo

Messrs. Bradlee/Simons: 5/21/75

     Today's puzzle: The foreign oil producers, we
report in our lead story today, are "expected" to
raise prices by $2 a barrel. We say that four
sources confirmed the expectation of a price increase and three of them confirmed the $2 figure.

     We also report that Frank Zarb, the administra-
tion's top dog on energy, was one of the four.
Question: Was Zarb, who should be the most authoritative source on such matters, one of the three
confirming the $2 figure?

     Well, let's see. We quote him as saying "it's
certainly not going to be healthy for our economy."
The "it" can be taken to refer to the subject of
the story, a $2 increase. Or it can be taken to
refer only to a price increase without a figure.
No help there.

     Let's try reading between the lines. If
Zarb was NOT one of the $2 sources, surely we would
have said so out of fairness to him and to the
reader. So Zarb WAS one of the three who confirmed
the $2.

     But wait a minute. If that is the case, which
of the four sources didn't confirm the $2? We quote
an oil executive in support of the $2 and later
refer to "oilmen" who anticipate a $2 rise. That in-
dicates that at least two, and possibly three, of
our four sources were oilmen and that they expect
a $2 rise. Maybe Zarb wasn't a $2 man, after all.

     Could it be that all four sources confirmed the
$2 figure, but we attributed it only to three be-
cause Zarb didn't want to be quoted on that point?
No, that would be dirty pool.

     Now let's go over the evidence again...Reading
the newspaper can be fun.

                       Charlie Seib

FYI: It Was Learned

The newspaperman's friend, It Was Learned, is back with us as the source of a story from the (we guess) Justice Department. The story is that for the first time since 1965 the United States government is tapping telephones in criminal cases unrelated to the national security.

It Was Learned has always been with us, in good times and bad, and it is a comfort to see him again. It is somehow appropriate that when the government decides to snoop via a telephone tap, it chooses It Was Learned to tell us about it. It is odd that when the budget produces a $6 billion surplus it is Mr. Nixon who tells us about that, or when the Mafia is expunged from our shores it will be John N. Mitchell, the Attorney General, who will tell us about that. Meanwhile, we shall make do with It Was Learned. For the bad news.

For the edification of those who may be unaware of the etymology, the family tree, so to speak, of the wellsprings of news, it goes something like this: Walter and Ann Source (nee Rumor) had four daughters (Highly Placed, Authoritative, Unimpeachable and Well-informed). The first married a diplomat named U. S. Officials, and the second a government public relations man named Reliable Informant. (The Informant brothers are widely known and quoted here; among the best known are White House, State Department, and Congressional.) Walter Speculation's brother-in-law, Ian Rumor, married Alexandra Conjecture, from which there were two sons, It Was Understood and It Was Learned. It Was Learned just went to work in the Justice Department, where he will be gainfully employed for four long years.

—February 12, 1969

Who Said That?

The Washington Post
Interoffice Memo

TO: Bradlee, et al.   October 14, 1970

FROM: Harwood

We report, in a 16-paragraph story today, that the United States is giving the Israelis new military equipment. Who said that? Take your choice:

"White House officials"; "White House sources"; "officials"; "White House officials"; "these sources"; "American sources"; "U.S. sources"; "White House officials"; "American sources"; "U.S. officials"; "it was noted"; "White House sources"; "the reason given"; "it was said"; "these sources"; "U.S. officials."

All those sources in 16 paragraphs.

What the story did not say is that the White House invited editors to a briefing by the President in Hartford, Conn.; that the briefing and the President's part in it were reported in The Washington Post on October 13. What the story <u>does</u> say is that certain "disclosures were made to news executives on a background basis in Hartford, Conn. on Monday, with a transcript made available yesterday. Under the rules, the officials cannot be identified or quoted directly."

If we could say on October 13 that the President briefed the editors in Hartford, why can't we say it on October 14? Whose "rule" does that violate?

And while we're at it, why don't we just say that the facts in our story came out of the transcript? Why go through all this tortured business of "American sources," "U.S. sources," "White House officials" ad infinitum? Are we trying to kid somebody or impress somebody or create the impression that "we" were present at the briefing?

The whole thing turns me off.

The Butz Story—and How It Grew

By Charles B. Seib

What is news? Wise journalists duck that one. Those less wise offer definitions ranging from the inane—"news is what happens"—to the arrogant—"news is what we say it is."

But even though they can't define the product, newspaper people pride themselves on their "news judgment," the ability to tell news from non-news. And their exercise of that claimed ability is what determines the content of your newspaper each day.

News is not only amorphous; it is sometimes downright spooky. Once publication has authenticated an event as genuine news, it can take on a life of its own, expanding like one of those blobs from another planet in a late movie.

Our case in point is the Butz joke story, which began its brief public career Thanksgiving morning [1974] and enlivened, if that's the word, a dull holiday weekend. Its aftershocks are still being felt. What happened was this:

Agriculture Secretary Earl Butz breakfasted the day before Thanksgiving with 29 reporters. These breakfasts are a Washington institution; their purpose is to milk information from officials and other public figures in a relaxed and friendly atmosphere. The Butz session was on the record—that is, the reporters could quote anything he said and attribute it to him—with one small exception.

The exception was a joke Butz told—a mildly funny, mildly tasteless joke he said he had heard at the Rome food conference. An Italian woman, the joke goes, is asked about the Pope's stand on birth control and replies, "he no playa the game, he no maka the rules."

It's not a good joke or a new one—the warm-up comic used a version at Frank Sinatra's New York concert earlier this year and it goes back a lot further than that. And it has a nasty ethnic/religious sneer to it. But there was a polite titter, and then Butz, who is slowly learning the facts of political life, asked that it be off the record. Just what was said in response is unclear; there are several versions. In any case, 28 of the 29 reporters didn't report the joke. But one decided that Butz's use of it was of public interest and that an after-the-fact request to go off the record doesn't wash unless specifically agreed to. So he used the joke in a column he wrote for the Thanksgiving morning edition of his paper, the *New York Daily News*.

In New York a *Daily News* editor, exercising that news judgment we mentioned earlier, directed that the item be lifted from the column and turned it into a two-paragraph story that appeared on page two of the paper with the headline: "Butz Raps the Pope." The Italian woman was gone and the punch line was attributed directly to Butz and presented as a dismissal by Butz of the Pope's position on population control.

Then the blob began to grow. Within hours, a spokesman for the New York Roman Catholic archdiocese wired President Ford to complain about the "crude, pointed insult" to the Pope and demanded Butz's apology or resignation. Members of Congress also protested. By Friday morning the story that had been worth two paragraphs had blossomed into a page one banner story for the *Daily News*. Other papers began climbing aboard, although not so flamboyantly. All three networks included an item on Butz's troubles on their evening news, giving the event the imprimatur that comes only with a mention by Walter Cronkite.

Friday was not one of Butz's best days. He tried to put the fire out by saying he meant no harm, but that wasn't enough. President Ford called him in for a little talk, after which he issued a formal apology.

The President's entry into the case escalated the story another notch. Saturday morning it made the front pages of the *New York Times* and the *Washington Star-News*. The *Post* had a teaser on page one and the story on page five. The networks reported the new development. The only bright spot for Butz was the fact that the *Daily News* gave the story only a secondary spot on page one.

So there you have the life history of a news story. It isn't quite dead; it takes a long time for such stories to die. But a quiet senescence has begun, punctuated by occasional editorial harpoons for Butz (including one from this newspaper) and outbursts like the one from a usually calm columnist who declared that every day Butz remains in office he advertises America's insensitivity to suffering.

Without in any way defending Butz as a humanitarian or as a public official, one must ask whether that miserable joke told over breakfast justified what followed.

True, the story developed as the hours went by. There were the protests to be reported, and the presidential dressing down. Also, it received additional momentum from the fact that just a few weeks earlier Gen. George S. Brown, chairman of the Joint Chiefs of Staff, got himself in trouble and drew a presidential rebuke—with remarks about Jewish influence on American foreign policy. But it still comes back to the old chicken or egg question: did the Butz story generate the coverage or did the coverage generate the story?

Whatever happened in the Butz case, the cause of balance and perspective and maturity in the press was not advanced. And everybody—the media, the indignant protesters, the stern President, and, of course, Butz himself—ended up looking faintly ridiculous. A Vatican spokesman must be credited with the sanest statement in the whole episode. In declining comment, he said, possibly with a touch of bewilderment, "All we know is what we read in the newspapers."

—December 13, 1974

It Takes Two to Tell the Tale

By Robert C. Maynard

One of the principles that has characterized the *Washington Post* investigative reporting on Watergate from its inception has been a rule that nothing told a reporter by one source is to be published until it can be confirmed by yet another independent source. "If one person will tell you," said an investigative reporter, "then it's not very hard to get it from another. There are no secrets in Washington."

As a result of that principle, very little of what the *Post* has printed about Watergate has ever been successfully refuted by the Nixon administration. At the same time, stories that later turned out to be true were withheld from publication because that second source couldn't be found.

But the best of principles often go awry, and this is the anatomy of one such story, pieced together as best it can be without violating those all-important confidences.

From the outset of the Watergate hearings, a familiar refrain among the embarrassed Republicans on Capitol Hill was that they would eventually prove that the Democrats were as guilty of "dirty tricks" as the Republicans.

During John Dean's painful week, several Republicans warned their Democratic colleagues to contain any temptation to smirk, for their embarrassing time was soon to come. When it didn't materialize by the August [1973] recess, notice was served that time would be set aside immediately after the recess for "Democratic dirty tricks." Nothing comparable to the Watergate break-in materialized.

Then, as if out of the blue, a four-column story marched across the front page of the *Washington Post* of December 20, its headline declaring: **Hunt Tells Senate Panel He Spied On Goldwater in '64 on LBJ Order.**

The story told of E. Howard Hunt, working with other operatives of the Central Intelligence Agency, spying on Goldwater "well before his nomination." It said he acted at the instruction of President Johnson, passed to Hunt through an intermediary.

The story went on to quote Goldwater himself as saying, "I knew 10 years ago what was going on" and he added that friends of his within the CIA and FBI had told him he was under the surveillance of both agencies during his disastrous campaign.

There at last, it seemed, was the stuff of which bipartisan scandal is made. That Hunt, the principal actor responsible for so much of Watergate, was also involved made it all the more compelling a tale.

Unfortunately, the bubble was burst 24 hours later. The headline then was: **Hunt's Role in 1964 Minor, Hill Unit Told.**

The second day story acknowledged:

"Watergate conspirator E. Howard Hunt's alleged 'surveillance' of Sen. Barry Goldwater during the 1964 presidential campaign consisted of having a secretary pick up press releases, speeches, travel schedules and other materials at Republican headquarters, according to reliable accounts of Hunt's secret testimony to the Senate Select Watergate Committee."

So, those who were expecting the long-awaited unfolding of the Democratic version of "dirty tricks" were to be disappointed once again.

Some editors have defended the first *Post* story against the charge that it was based on a single source by saying that the unnamed source was one, and Goldwater was the second. Therefore, it has been argued, the story didn't violate the paper's wise principle of requiring two independent sources.

The trouble is that Goldwater apparently was not an independent source, but received his information from the same person the *Post* quoted. Apparently, Goldwater learned of the Hunt disclosures from a source within the Committee and tipped an editor of the *Post*. The editor passed the tip to a reporter who wound up facing Goldwater's source. The reporter then went to Goldwater for more elaboration.

Thus, the *Post* was in the posture of reporting two sources for the story, when in fact it had only one, a violation of its own rule, a rule that had served it well for more than a year.

An explanation has been offered by *Post* editors and reporters, and it is that there was no way to tell for certain that Goldwater's source was also the *Post's* single source.

The business of printing stories based on anonymous sources is a dicey one under the best of circumstances. In Watergate, it is an incredibly tricky game. Those who know it best develop a smell for a bad pitch.

In this story, waiting a day to check further and to learn—as it later became possible to do—the content of the transcript would have prevented the *Post* from having to back away from the story in 24 hours.

—January 17, 1974

134

The Use and Abuse of Unattributed Information

By Richard Harwood

On March 26, 1971, an editorial appeared in the Richmond, Ky., *Register* under the title "Advertising Makes It Go." It was inspired by a critique of the advertising industry prepared by Mrs. Virginia Knauer, the President's adviser on consumer affairs. The editorial made the point that "one should not lose sight of the fact that advertising is an indispensable feature of the free market."

On March 27, the same editorial appeared in the Marion, Ind., *Chronicle-Tribune*. It appeared on April 5 in the Williamson, W. Va., *News;* on April 8 in the Towson, Md., *Jeffersonian;* on April 13 in the Galax, Va., *Gazette;* on April 14 in the El Dorado, Ark., *Times;* and on April 15 in the Washington, Pa., *Observer-Reporter*. Various other newspapers across the country used the editorial at approximately the same time.

From this pattern of coincidence, one might assume that the Richmond, Ky., *Register* exerts considerable influence on the American press. But that assumption would be wrong.

"Advertising Makes It Go" was written in Hillsboro, Ore., by E. Hofer & Sons, a company that has been producing editorials for American newspapers since 1913. Each week it mails out material to 10,000 daily and weekly newspapers, material that is specifically designed to create favorable attitudes toward capitalism in the United States.

The Hofer service is supplied free of charge to the free American press. The company is able to do this, Lawrence Hofer of the founding family explained, because it is underwritten by large industrial groups—oil, electric utilities, timber, shipping, railroads, chemicals, pharmaceuticals—and by such private professional groups as the American Medical Association.

The arrangement is simple. Hofer develops material on matters of concern to industry—environmental questions, for example—and then finds "an industry group to support us" in providing the material to newspapers.

It is apparently a highly effective propaganda device. Hofer estimated that from 300 to 2,000 newspapers publish the company's material each week. Frequently it appears, as in the case of "Advertising Makes It Go," as the considered judgment of American editors.

There is, in this operation, no deception on Hofer's part. The newspapers receiving the service are informed each week that it is subsidized by industrialists who wish to promote a sympathetic view of free enterprise in action. The deception is on the part of the newspapers; the people deceived are the readers who are unaware that they are consuming paid propaganda.

This sort of thing has been going on in American journalism for many years. In some cases—E. Hofer & Sons, for example—newspapers are witting partners to the act of deception. They plead poverty and lack of staff and fill up columns with whatever material or propaganda comes to hand. In other cases, newspapers are used unwittingly for propaganda purposes, as a Senate committee discovered in an investigation of foreign lobbying activities a few years ago. One subject of the investigation was the International News Service, a now-defunct competitor of the Associated Press and United Press. For $6,000, the committee found, INS officials agreed that their foreign editor would produce favorable columns about the Trujillo regime in the Dominican Republic. These columns were distributed for three months to INS clients throughout the country. In another case it was discovered that the *New York Herald Tribune* (also now defunct) and the North American Newspaper Alliance were distributing stories written by a paid agent of the Nationalist Chinese Government on Taiwan.

The objections to practices of this kind were recited some 25 years ago by the Hutchins Commission on Freedom of the Press:

"Whether a unit of the press is an advocate or a common carrier, it ought to identify the sources of its facts, opinions and arguments so that the reader or listener can judge them. Persons who are presented with facts, opinions and arguments are properly influenced by the general reliability of those who offer them. If the veracity of statements is to be appraised, those who offer them must be known. . . . If (full and free) discussion is to have the effect for which democracy hopes, if it is to be really full and free, the names and the characters of the participants must not be hidden from view."

Those platitudes, no doubt, would win a ringing endorsement today from the American Newspaper Publishers Association and from the American Society of Newspaper Editors. These same groups would probably deplore the unattributed use of such things as Hofer editorials or Dominican propaganda because the deception is so obvious.

But there is a related and subtler problem of "sourcing" that neither publishers nor editors nor reporters have been willing to tackle. This is the problem of unattributed information that *we* seek out and publish every day. It comes from "informed sources" and "high government officials" and "reliable authorities." The reporters involved know who these sources, officials and authorities are; sometimes their editors know. But the reading public never knows and is thus unable to judge for itself their reliability, veracity and character. Do they represent, like the hidden clients behind "Advertising Makes It Go," self-serving points of view or propaganda interests? Are they always quite as "informed" as we tend to imply? Do they have motives other than disinterested service to the public? Are they genuinely credible men and women?

Under the present system those judgments are made by a handful of newspaper people and we give our readers few clues about the nature and interests of our sources. So the public has virtually no information about the "sources" who are speaking to them through us. The result is a faulty and, in some cases, corrupted communications process as our experience in going to war in Vietnam has shown. We told the people what was happening but we told them, too often, through the mouths of anonymous "officials" and "authorities" and not many people were listening to messages diluted in that way.

Several years ago the executive editor of this newspaper, Benjamin Bradlee, made a speech out in California in which he said that "the abuse of unattributed information . . . is a professional disgrace, an identifiable . . . roadblock in the way of newspapers and news services trying to make public affairs understandable. . . . Why then do we go along so complacently with withholding the identity of public officials? I'm damned if I know. I do know that by doing so, we shamelessly do other people's bidding; we knowingly let ourselves be used for obvious trial balloons and for personal attacks. In short, we demean our profession."

Ringing words. But the practice of publishing unattributed news, like the publishing of planted editorials in the country press, goes on unchecked — needlessly, in many cases — because it suits our convenience and interest; it makes the job easier. But there is real reason to question whether it always suits the public convenience and interest and whether it is not time for a change.

—July 19, 1971

Supplements and a Sleight of Hand

The Washington Post

Interoffice Memo

Messrs. Bradlee/Simons: 2/11/75

The Post--and a lot of other papers--should
take a hard look at the practice of putting out so-
called "advertising supplements" like Sunday's
"Housing '75" section.

Having dealt with this sort of thing in my
previous incarnation, I think I know the ration-
ale: Because there is an "advertising supplement"
label on every page and because special headline
and body types are used, everybody knows that this
is not a product of the Post's editorial department
and that usual journalistic standards do not apply.
Good try, but baloney.

It may be that the reader consciously or sub-
consciously notices the difference in type faces.
But I don't agree that he therefore also knows
that this is something other than a product the
editorial department of the Post stands behind. He
has been too thoroughly conditioned to accept the
headline-and-columnar-body-type format as charac-
teristic of editorial material. I don't think he
makes the distinction we try to signal by using
different faces. By the same token, the "advertising supplement" labels don't do the trick. Of
course he knows it's an advertising supplement on
real estate. But that doesn't mean he gets the important part of the message: What looks like
editorial copy is really something else.

This unconvincing sleight of hand has bothered
me for a long time. I decided to comment on it
after I received a phone call Sunday morning from
a reader (also a friend). She was indignant about
"Housing '75." Why was the Post pushing people
into buying homes as quickly as possible? Why was
it presenting only one side of the story?

(more)

138

When I tried to point out that this was not
to be judged by the standards usually applied to
editorial matter, she would have none of it. So
far as she was concerned, it was the Post talking
to its readers, and normal journalistic standards
should apply.

Now this was a highly intelligent woman--the
widow of a newspaperman, a Library of Congress
staffer. It wasn't that she didn't understand
what I was saying, she just didn't accept it. And
I don't think she is alone.

What are we dealing with here? Take a look at
the lead article in "Housing '75" by a free-lancer
who did this work for the ad department. The
article is headlined "Pros and Cons of Buying
Homes." I challenge anyone to find a single "con"
in the whole three-column piece. The buy-now
thrust was strong throughout the section: "Area
May Be Headed for Housing Shortage," "Money Available to Qualified Borrowers," "Home Prices to
Rise," and so on.

The problem is not limited to real estate
special sections, of course. Camera, auto, hi-fi,
shopping mall sections have all appeared in the
same format. It may be a little more serious when
you're dealing with real estate, though, because
of the importance of housing and its cost in the
lives of all of us.

I know how this sort of thing comes about.
At least I know how it used to come about at the
Star:

Ad Manager: "Charlie, we think we can sell a
pot full of ads for a condominium section. Would
you fellows be willing to put one out?"

Seib: "Okay. But I should warn you that any
section we put out in this department is going to
have to deal with the pitfalls of buying condos
and the problems being caused by the conversions
of rental apartment houses and things like that."

(more)

Ad Manager: "Well...maybe we'd better ask the promotion department to work with us on it as an advertising supplement."

Seib (with relief): "Good. But be sure it's clearly labeled, and don't use our regular type dress."

Another problem solved. But not really. You still end up with something that's a little like a special Watergate section written and edited by the folks of the Nixon White House.

I don't have a solution. I know these sections are big revenue items. All I can say is that I think we're kidding ourselves with the present approach. And raise the broader question: Is it right in the long run--however convenient it may be in the short run--for this department to abdicate responsibility for non-ad space in the paper?

I can suggest one approach that might be a partial solution: Make up the special section just as tightly as it can be made up and fill the remaining non-ad space with neutral service material: A glossary (we did run one of those Sunday), tables on mortgage costs, lists of savings and loans and their position on mortgages, how-to stuff on signing a contract, etc. Or go back to the old way, and have this department put out a balanced, useful report on the real estate situation--one in which a story purporting to list the "cons" would actually list them.

I don't know what problems these approaches would raise for the ad salesmen. I suppose the second route would raise manpower problems in this department.

My main message is, let's not suppose that ultra Bodoni headlines and sans serif body type get us off the hook.

Charlie Seib

Discrimination in the News and in the Newsrooms

Retrospective: The Hard Journalism of Tom Fortune

By Colman McCarthy

Thanks to digging biographers who know an eager audience awaits the buried treasures of history, we have been learning much recently about William E. DuBois, Marcus Garvey, Frederick Douglass and other Negroes of bravery who have influenced American life. We need to know about their thoughts and their past times—the mid-19th and early 20th centuries—because we are still confused about the American Negro in present times. Many are confused not only about the feelings, rights and responsibilities of these 22 million citizens but even about their correct name. Linguistic fashion, as fickle as clothes designer fashions, prefers "the blacks" right now rather than "Negro." Yet, as Prof. J. Mitchell Morse of Temple University said in a recent essay, when British colonialists and white trash wanted to insult their slaves, the term black was used. Black was ugly, Negro was beautiful.

Along with DuBois, Garvey and Douglass, the historical richness of American life 100 years ago runs deep with men and women whose genius went unrecognized because they were the wrong color, and that made all else about them wrong, too. Few illustrate this better than T. Thomas Fortune, an ex-slave who from 1885 to his death in 1928 was a journalist of power and nerve. Fortune is an unknown name today, perhaps because he left behind no important books or followers, perhaps because so much of his energy was used surviving mental illness, destitution, a flawed marriage. Then also, he refused to adopt the role that whites love to assign blacks—"spokesman for his race." Better to deal with a spokesman than the social sufferings of the millions he speaks for. Most of what we know of Thomas Fortune, whose hard journalism spoke only for himself, can be found in the recent and excellent work of scholarship by Prof. Emma Lou Thornbrough of Butler University in her biography *T. Thomas Fortune.* The University of Chicago Press published the work as part of its series on Negro American biographies and autobiographies.

No profession was more closed to blacks during the Reconstruction than newspapering. A white press flourished, but Fortune had no way of entering it. His first job, after leaving the Deep South at 18 and a youth of devouring books, was in the printshop of *The People's Advocate,* a Washington, D.C., weekly. Fortune was a Howard University student—three years of formal schooling had qualified him—and began a column. The paper paid little and he left soon for New York and another paper. In the 1880s, Negro weeklies—always four pages—had small circulations, small staffs and small chances for survival. One exception, if only on the last count, was the *Globe,* and Fortune wrote for it.

Opinions interested him more than events, so he became an editorial writer. The reasons for a Negro press, he wrote, were "that white men have newspapers; that they are published by white men for white men; give, in the main, news about white men, and pitch their editorial opinions entirely in the interest of white men. . . . Can we reasonably expect other men to use their lungs to cry out for us when we are wronged and outraged and murdered? If we do, let us look at the white papers of the South and learn from them the necessary lesson, that the only way we can hope ever to win our fight is to arm ourselves as our opponents do, support those newspapers alone that support us, and support those men that support us."

The *Globe's* prestige came from its editorial page. Prof. Thornbrough noted that throughout Fortune's life "he held the view that the editorial page was the most vital of any newspaper. When at one point it was necessary as an economy measure to reduce the size of the *Globe,* he announced that other matters would be decreased, but the editorial page would remain intact."

Like any editorial writer worthy of his independence, Fortune could rankle people not only on one side of an issue but on both sides. When Frederick Douglass married a white woman, Fortune criticized those Negroes who opposed intermarriage. Negroes, he wrote, "are always prating about the unreasonable prejudices of other people and yet show, when occasion presents itself, prejudices just as narrow and unreasonable." As for whites, "we are surprised at the amount of gush which intermarriage inspires in this country. It is in strict keeping with all the sophistries kept alive by the papers and the people about the colored people."

Fortune again took them on two at a time when he denounced the Democrats as "the party of stupidity" which "learns nothing and forgets nothing" and denounced the Republicans as "a mean, cunning, treacherous organization." Fortune correctly saw what men like Jesse Jackson and Geno Baroni are talking about now: "The hour is approaching when the laboring classes of our country, North, East, West and South, will recognize that they have a common cause, a common humanity and a common enemy. . . . When the issue is properly joined, the rich, be they black or be they white, will be found on the same side; and the poor, be they black or be they white, will be found on the same side."

Fortune was a close friend of Booker T. Washington, a strange alliance in view of Fortune's total rejection of Washington's "get along" philosophy. As a way of scorning accommodationism, pushed from Tuskegee, Fortune founded the Afro-American League. The term *Afro* is now common, but in 1890 he wrote: "There are some laws which no self-respecting person should be expected to obey. No man is compelled to obey a law which degrades his manhood and defrauds him of what he has paid for. When I willingly consent to ride in a 'Jim Crow Car' it will be when I am a dead Afro-American." Independent from Washington's "get along" view, Fortune never joined with Marcus Garvey's "get out" belief, the back-to-Africa movement, either.

The *Globe* went bankrupt and Fortune started, as sole owner, the *Freeman,* and still later went to the *Age.* He continued to write thundering editorials, as was the style then, but he also learned the art of understatement in which the reader is served more by explaining subleties and shading than by denouncing evils, which any bigmouth can do.

Inevitably, Fortune was seen as an agitator. In 1900, following a speech, in which he said that for every Negro killed in a riot at Wilmington, Del., a white should have been killed, the white press took that one loose remark as an excuse to devastate all of Fortune's thinking. A *Washington Evening Star* editorial said Fortune was an enemy of his own people, that he should be surpressed. The *Washington Post,* also hostile to Fortune, joined in. When someone suggested that Fortune and the editor of the *Post* should reconcile their differences, Fortune replied: "Get together? Not much. There is no man or combination of men who can construct a platform on which the editors of the *Age* and *Post* could stand two minutes without a hand to hand fight."

Throughout his life, Fortune had no money and little job security, and lived with constant mental and physical pain; all that, plus racism. Toward the end of his life, in 1927, he was called "the beloved dean of Negro journalism" by the National Negro Press Association. But what could the honor have meant, when he was so little honored by a steady income or steady audience? He was worn out and soon to die. To the end, he kept his newspaperman's skepticism, in this case, a suspicion about the good will and cooperation of whites. On his death, the *Amsterdam News* called Fortune "a young old man, a New Negro, who loved America, while recognizing much in it to hate."

—November 14, 1972

Perspective: A Black Journalist Looks at White Newsrooms

By Robert C. Maynard

> ". . . the total professional figure nationally (for all minority group members in daily newspaper journalism) may reasonably be estimated at approximately 300 — or three-fourths of 1 per cent of total writer-photographer-editor employment."
> — *From a report to the American Society of Newspaper Editors by its Committees on Minority Employment and Education in Journalism.*

If the figures for minority participation in American newspapers are not shocking in and of themselves, I invite you to imagine how those white newsrooms appear to the eyes of a black journalist. What he sees is not just a pervasive whiteness that can only suggest racism in the raw. He also sees hypocrisy in this. Not just because newspapers are pious in their platitudes about racism and injustice in some other fellow's barnyard, but for another and more fundamentally disturbing reason. If government infringes on some right of the media, those who own them waste no time in reaching for the First Amendment to remind the government, or any other interloper into the arena of the free press, of where exactly to get off. And properly so. What is forgotten in these times is that we have some other Amendments — the 14th for some reason comes readily to mind — that would make a stranger to these shores assume something very different about the performance of American institutions with regard to the hiring and promotion of minorities.

So it should not be surprising that there are mornings in the lives of America's black journalists when the world seems not only to be colored white. It also appears to be colored contradictory — if not downright hypocritical.

Yet it is also fair to say that it is a world filled with challenge. There is no place to go with figures such as these, except up. That is one of the small comforts of the times. After all, before the advent of the urban uprisings, which demanded the hiring of people who could at least gain safe passage to the site of the story, that percentage was probably one sorry fifth of what it is today.

Because we were mostly hired to face down the urban rebellions, the black journalist's position was in yet another way unique. To the police, he was a nosy snoop appearing on the scene of disturbances to ask the kinds of questions police officers are not accustomed to being asked. I remember once during a disturbance in Washington that I asked an officer a pretty simple question — his name. He raised his nightstick and said,

"I'll give you 10 seconds to get out of my sight. Then, I put your light out. You can get my name from the hospital when you wake up." It makes it hard to maintain one's professional composure under such circumstances.

Then there were the young blacks who were certain our purpose was to "spy for the man" and they were often just as hard to deal with. By the time a day in the street was over, between the hostile white police officer and the hostile and angry young black, a black journalist headed back to the newsroom in search of some sanity and reason, virtues our media prize greatly. But unfortunately to many a black reporter, we were all to discover times within our own offices when the heat of crisis had all but overtaken those of our white colleagues barricaded inside, wondering if indeed Armageddon had arrived. Even in the quiet moments, it seemed to us then that many of our colleagues had lost their perspective in the midst of chaos.

It was then that many of us looked about to ask where the blacks who knew and understood the city were working during those times of urban stress. They were all out on the street eating tear gas and ducking bricks and nightsticks almost simultaneously. The writers, the editors, the people with ultimate responsibility for portraying the event to the world were all white.

Ben Bagdikian, in an article about the internal agony of one newspaper, the *Washington Post,* noted that institutions must be qualified, too. That they must be capable of discerning their staff needs wisely. And that this discernment must be racially sensitive. I raise that point because I am among the least convinced that the problem of finding "qualified" blacks accounts by itself for these appalling statistics.

When white editors are faced with the challenge of making judgments about white candidates for newsroom jobs, they seem to be able to do that with very little problem. But when they must make the same judgments about blacks, it's Jackie Robinson or no go. They want a surefire hitter, a dynamite dude, a winner in all fields. Much as that is racism, it is also a function of the uncertainty that racism produces. If you know no blacks, on what basis would you judge the first one you had met?

Nothing speaks more clearly than that does to the need for more blacks in the management of the mass media. You are familiar with what I call, at the risk of coining a terrible sounding phrase, the myth of unfireability.

In the report on minority employment, white editors seem to be saying that they not only cannot make sound judgments about what constitutes a "qualified" black or minority journalist, but they also seem to feel that if they did make what we shall all assume was a genuine mistake in judgment that they would not be able to undo it. In effect what we are hearing is that it's better to have no blacks at all than to hire a black who doesn't work out and run the risk of a discrimination suit if he has to be let go.

Aside from the amusing aspects of such a faulty piece of logic, it has about it an unquestionably self-fulfilling aspect. If those are the attitudes that prevail in the newsroom, so little communication is probably taking place that most blacks — except for the Jackie Robinsons of our business — would probably be surefire losers.

What, then, is the answer? Surely, it is simple and logical. There must be blacks in the management structures who can help in making judgments about new personnel, assist in their training and help take the heat for the failures that occur. And those, I suspect, would be kept to a bare minimum.

That is not the sole reason minorities must be brought into the management structure of the mass media. The equally important other reason is that the picture of America as seen through the lens of the mass media is badly distorted. In a society wracked by the problems of race, white voices dominate and white hands control the final outcome of the product. That is not just unfair to blacks and other minorities. It is unfair to whites as well because they are not getting their money's worth from their newspaper. It is this, I think, that hinders the fulfillment of democracy.

And last, I must add a personal note about this problem of qualifications. When I began at age 16 to become a journalist, it was not a calling that cared very much about college degrees. In fact, I remember the first editor who sized me up and decided to take a chance on me. I told him I had no college degree. "Look," he said, "skip all that. Can you write or can't you?" Had he and a few others like him not decided they could make a decision, I, too, would no doubt find myself today among the ranks of the "unqualified." It is a galling and terrifying realization in a multicultural society.

— April 26, 1972

Discriminating News

The Washington Post

Interoffice Memo

Messrs. Bradlee/Simons: 4/7/75

A reader was sharply critical of our failure Saturday to say that whites were excluded from the African Heritage Studies Association meeting at which Barbara Sizemore made an anti-white speech.

He noted that the Star story mentioned that fact--and that its white reporter was barred from the meeting. (Today in a Style piece we refer to the association's "long-standing rule" that only blacks can attend its conferences.")

The reader also questioned the Post's decision to give coverage to a meeting operated under a racial exclusion policy. I can't go along with him on that; we've got to report the news, no matter where it is made. But I think the fact that Mrs. Sizemore was speaking at a blacks-only meeting was news and should have figured prominently in the Saturday story.

--0--

A reader called to protest a common practice exemplified in our story today on the jostling of Ted Kennedy in Boston. We refer to South Boston as "a working class predominantly Irish neighborhood." He objects on a number of counts.

First, he says, it is an ethnic identification that is out of our normal pattern (we also refer to East Boston as predominantly Italian in the previous paragraph). Second, he says, it glosses over the fact that the so-called "Irish" are second and third generation Americans and in very many cases are no longer of pure Irish extraction.

Third, he says, many people read "Irish" to mean "Catholic"--bringing a religious element into the story by the back door. And finally, he says,

(more)

despite the use of the escape word "predominantly,"
the effect is to portray South Boston as all Irish
and all working class, which is a gross over-
simplification.

Nit-picking, maybe. But his protest has at
least a cautionary value in reminding us of the
sensitivity of some readers to such generalized
characterizations.

Charlie Seib

Racism

The Washington Post

Interoffice Memo

TO: Bradlee, et al.   September 30, 1970

FROM: Harwood

Sonny Sixkiller, the American Indian who is the
subject of Ken Turan's story today, expresses mildly
his irritation with the publicity blizzard that uses
all of the racial cliches and stereotypes about
Indians. Unfortunately, the cutlines reflect those
same cliches and stereotypes--"brave warrior,"
"whoops of praise." This is insulting, patronizing
language and the tragedy of it, I suspect, is that
it is all unconscious. The cutline writer didn't
know what he was saying.

We have grown sensitive--we WASPS and Jews--to
slurs against black people. We take Agnew to task
for talking about Fat Japs and Polacks (although
Polish jokes are still Chic at cocktail parties).
We may even be more sensitive than in the past to the
sensitivities of Mexican-Americans and women. We
should be sensitive to the Indians, too.

Sexism and the Media's Changing Standards

By Ben H. Bagdikian

Readers of the *Washington Post* who got their paper before 1:30 a.m. Saturday, March 25, 1972, (an edition with one small dot in an upper corner of most pages) saw a Style section dominated by a six-column photograph of the rear view of about 13 Playboy Club Bunnies, emphasizing legs, thighs and buttocks in the usual chorus-line cheesecake.

Readers who got their papers after 1:30 that morning (in editions with three small dots in the corner or dots plus an "R" meaning "replate" for late news) never saw that photograph. Instead, there was a different shot showing a front view of Hugh Hefner, entrepreneur of Bunnyism, fully dressed, escorting the 1972 Bunny of the Year whose front view displayed a more modest (if that's the word) aspect of the female frame.

What had happened was not an unusual event in a paper like the *Post,* an argument among editors on the subject of sexism in the news. That is, whether this photograph exploited the sexual attributes of women for the stimulation of males, treating women as sex objects rather than human beings with some other reason for being in the news. And whether sexiness unrelated to news has any place in the paper in the first place.

The treatment of women in the news is a subject of turbulence in every newspaper and magazine that has a discernible sign of life. Many women are objecting to being treated in sexual references not used for men, and every general publication goes through constant argument. Publishing is an ocean of males who now feel surrounded by tiny islands of indignant females.

This was a particularly intriguing case because on the same day, the woman-oriented magazine, *Cosmopolitan,* had made some kind of publishing history by printing the first photograph in a general circulation magazine of a full-body nude male, comparable to the usual practice with women by *Playboy.* The idea, one assumes, was to give women readers their male pinup, in this case television actor Burt Reynolds dressed only in a smile and a cigar, with one hand strategically placed.

At a 3 o'clock conference of Style editors (all male at that point) it was decided to satirize both events. There would be an account of the exploitation of females and of males. One would be the story on the Bunny award as written from the scene at McAffee, N.J., by *Post* writer Sally Quinn, and photographed by Matthew Lewis, inevitably showing the Bunnies in their fragments of satin. The other would be a wire story telling of the *Cosmopolitan* episode with a reproduction of the relatively discreet nude photo of Burt Reynolds.

At the 3:15 plenary news conference of *Post* editors, Executive Editor

Ben Bradlee was enthusiastic about the idea of satirizing the Reynolds photo.

Shortly after 6, the page one conference of editors looked at the projected paper for the day, Bradlee actually saw the photograph of Reynolds and he changed his mind, saying it was in bad taste. Style editors remember other male editors adding that it was also ugly, the women editors surmising that of course a man might think a male nude ugly but a female nude not ugly. Bradlee vetoed the *Cosmopolitan* nude, though not the story about it.

When the first edition arrived from the pressroom at 10:30, with the big rearward photo of Bunnies but no Reynolds picture, the argument started.

Mary Wiegers Russell objected. (In the informal nature of much of the *Post* operation, editors, sub-editors and reporters often get involved in discussions if not always final decisions.) She felt that if ridicule of the use of a nude male was dropped, the same should be done with the leggy exposure of the females in the big Bunny picture.

"If we want to run both, fine, though I think it's probably degrading for both sexes," she explained later. "The men were offended by the male cheesecake. . . . Yet any woman who would react that way to a female pinup would be labelled a square or a prude. Running pictures of a nude ballet or any other situation in which the human body is treated with dignity doesn't bother me. Running pictures in which it is cheapened does. And up till now I think the female has borne the brunt of this cheapening."

Joel Garreau, assistant Style editor for graphics, defended the picture as an appropriate illustration of the staged blatant sexism being reported in the Quinn story. But Thomas Kendrick, managing editor of Style, after conferring with Style editor William Cooper, at his home, agreed to pull the big Bunny shot on grounds that the satirical point was lost when the male nude was dropped. So the makeup was changed between editions. Like Muhammad Ali and Niagara Falls, the *Post* seldom stands still.

The beefcake-versus-cheesecake controversy was only part of the continuing change in standards of treating women in the news, in many ways comparable to the treatment of minorities. It has been a cliche in journalism to describe women in terms of their physical attributes, especially sexually attractive ones. "Shapely, trim-legged Mrs. Jones took the stand . . ." but never, "Big-shouldered, slim-hipped Ralph Dogood announced his candidacy today. . . ."

That habit left the *Post,* or at least started the process of disappearing in June, 1970, when Bradlee circulated a memorandum forbidding irrelevant sexual references for women whose counterparts were not also used for men, like "divorcee" or "grandmother" or "housewife" or adjectives like "vivacious" and "pert" and "cute."

"Stories involving the achievement of women are often implicitly condescending," he wrote. "They imply 'pretty good for a woman'. . . . It is the policy of the *Washington Post* to make the equality and dignity of women completely and instinctively meaningful."

There are other serious issues of sex, like the hiring, promotion and pay of women journalists compared with men, and want ads that some women complain list the best professional jobs only under male headings. Neither is there much doubt that the trade as a whole continues its traditional momentum of a male preserve that keeps photo editors' desk drawers filled with girlie pictures for the boys to slaver over between coffee breaks.

In September, 1971, UPI asked its client editors, "Should revealing photos of well-endowed women be transmitted in news agency picture services even when they are not related to the news? Do they really get printed or simply passed around for in-house delectation?" The overwhelming response from around the country was that the editors would never think of printing such pictures in their family newspaper but that they hoped UPI would certainly keep sending them. Marv Sussman, picture editor of *Newsday,* on Long Island, wrote back, "We all enjoy a good cheesecake shot. The ones I get make the rounds and end up on bulletin boards, rarely in the paper."

Don Hadley of the Geneva (N.Y.) *Times,* said, "Of course we don't run them. . . . Of course we pass them around the newsroom." Don Green of the Wooster (Ohio) *Daily Record* replied, "Bring on les girls! Who cares about publication?"

What happened at the *Post* with the Bunny shots was not cosmic. But the problem of changing standards is not an easy one to cope with. At the turn of the century, a peek at a lady's ankle below her floor-length gown was enough to set male temples to pounding. A paper printing a picture of a woman in a bathing suit revealing naked kneecaps would be denounced as indecent.

One difference today is that the entire social scene is changing more rapidly than ever. A paper that stands still may be displaying a culture most of its readers ignore or dislike because they have been educated by some other medium like television, movies, magazines, candid talk at home, school, church and on the back porch.

Women and many men insist that when it comes to treatment of women and sex in the media, the bias arises because it is a male-dominated profession. One response to the UPI poll was a prediction from K. F. Melville, assistant city editor of the Morgantown, W. Va., *Dominion-Post,* who said: "You will find that most editors receiving UPI 'girlie pix' don't use them but also do not object to receiving them so that they may be passed around the newsroom. This will probably be your finding because most editors are men." Melville added that the wirephoto girlie pictures were "insulting, demeaning and totally disgusting."

The K. F. in K. F. Melville stands for "Kathleen Fey."

—April 17, 1972

151

Conflict of Interest and Ethics

The No-Man's-Land of the News Business

By Richard Harwood

On March 24, 1971, a full-page advertisement was published in the *Washington Post* by the National Citizens Committee for Revenue Sharing. This newly formed lobby listed among its sponsors various politicians, businessmen, educators and the editor-in-chief of a major American newspaper — Erwin D. Canham of the *Christian Science Monitor.*

On the same day, the Washington-Baltimore Newspaper Guild, an AFL-CIO union, adopted a resolution of support for the antiwar demonstrations scheduled to be held in Washington on April 24.

Out in Chicago at about that time, 38 members of the *Chicago Daily News* reporting and editing staff and 61 members of the *Chicago Sun-Times* staff bought advertisements in the two newspapers to express their opposition to the re-election of Mayor Richard Daley.

A few days later an antiwar lobby — the National Peace Action Coalition — published an advertisement in the *New York Times* urging support of the April 24 demonstration. The signers included — besides politicians, educators and entertainers — Gerald Walker, who was identified as the editor of the *New York Times Magazine.*

On April 9, a news story reported that the publisher of the *Cincinnati Enquirer,* Francis L. Dale, would be the chairman of a citizens committee to promote the re-election of President Nixon.

In February, Tom Wicker, a columnist and associate editor of the *New York Times,* made a stirring antiwar speech at a Cambridge, Mass., teach-in: "We (antiwar forces) got one President out and perhaps we can do that again."

His speech inspired a number of Boston journalists to action and 171 reporters, editors, television and radio correspondents sent a telegram to the President and to various congressmen declaring that "each day our military remains in Indochina is a further crime against mankind. As men and women of the American news media, we feel we must speak out."

They were tacitly encouraged in this effort by the editor of the *Boston Globe,* Thomas Winship, who had said that there are "one or two fundamental issues which come along in a lifetime which have such overriding moral importance that you just can't be neutral. Vietnam is one of them. . . ."

Developments of this sort in the news business are rather commonplace these days. They are noteworthy for a variety of reasons. They reflect, to begin with, the no-man's-land of journalistic ethics and the utter confusion in this business over such simple concepts as conflict of interest.

It is rather generally accepted among newspaper people that financial corruption is probably sinful, that editors and reporters ought not take money or other things of value from people and organizations that are in the news. On some newspapers (this one included), the acceptance of a bribe — for that is what it is — is a firing offense. But not on all newspapers, because our collective sense of ethics remains primitive and is tempered with practices out of the past. The *Denver Post* recently proposed to abolish all "payola" in the newsroom: there would be no more gifts, free trips, free tickets to entertainment events, free junkets and so on. The proposal produced a great outcry among the editing and reporting staff and resulted in a compromise that left it up to the individual to decide what gifts he should accept: in other words, "payola" was legitimized.

It is also accepted rather widely in this business that news people ought not get involved in "politics," that it is improper, say, for your political editor to serve as a delegate to a political convention, to write or make speeches for political candidates and so on. On some newspapers (this one included), the rule is inflexible. But not on all newspapers. One of the editors of a Chicago daily once managed a local political campaign while serving as a Washington correspondent. Publishers and editors in many cities are up to their necks in political activity, and not merely through their editorial pages. Every roster of delegates to the Republican and Democratic national conventions contains the names of newspaper owners or executives or writers. In some cities and states they are party kingmakers and strategists and financiers. To bring it closer to home, the late Philip Graham, as publisher of this newspaper, played a prominent role in the 1960 Democratic National Convention, as the country learned much later from Theodore White's *The Making of the President.* So here again, what ought to be an ethical plateau for this business is in fact an ethical jungle.

Today there is desultory discussion among editors and reporters over the proper limits of "involvement," whether — in the fine phrase of J. R. Wiggins, former editor of this newspaper — one can "reasonably ask the privilege of being on both sides of the footlights, actors on the stage and critics in the audience at the same time." But there is ethical bankruptcy in the news business on that issue as on other conflict of interest questions.

What is ethical on the *Daily Bugle* is unethical on the *Daily Clarinet*. There is even conflict and confusion within given newspapers.

Editor Winship in Boston sternly opposes the involvement of his staff in "politics" and openly approves of staff involvement in antiwar activities. Editor John Hughes of the *Christian Science Monitor* strongly disapproves of staff involvement in causes and political movements of any kind. Yet Editor-in-Chief Canham of the *Monitor* lobbies publicly for revenue sharing, has served as president of the U.S. Chamber of Commerce and has been involved in many other causes, organizations and government assignments. William Woestendiek was fired last year from his job as editor of a WETA-TV news show because his wife took a job as a press agent for Martha Mitchell. One of his colleagues on the show was not fired even though her spouse was a press agent for a Democratic senator. And the board chairman of the station, Max Kampelman, retained his position despite his long and continuing involvement in the political fortunes of Hubert Humphrey.

A hundred years ago newspapers in this country, by and large, were political propaganda sheets, house organs for parties and factions. They did not expect to be taken seriously by their enemies or by a mass public seeking information on which to arrive at reasoned judgments about public men and public issues. It is only in this century and especially in the last 30 or 40 years that the "free American press" has tried to rise above its shabby origins. It yearns now for "status," "influence" and "respectability"; it wants to be taken seriously. Above all, it wants to be *believed* because its power, its influence, its status in American life rests on that single and fragile thread — *public belief.* Without believability — "credibility" is the popular word — a newspaper is simply another business enterprise, and a hollow and pretentious one at that. Without believability it is as pitiful as the discredited politician who cries, "Follow me!," only to be greeted with mocking laughter.

Newspapers and the people involved in their production cannot have it both ways. They are no longer confronted with an illiterate or indifferent audience. Their audience of the 1970s is educated, aware and concerned. It is not tolerant of publishers or editors or writers who compromise themselves financially and politically and then parade their "integrity" and "fairness" in demanding the respect and influence that comes with *belief.* The audience, in those circumstances, will not believe.

Nor will the audience be bullied or brainwashed into belief through the labors of newspaper "image committees" or self-serving "press councils" or payrolled house critics such as me. The remedy is in ourselves as journalists, in the self-discipline we are willing to accept, in the ethical standards we are willing to observe, in the example publishers and editors are prepared to set.

A *Wall Street Journal* reporter got into this debate some time ago and declared that newspaper reporters have as much right to picket the White

House as do publishers to lobby and fraternize with Presidents. Of course they do. The possession of a press card limits no one's rights as a citizen. Journalists may go into the real world and run for public office — and some of them do. They have the right as citizens to wheel and deal within the law, the right to lobby and to exploit to the fullest the very unique privileges that come with the ownership of printing presses and press credentials. But if they choose to have it both ways, if they choose to be both actors on the stage and critics in the audience, they will pay the ultimate price of diminished public trust.

—April 16, 1971

The Reporter: Professional Observer vs Participating Citizen

By Ben H. Bagdikian

It's ironic that the AFL-CIO refused to endorse a presidential candidate for the first time in its history the same week that the Newspaper Guild, thought of as the reporters' union, did endorse a candidate (George Mc-Govern) for the first time in its history.

But for newspapermen it is more than an ironic coincidence in time. It raises again the tough issue of the conflict between the reporter as professional observer and the reporter as participating citizen.

If the steelworkers' union can endorse a presidential candidate it thinks will be best for the well-being of the union member, why not a reporters' union? If the security of both will be influenced by the kind of President that leads a country for four years, why can't the reporter be as much an organizational pro as a pipefitter?

The problem that is usually talked about is that the pipefitter won't be suspected of cutting threads in elbow joints any differently because his union said it prefers one candidate over another, but a reporter, whose work may find him reporting on Richard Nixon, could ply his trade differently because of his union's commitment to George McGovern.

The argument for a public endorsement by the Guild runs to support for national policies that are seen as beneficial for its members. Charles A. Perlik Jr., president of the Guild, said:

"If we can demand a 'voice' in the quality of the products our members' labor produces, what's wrong with demanding a 'voice' in the quality of governments which structure, manage and dominate our lives?"

The case against the endorsement by some Guild members was expressed in a petition some Washington reporters published as an ad:

"The Guild has no business interjecting its members into a partisan political role. Its efforts to do so demean us as professionals whose hallmark is fairness. It ties us to a political decision we personally may or may not favor."

But there are two factors not being talked about that need to be recognized: one is that the unanimous vote of the international executive board is misleading as a measure of reporters' feelings, and the other is that the vote has little practical news consequence.

The issue first came up at the Puerto Rico convention of the Guild in the form of a recommendation by an official Guild Committee for endorsement of a presidential candidate. It is a 19-member committee and the vote was a narrow 10 to 9, in favor. Then on the floor, a roll call vote on a direct endorsement of McGovern was defeated 201 to 148.

A second motion, authorizing the international executive board to endorse a candidate after both major conventions, carried 226 to 124. (The IEB apparently took the Nixon nomination for granted and went ahead before the Republican convention.)

But the makeup of the 226 majority is interesting as a sign of the complications in this branch of journalism. The major blocks of votes that put it over were 11 from Boston, 10 from Cleveland, 14 from Los Angeles, 14 from Philadelphia, 16 from San Francisco-Oakland, and the crucial 68 votes from New York. A reversal of votes by the New York delegation or a group of the others would have defeated the endorsement authorization.

The general impression is that "reporters" had voted to endorse McGovern. The Newspaper Guild is known primarily as a reporters' union but in fact slightly less than half its members are journalists — writers or editors and other news department employees. The others are workers in commercial and other departments of a newspaper — ad salesmen, circulation workers, clerks. It has always been an issue whether the Guild should include nonjournalists. Journalists, though sharing everyone else's economic problems of sending children to college and paying the rent, have working needs peculiar to their trade not shared by commercial workers. On the other hand, a union solely of reporters lacks power at bargaining time, not only because of smaller numbers but because a strike solely of reporters can be circumvented by executives pasting up wire service copy; reporters need other workers in absolute alliance.

So the vote to endorse was not so clearly a reporters' vote. The crucial New York vote, for example, was cast by 18 delegates under the unit rule, meaning a majority of the 18 would decide how all 68 votes would be cast. Tom Lask, of the *New York Times* book section, headed the delegation and under the rules does not vote except to break a tie. He said that of the 18 delegates, 5 or 6 were working journalists, about the same number nonjournalistic employees in the news department, and about a third from commercial departments. In the caucus the vote was "close," he said. He did not vote but if necessary would have in favor of the endorsement.

The 14 votes from Los Angeles were all from the long-struck Hearst *Herald-Examiner* (the *Los Angeles Times* is nonunion) and were cast by two delegates, one a worker in classified ads, the other from circulation. The 10 Cleveland votes were cast by six delegates, half of them not working journalists. The 14 Philadelphia votes were cast by seven delegates, one a photographer, one a reporter, one a full-time employee of the union local, and four from nonjournalistic departments.

The chief argument against the endorsement is that it makes reporters vulnerable to additional attack for alleged bias. It has already been seized by enemies of the press and used in precisely that way.

This is a public relations argument and it has meaning. But it is not a real problem in terms of how the news is actually covered. There are fair reporters and unfair reporters and neither are influenced in their behavior by a vote taken by the international executive board of the Newspaper Guild.

If the argument is seriously made that the vote by the IEB is bad because it will influence the political reporting of reporters, then there is another matter that these same critics need to face:

Most publishers of newspapers are going to endorse Nixon (80 per cent of endorsing publishers in 1968 did and 85 per cent when Mr. Nixon ran in 1960). These are the men who pay the reporter his salary, decide on his promotions and make or break his career. If it's believed that the union chieftains can tilt the reporter one way, it is as logical to suppose that the reporter's concern for his own career will tilt him his publisher's way.

It is hard to see any definite gain for the Guild or reporters or even Mc-Govern. McGovern won't benefit since he'll be accused by his opponents of being the undeserving recipient of sympathetic reporting from a politically biased press. Reporters won't be influenced one way or another since Guild members, like the rank-and-file of most American labor unions, have been indifferent toward the political opinions of their leaders.

The more basic problem is that the endorsement by the Guild erodes the philosophy that whenever possible reporters should stay out of the scenes they report. This is not a rule that applies to advocacy journalists for publications serving special audiences. But it is real for the straight news reporter whose audience is an entire community. A reporter wearing a "Down with Mr. X" button on his lapel, real or symbolic, while he interviews Mr. X, does not get representative answers from Mr. X — or from Mr. X's political opponents. One suspects that the most vigorous objectors to the Guild's endorsement are not the reporters who dislike McGovern but the ones who are most deeply engaged in political coverage and know from personal experience how journalistically crippling the endorsement could be.

—July 24, 1972

Should the Media Buy News?

By Charles B. Seib

The CBS television network paid H. R. Haldeman, President Nixon's chief of staff in happier times, a sizable sum—$25,000 is the lowest estimate—for submitting to an interview that was broadcast in two one-hour segments in March [1975]. Since then, there has been much discussion centering on this question: Should the media buy conversations with public figures, particularly public figures who have been found guilty of crimes?

Traditionally, newspaper editors have recoiled from paying news sources with a moral horror that is a little puzzling in a business where, for example, the stolen document is not unacceptable—provided your own staffer did not do the stealing.

On the other hand, the exclusive magazine article and the celebrity book have long been staples in the world of big-time media spending. The bosses of CBS, in defending the deal with Haldeman, put it in that category. They weren't buying news, they say, although they hoped the broadcasts would be newsy; they were buying a "memoir."

The network is defensive about the Haldeman purchase. There are assurances that it was carefully considered and was admittedly a "close call" and that the whole subject is under review. Nevertheless, we probably can expect more of the same all through the media.

In terms of dollars, the Haldeman interview appears to have been one of television's great bargains. The highest figure mentioned in the speculation about what he was paid is $100,000 for what boiled down to two hours of viewing. I am told by a network official that an hour-long shoot-'em-up can cost as much as $300,000 to make. Perhaps Haldeman didn't have the pulling power of Mannix or Columbo. But by any measure the interview was an inexpensive way to fill air time, and with material that could be billed as straight from the den of iniquity.

Assuming that I am right in feeling that for economic reasons, if for no other, we are in for more such "memoirs" on television, and perhaps their counterparts in the print media, I would like to make a Modest Proposal for the Protection of the Public. Let it be required that the purchased interviews be preceded by this information:

1. The price paid to the subject and exactly what it covered—the "discussion" prior to the interview (there was reported to be 44 hours of this in the Haldeman case), the length of the interview itself, home movies (as in the Haldeman case) or other trimmings. If family members—or the dog—come extra, the audience should be told that too.

2. The restrictions, if any, on the interviewer. Were some questions or areas ruled out of bounds in advance?

3. The way in which the interview was edited for viewing (or publication). Did the subject take part in the process? Could he insist that certain passages be retained in the edited version?

(I am assured by a CBS executive that Haldeman put no limitations on the questioning and that he did not take part in the editing. CBS steadfastly refuses to tell how much Haldeman was paid or to comment on the amounts that have been mentioned.)

But even if these or similar ground rules were adopted, the purchased interview would continue to have certain inherent problems. In theory, a tough interviewer (and Mike Wallace, who did the Haldeman job, has a reputation as one of the toughest) can dig deep. But experience, certainly confirmed in this instance, has shown that television interviews, particularly of highly placed or highly paid subjects, tend to come out bland, dull and even fawning.

At times the transcript of the Haldeman interview resembles the less coherent moments in those memorable little talks in the Oval Office. Try this as an example of high-level communication:

WALLACE: Mr. Haldeman, why did the White House need the plumbers—Gordon Liddy, Howard Hunt, Anthony Ulasewicz, Jack Caulfield, Donald Segretti—all of what John Mitchell described as "the White House horrors"? Why did you need them?

HALDEMAN: Well, you're bug—bungling—bun—bundling into a—a bag a lot of different apples and oranges and carrots.

WALLACE: But they all—they all worked for, in, around, on the payroll of the White House.

HALDEMAN: I—I don't—Well, let's see, maybe they all did.

WALLACE: They all did.

HALDEMAN: No, Liddy never worked—yes he did—

WALLACE: Yes, he did. He was in the plumbers.

HALDEMAN:—he worked for the plumbers. You're right. You're right. Okay, let's take them one at a time. The—One of the problems we've got here is that all those things keep getting jungled—jumbled into the—this bag and—and then added to Watergate, and it all comes out as—as a—as an integral whole, which it is not. It was not at the time.

WALLACE: Well, these all worked for the White House. They were all on the payroll of the White House. They were all engaged in gumshoeing or wiretapping or—Some of them have gone to jail. Why did the White House need that—

HALDEMAN: Well, let's—let's—

WALLACE:—with your accomplishments?

HALDEMAN: Let's take them bit by bit. Why—why it needed the plumbers—

WALLACE: Was for leaks?

HALDEMAN:—has—has been covered ad nauseam, I guess—
And so on.

160

Well, dullness is not entirely unknown to television, or the print media either, and the viewer and the reader always have the option of turning off, literally or figuratively. But there is another element of the superstar interview that raises a more serious question—the element of monumental self-service. This runs through both installments of the Haldeman interview and reaches its purest form in the closing minutes of the second one:

WALLACE: Mr. Haldeman, Dean confessed. Krogh confessed. Colson made a bargain with the prosecutor. Magruder. All of these fellows who worked either for you or with you. Has it never occurred to you to do the same?

HALDEMAN: I have to assume, Mike, that each of those people felt he was guilty of what he confessed of. If I felt I were guilty of any crime for which I have been charged, or any other crime, I'd confess to the guilt of that.

WALLACE: It has never occurred to you that it might be wise at this moment to take your losses, get it over with and start a new life?

HALDEMAN: Yes. It has occurred to me. If there were, in fact, a charge to which I was guilty, I could in good conscience plead guilty to it. And there is an enormous temptation to do that and to want to take the guilty plea under the kinds of pressures that have been put on us . . . But on the basis of living with yourself, you've got to be able to, I at least, I can't speak for anyone else, I've got to be able to know that I'm in a truthful and honest position. And a plea of guilty would not be truthful or honest on my part and so I can't do it.

The Modest Proposal I outlined is meant seriously (although I have no illusions that it or a less drastic proposal by the National News Council will be adopted), but in view of the above I can't resist the temptation to make a facetious amendment:

Let there be established a National Memoir Council to preview purchased interviews and make sure the public interest is protected. If the council finds clear-cut evidence of self-service by the person interviewed, it shall order a rebate, to be reported at the beginning of the broadcast or article. In the Haldeman instance, it might have gone like this:

"Mr. Haldeman received $50,000 (or whatever it was) for his presence, conversation and home movies, but he was obliged to refund $7,500 for the self-serving protestation of innocence you will hear in the closing minutes of the second broadcast."

Perhaps provision could even have been made for a beep at the appropriate moment, so the viewer could give the volume control a twist and, in effect, share in the rebate.

—April 26, 1975

How Valuable Are Codes of Ethics?

By Charles B. Seib

Patrons of the news business—members of the public, in other words—often ask why the press doesn't have a code of ethics to govern its behavior. The implication, of course, is that some definition of ethical standards is desperately needed.

The fact is, the press has not one but many codes of ethics. They are all high-minded, sincere and of minimal value. Sigma Delta Chi, the journalistic society, has one; the trade organizations of editors have them; various segments of the business—the sports writers and the business writers, for example—have them.

Many individual newspapers have their own codes of ethics or rules of conduct. These tend to be more specific and less rhetorical than the journalistic organizations, and therefore more useful. But these house rules have recently run into trouble. National Labor Relations Board administrative law judges have found that rules of conduct affect conditions of employment. Therefore they must be arrived at, say the judges, through collective bargaining on papers that have unionized editorial departments. The day of the editor posting the rules of the game as he sees them may be about over.

Not even the most militant unionist could find much to object to in the various industry-wide codes of ethics. Who can argue with the Associated Press Managing Editors' assertion that a good newspaper is "fair, accurate, honest, responsible, independent and decent," and that truth is its guiding principle? That must be the most unobjectionable statement since the Boy Scout oath.

But when the codes get the least bit specific, their main problem—lip service—surfaces.

The APME code provides: "News sources should be disclosed unless there is a clear reason not to do so. When it is necessary to protect the confidentiality of a source the reason should be given."

In practice, the unidentified source pops up everywhere. He has become a standard character; he gives the cachet of inside dope.

And how often lately have you seen a reference to the ever popular "informed source" or "highly placed source" or just plain "source" followed by the reason the reporter can't tell you who the source is?

Or take the matter of corrections. The APME code provides that all "substantive errors" (different from old-fashioned ordinary errors, apparently) should be corrected "promptly and prominently." The American Society of Newspaper Editors says the same thing about "significant errors of fact, as well as errors of omission."

But as every journalist and patron of the media knows, correction is a sometimes thing. Promptness is likely to be related to the danger of a law suit. And prominence is too often taken to mean a few lines at the bottom of an inside page.

The newest journalistic code of ethics is the one from the ASNE, the most prestigious of the journalistic trade organizations. Called "A Statement of Principles," it has the usual lofty references to the responsibilities imposed by the First Amendment and the need for the highest ethical and professional standards.

But two quotations from the ASNE code point up the limited use of such documents when the chips are down. Under Freedom of the Press, it says: "Journalists must be constantly alert to see that the public's business is conducted in public." And under Fair Play, it says: "Journalists should respect the rights of people involved in the news."

Certainly no one could argue with either of those statements. Yet in practice there is a conflict between them that is at the heart of the free press—fair trial controversy between the press and the courts.

The first statement is based on the press's insistence that it has the right to publish anything it feels to be in the public interest. Most journalists would say that this includes the past record of a person arrested for a crime or the fact that the arrested person has made a confession to the police. But a growing number of judges are issuing what they call protective orders and the editors call gag orders based on the second quoted statement—the one about the rights of the individual.

The judges are saying that publication of certain information—a man's past record, perhaps, or the fact that he has made a confession—can endanger his constitutional right to a fair trial. Some of them are even issuing orders against publication of material made available in open court.

The free press-fair trial dispute is a tough one, concerning as it does an apparent clash between two sections of the Bill of Rights—the First Amendment guarantees of a free press and the Sixth Amendment guarantee of a fair trial.

All the codes of ethics in the world are not going to resolve it. The most they can do is to set standards of integrity and responsibility under which a solution can be worked out.

Which brings us to the fact that, in the clinches, written codes are of limited value. There it boils down to the good judgment, the good will and the personal standards of the editors and reporters who make the minute-by-minute decisions that result in the country's daily budget of news.

—December 13, 1975

A Reporter's Ethical Dilemma:
The Story of a Missed One-Foot Putt

By Colman McCarthy

Chuck Thorpe is a young professional golfer, a black athlete competing in a country club sport long dominated by whites. Known for his power off the tee, Thorpe occasionally has power of the mouth, boasting of his skill, like Muhammed Ali. Some of the vets don't like his big talk; a white rookie can brag, because that's self-confidence, but when a black pops off, it is arrogance.

I have known about Thorpe because he played in the Washington area for awhile, before he qualified for the tour at the Professional Golfers Association player school in Florida. When he played at the 1972 Westchester golf classic, the richest mother lode of the tour, I went to watch Thorpe play, with the idea of writing about his tour experiences. I didn't catch up to Thorpe at Westchester until the 15th hole of the second round. By the end of the day, a series of unlikely events had thrown Thorpe and me into a tense drama involving both the ethics of his profession and mine. Thorpe was disqualified from play and I had a story far different from the one I planned. Each of us, however painful, met standards we should automatically expect from others in a like situation.

When I found Thorpe, he had only four holes to play. He had just bogeyed 15 and 16 from sloppy shotmaking but was still one over par, a score that would be close to the cutoff for the final 36 holes. At 17, an easy and short par four, Thorpe, either tense or lazy, flubbed his second and third shots to reach the green. His playing partners, Dick Crawford and Roy Pace, were closer to the cup, so Thorpe putted first, from about 25 feet. He stroked it close, a mere foot short of the cup. Then, hesitating — he was in Pace's line and not sure whether to putt out or mark — Thorpe jabbed at the one footer. He missed. His score was six. On the 18th, Thorpe rallied for a birdie four. The gallery that trailed him — I was about 20 per cent of it — cheered at the home green because the birdie put Thorpe at 146 — 72 on Thursday and 74 on Friday — a score that might make the cut. Following the round, I interviewed the tall and muscular player — he is one of 13 children from a small North Carolina town and learned golf by playing on caddy's day at a white country club where his father tended greens.

An hour later, I happened to look at the official scoreboard off the 18th fairway. Thorpe's score was posted as 145, with a five on the 17th, not a six as I saw him take. I waited another hour to see if the correction would be made but the five stood. Whatever the cause, a rule had been broken. The PGA requires one player to keep the score of another and at the end of the round both players check their own scorecard hole by hole for accuracy. Mistakes are occasionally made—the DeVicenzo case at the Masters in 1968 is well-known—but disqualification is the automatic penalty when a lower score is substituted for a higher one.

With unwelcomed suddenness, I faced the painful fact that no one else had noticed the error and that Thorpe's fate at Westchester was at the mercy of my judgment: be silent about the rule infraction or go to a PGA official to report it? If Thorpe's score was 150 or 153, it would have made no difference—he was out anyway. But his 145 as posted appeared likely to be the cutoff. By day's end it was; Arnold Palmer, 1971's winner, was at 146 and he packed off in his usual dejection.

I had gone to the tournament as part of a vacation, a rest from typewriters and editors (and they a rest from me), with no intention of reporting, much less getting involved in a conflict. But how do you hide? True, to be silent meant Thorpe would play the final 36 holes, be guaranteed a few hundred dollars at least and perhaps—if he played well—many thousand. He would also be exempt from the ordeal of Monday qualifying at the next tournament. Looking the other way also meant boosting my fan sympathies for Thorpe, a rookie athlete in a lonely and harshly competitive sport, a self-taught player with few of the breaks of the average tour pro who learns the game at a country club and perfects it in college. Even the foolish way Thorpe missed the one footer at 17 earned him sympathy: a mistake other pros make early in their amateur days and junior tournaments. The experienced and careful golfer, knowing a tap-in putt equals on the scorecard a 300-yard drive, does not rush his pace to get out of another player's line, as Thorpe did. Instead, the ball is marked and holed out later in full concentration. This is a lesson the fair-haired Jack Nicklauses learned in leisure at age 18, but which Thorpe, denied entrance to early doors, was learning on the job.

The main trouble with letting Thorpe's error stand was my uneasy feeling of paternalism; go easy on him, he's a black, whites have stepped on him enough already, what's one stroke out of 146? In context, this was reverse racism, as muddled as the straight kind. Black players worked hard to get into pro golf and to favor them now by relaxing the rules is really to keep them "in place," exactly what many whites have always done.

Before deciding to tell the PGA officials about the 17th hole score, I tried—unsuccessfully—to find Thorpe. He was neither at the club or his hotel. I found Crawford, though, who had kept Thorpe's scorecard. By chance, Crawford was also involved in a dispute. He was penalized two strokes for being late at the first tee; his clubs were stolen from the locker room and in hunting around for a new set he showed up late for his starting time. Crawford, distracted all afternoon by the PGA's dogmatic penalty—why doesn't the PGA make an exception for lateness when the reason is valid?—said he wasn't watching Thorpe on 17 and put down a five believing Thorpe made the "gimme." In the scorer's tent following play, Thorpe, surely dejected by his play and perhaps distracted by Crawford being victimized by both a thief and the PGA (Crawford missed the cut by two strokes, the same two he was penalized), may not have noticed his inaccurate scorecard.

With the intention of correcting an oversight (the missing missed putt) and not exposing cheating — I don't believe Thorpe had surrendered honesty in any way — I went to a PGA official in late afternoon. The third member of the threesome, Roy Pace, an unknown Texas pro who played well at Westchester, was present and confirmed Thorpe's six. A few hours later, the PGA located Thorpe. Apparently, the golfer confirmed that his score was really a six on 17, not five. The young black professional was disqualified and thrown into temporary joblessness.

If only Thorpe had made that tap-in putt — for his profit and my relaxation. I don't know if the PGA told him or anyone else about my involvement. Probably not. The officials like to boast that pro golf is unique as a sport of honor and spreading talk that a reporter saw a rule violated would only raise questions. Actually golf is no more or less honorable than any other sport in which athletes hungrily compete for big money. It is also mysterious why the PGA allows players to keep score; why don't official scorers keep it, as in other pro sports?

My hope now is that Thorpe will go on for both a successful year and a rewarding career in the game. Perhaps it is better he committed the errors he did — hasty putting and careless score-checking — at Westchester now than later on, say, in the U.S. Open or the Masters. Thorpe has the talent to win both. If he ever does, I will be one of those who can say I knew Thorpe when he was on the way up. And I didn't stop his rise by a "helpful" look the other way.

— August 20, 1972

The Big Business of Being a Newsman

Speaking Out–for a Fee

By Stephen D. Isaacs

Over the years, journalists have been ever ready to broadcast and write about the outside income of senators and congressmen.

Each May 15, when senators have to file their sources of outside income, eyes bulge at some of the fees the legislators command for speaking engagements, sometimes as high as $5,000 per talk.

It turns out, however, that although the sums aren't filed anywhere in public view, the media in Washington and in New York have quietly spawned an industry-within-an-industry with tidy profits accruing from newsmen's zipping out to the airport, hopping aboard a jet going somewhere to make a lecture, speech, appearance or whatever — at a relatively high tab.

Columnist Jack Anderson, for instance, makes so much at the business of lecturing that he takes no income from his column. Instead, he puts the profits from the column back into it, he says, in the form of salaries for his assistants, and lives off the lecture circuit.

Anderson tries to give one speech a week during the speaking year, which runs from September through early June. At Anderson's minimum fee of $2,500 a speech, plus his expenses, that adds to a tidy income. As Anderson says, "I'm just the son of a postal clerk, so that's big money to me. I live very well, thanks to these lectures."

Anderson is a current star on the lecture circuit, with investigative reporters and reporting now in fashion. So are Carl Bernstein and Bob Woodward of the *Washington Post,* who have been greatly in demand because of their reporting of the Watergate scandal. But even their fee, rang-

167

ing up to $2,000 per appearance, is less than some of the big stars of the circuit.

One of the biggest is columnist Art Buchwald, who makes between 35 and 40 paid speeches a year, and his fee is from $3,000 to $3,500 per appearance. Buchwald turns down many offers.

He is particularly fond of small groups of businessmen, increasing numbers of whom will hire him "to get you in the room, to get the hot poop. I've done about three at '21' (a fancy New York restaurant)—they've been brokerage houses and they entertain their best customers. There's 60 or 40 or 50 people at each one, and that is so beautiful because you can get such a great meal and you're out by 10 o'clock. And then, for your sins, you have to go to Missoula.

"It's not just the dough," says Buchwald. "It gets me out of Washington, and I go to places you wouldn't go to under any other conditions. . . . It's a great way to get out of the city and talk to people. I get a lot of ideas from it for the column and by osmosis. It's very stimulating. Then, it's an ego trip. You go out and speak to people who read you. Yeah, it has great compensations besides the dough, which I don't object to."

Tom Wicker of the *New York Times* says he does it both for the money (usually around $2,000 per speech) and for the input audiences give for his columns. The question-and-answer sessions after the speeches, says Wicker, "give you some sense of what people are interested in. I get asked questions and get challenged sometimes on points that hadn't ever occurred to me. I find quite often that in Q and As with audiences, they either raise a point in your mind you hadn't thought about or they force you to formulate an answer to something. I often find that is a seed of a column.

"So that sort of thing is useful for me to do. I grant you that I make a lot of talks just because I'm being paid to do it. If there were a law that prevented speakers from being paid, which would probably be a good law, I suppose I'd do half of what I do now."

Another busy journalist-lecturer is James J. Kilpatrick, who made between 40 and 45 lectures in 1973 and is trying to "cut it down to about 25 or so this season."

"It's a very lucrative business and it's good for me," says Kilpatrick. "I'm not going to give it up entirely. But there are a whole lot of tensions involved in this thing, chasing around the country, catching the planes, being away from my wife and my place in the hills I like so much."

Kilpatrick, too, finds the give-and-take with audiences to be a boon journalistically. "It's very useful," he says, "and most of the time I enjoy it." He spent a recent Tuesday in Chillicothe, O. (at the University of Ohio) and the following day in Oshkosh, Wis. (at the University of Wisconsin). "Oshkosh didn't go too well," said Kilpatrick. "I was boffo in Chillicothe. That was a great one."

Kilpatrick believes that he is relatively popular as a campus speaker because of his political outlook.

"I know what I have going for me," he says, "which is that I am a front-office or token conservative on most of the college or university speaking schedules. At the University of Delaware, they had a series of 23 or 26 lectures and Phil Crane and I were the only two conservatives on the whole damned list.

"I discover wherever I go that I'm following on the heels of Dick Gregory and Julian Bond and Harrison Salisbury and Walter Mondale and Gaylord Nelson and on down the line. Ordinarily, I will be the only conservative in the whole speaking academic year or often the only one in two years. I have a little something going for me on that. I don't have to be good. I just have to be alive.

"Then they go to the trustees and say, 'What do you mean we've got nothing but radicals and far-out left-wing liberals on our speaking schedule? Look: Kilpatrick. There he is.' I'm the raisin in the dough."

Not every newsman can do lectures, or is wanted as a lecturer. In general, television personalities are more sought after than print journalists.

Harry Walker, head of one of the biggest lecture-booking bureaus in the country, says that Anderson's big fees (Anderson has been a Walker client for 26 years) are the result of his exposure.

"The lecture business follows the economic trends of our country," says Walker. "It's easier to book a television correspondent than a columnist. They are seen by your clientele, who want to see the person in the flesh.

"Unless a columnist is in 400 or 500 newspapers, there isn't that much exposure. People just don't read bylines. Who notices the name? They'll remember Marvin Kalb (another Walker client) because they've seen him on television. I've represented Max Lerner for many years and he's probably one of the 10 best speakers in the United States. But it isn't as easy getting him a date as it is for a Kalb, a Brinkley or a Reasoner. I've had Hans Morgenthau for more than 15 years. We get $1,500 for him. How would you compare his background and training—he's probably the leading political scientist in the country, so provocative and so learned— with some of these people who get twice as much or more?"

Kilpatrick, who gets between $1,000 and $1,500 per speech, feels that, in effect, that is the way the cookie crumbles. "It's an aspect of the free marketplace and I don't knock it. I'm getting much higher fees now, since I have been doing the CBS '60 Minutes' thing, than what I was getting when I was editor of the *Richmond News-Leader.* But then I was getting higher fees when I went into national syndication than I was getting in Richmond. There are an awful lot of lecturers kicking around who are all hungry for the engagements."

"This is getting to more and more of a celebrity-affair type of thing," says Robert Keedick, head of the nation's oldest booking agency, the Keedick Lecture Bureau, Inc. "They go to see the personality. They'd rather be entertained than have a real weighty, thought-provoking discussion."

Television commentators, says Keedick, "as a general rule, don't have the background" of some of the learned speakers, yet talk on the same subject, "and yet they get paid umpteen times as much."

Walter Cronkite takes very few lecture dates a year and his lawyer would not divulge just what his fee is. Nor would David Brinkley's office, but he is understood to get a fee in the $3,000-$3,500 range. Brinkley does about 30 speeches a year. Harry Reasoner says he does about a dozen dates a year, at a minimum of about $3,000 per speech, and says, "I used to do twice as many."

A college or a corporation or a community group can pick from a huge assortment of newshounds. Boston's American Program Bureau, run by Robert Walker, offers 36 of them, ranging from Bernstein and Woodward and Kilpatrick to most of the television correspondents in Washington and *Rolling Stone*'s Hunter Thompson.

W. Colston Leigh's offerings include R. W. Apple of the *New York Times,* Buchwald, Nancy Dickerson, Elizabeth Drew, Drew Middleton, Harrison Salisbury, Daniel Schorr, Hugh Sidey, Sander Vanocur and Garry Wills, among others. Leigh's brochure offers Evans and Novak as a team, or individually, and he offers Max Lerner and Reid Buckley as a debate, with the topic as either "Will the American republic survive into the 21st century?" or "Liberalism: doom or hope of society?"

Keedick offers Wicker, Charles Bartlett, Jimmy Breslin and Norman Cousins. Harry Walker, Inc., ranges from Anderson to Brinkley to Bill Moyers to Carl Rowan to Barry Sussman to Bill Monroe to John Hart.

Between them, Evans and Novak do about 40 speaking dates a year, according to their agent, Leigh, and most are to business groups. They get from $1,500 to $2,000 per speech. "We do very few colleges," says Novak. "They really want your life for a day."

Evans and Novak also publish an every-other-week newsletter (called the Evans and Novak Political Report) which sells for $60 a year to about 1,500 subscribers, most of them businessmen, on inside-Washington goings-on. They also put on two day-long seminars each year at the Madison Hotel for businessmen (each seminar is limited to about 65) who pay $200 each to hear Evans, Novak and various government officials and politicians they hire to speak.

On the other hand, Harrison Salisbury of the *New York Times* concentrates on campuses, taking about 80 per cent of his 30 or so speeches a year (at $1,000 to $2,000 each) at colleges. Salisbury's speeches focus on the relationships between China, Russia and the United States.

Some Washington and New York journalists are surprised to find they are offered in speaker-bureau brochures, as was Peter Lisagor when told his picture was in that of the American Program Bureau.

Lisagor, Washington bureau chief of the *Chicago Daily News,* said, "I had thought I wasn't listed in anybody's brochure. No one is selling me and it's been some years now since I've had what is normally known as a lecture agent."

Lisagor says he's had "bad experience" with agents and, more importantly, "I don't have the time to make a hell of a lot of lectures. There are not a hell of a lot of people clamoring for me to lecture, since I'm not a folk hero."

He defined "bad experiences" as having the lecture bureau "taking one third of your fee, and your having to pay your own transportation. It doesn't leave you with very much, and when you consider the transport and my particular problem to try to find the time to do this, it just seemed to me to be too much of a hassle."

Columnist Joseph Kraft also finds it too much of a strain. "The year before last and last year I did some," he says, "on the big-fee basis and I did find it a strain, particularly since I had to write all the time." The trouble, he says, was the physical effort of the travel and of the luncheons and parties and having to commit yourself to a particular date long in advance. "You can't change it in case there's a Watergate development or a Middle East war," he says. "That really was central."

Buchwald says his predictability, the fact that his column is not circumscribed by news events, makes him a lecturing success. "I can say eight months in advance, 'I'll be there at 4 o'clock on July 6' . . . I've never canceled any."

All of those on the big-fee lecture circuit say that the business is not the picnic that it might appear to be. "It's hard work sometimes," says Wicker. "Recently I went down to make a speech. This happened to be one of those community forum things. The first thing I was invited out to a restaurant nearby the auditorium for cocktails and dinner with the committee that ran this thing. This turned out to be about 25 people and so, for a solid hour and a half, I did nothing but answer questions, every question directed at me. . . .

"For two drinks and a reasonably decent meal, I talked almost nonstop for an hour and a half. Then they hauled me over to the auditorium, that's fine, and there's a nice crowd there and I say my say and then questions and answers there. Then they drive me back to my hotel, which is a half-hour drive and, believe it or not, they bring in a man and wife who I hadn't met before and I have to talk for another half an hour on the way back to the hotel because they never stopped pouring those questions on me.

"So I got back to my hotel that night at 10:30 and, having had a fairly long trip to get there that day, I was fagged out. I earned my fee that night."

That's why, Buchwald says, he loves to do conventions, because the conventioneers don't want to socialize with the speaker. "They don't want to know from nothing," he says. "They just want you to do your thing and get the hell out."

But with women's groups, he says, "you come in the night before and someone's got a dinner party for you or a cocktail party. Then the next day you have to give your talk and they give a luncheon for you, and you're really working.

"At colleges it's the same. The kids meet you at the airport and you're talking until the time you go on, and then you're talking, and when you get off you're talking, and that's really exhausting. They just chew you up, and they're nice, you have to be nice about it. In fact, if you don't like people, it's really tough to do."

A consistent problem is that speakers get asked the same questions repeatedly. "It's great on the stage," says Buchwald, "because you get the same questions and you come out, pop, with an answer, and it's very funny and everyone thinks, 'Gee, he's good on his feet.' Well, you've been asked the question a hundred times and the ad lib is just right there, but when it's really tough is all during dinner and after dinner and cocktail time. That's where people earn their fees."

In general, the journalists doing the lecturing feel that the money is often secondary to their need to see people outside of Washington and New York, and to get a feel for the mood of the nation. If the lectures didn't pay so well, they might not do as many as they do, but they would still do some. Hugh Sidey, Washington bureau chief of *Time*, who does about 20 to 30 speeches a year for between $1,000 and $2,000 each, says:

"It's a pretty good educational device. If I didn't do this that way, I'd have to go out and do it some other way."

—January 27, 1974

Comments on
the Columnists

The Columnists' Inflated Rhetoric

By Benjamin C. Bradlee

"**I**n these difficult years, America has suffered from a fever of words; from inflated rhetoric that promises more than it can possibly deliver; from angry rhetoric that fans discontents into hatred; from bombastic rhetoric that postures instead of persuading."

Thus spoke Richard Nixon in his Inaugural Address, January 20, 1969. The passage has become something of a favorite of editorial writers, criticizing the excessive rhetoric of the Vice President [Spiro Agnew] and logically so.

The President's remedy was a suggestion that we all lower our voices. He described it as a simple thing. But it has proved otherwise, and not just for the Vice President — or for editorialists, whose weakness for polemics is well-known, if not traditional. Increasingly, it seems the raising of voices is an occupational hazard for some newspaper columnists.

Some months ago, I read a couple of my favorite columnists with the President's advice in mind, and came up with a new perspective.

"ugly facts" . . . "ever-darker plight" . . . "deeper and deeper peril" . . . "unprecedented losses" . . . "vastly more effective" . . . "immensely dense" . . . "desperately grave" . . . "cruelly heavy" . . . "the fiercest sort" . . . "equally critical."

These were the words of the stylish Joseph Alsop on a single day, and he was writing, not about Vietnam or guerrilla warfare in the ghettos, but about the presence of Russians in Egypt.

Same day, same page, I read as follows: "agonizing shock" . . . "hammered home" . . . "deeply foreboding" . . . "stunned to learn" . . . "severe

structural deficiencies" . . . "flagrant example" . . . "immense stakes" . . .
"massive help" . . . "crash registration" . . . "vastly more money."

This was Evans and (or) Novak talking . . . about politics in California.

A few days later an Alsop column included these phrases: "immensely
long-headed" . . . "enormous gamble" . . . "real fury" . . . "disastrous intervention" . . . "extreme resentment" . . . "immensely honorable" . . .
"deeply tragic" . . . "very heavy" . . . "very high" . . . "very active" . . .
"very timely" and "very deep."

The same day, Evans and (or) Novak were in similar form, thusly:
"really dead" . . . "immensely successful" . . . "hopeless plight" . . . "high-
volume reaction" . . . "highly sensitive" . . . "major offensive" . . . "dimly
perceived" . . . "powerful appeal" . . . "maximum embarrassment" and
"minimum cost."

In the ensuing months, somehow I got sidetracked from this esoteric research. To paraphrase President Kennedy, one read as much of Agnew,
Alsop, Evans and Novak, but perhaps one enjoyed it less.

But yesterday, the research urge came back, with a vengeance.

"extraordinary coincidence" . . . "total secrecy" . . . "cold response"
. . . "extremely hard-line" . . . "traumatic process" . . . "diplomatic bul-
lets" . . . "sharp anger" . . . "unfair pressure" . . . "outrageous interference" . . . "suspenseful moment."

Evans and (or) Novak were back — or still — in high gear, and right next
to them was Alsop in similar form:

"dreadful years" . . . "stormtroopers attack" . . . "exceedingly odd"
. . . "exceedingly leftwing" . . . "bitter attack" . . . "ugly face" . . .
"nakedly displayed" . . . "wooly-minded" . . . "quite irreplaceable."

Meanwhile, of course, back in Jackson, Miss., Springfield, Ill., Boston,
Mass., and Richmond, Va., the Vice President's drumbeat rolled on. His
best rhetorical tool recently has been sarcasm . . . "the first-strike capabil-
ity of the *Washington Post* and the *New York Times*" . . . "blessed as we
(in the "northeastern zone of revealed truth") are each morning with the
editorial guidance of our betters." But he is no slouch with the rhetorical
phrase . . . "master of sick invective" . . . "summertime soldiers" . . .
"sunshine patriots" . . . "late-blooming opportunists" . . . "professional
pessimists" . . . "he lies in his teeth" . . . "bludgeoning the unconvinced"
. . . "brutally counter-productive" . . . "slaughtering a sacred cow."

Is any or all of this by any chance the "inflated rhetoric that promises
more than it can possibly deliver," or even the "bombastic rhetoric that
postures instead of persuading"? One is forced to conclude that it is.

— May 27, 1971

License

The Washington Post

Interoffice Memo

TO: Bradlee, et al.   September 30, 1970

FROM: Harwood

In his Monday column, Nick Von Hoffman quotes a movie character: "When I met your daughter, she was balling her way up the aisle at the Fillmore, and every now and then she used to try an old cod." The meaning of all that is that the girl screwed her way through the neighborhood.

Nick, we tell our readers, is the voice of the New Culture. Does that mean he is going to speak the literal language of that culture in The Post?

I think we do not permit that sort of thing in other sections of the paper. Which leads to the question: Is there one standard for Nick and another standard for all the rest, including syndicated columnists? We do, after all, edit the columnists on grounds of taste.

Editing Columnists

The Washington Post

Interoffice Memo

Messrs. Bradlee/Simons   1/22/75

     Last week I reported a protest on a Jane Bryant Quinn column that made an all-encompassing charge against real estate brokers. As a result, an editor has asked whether I think columnists should be edited. "Should they get away with the sweeping generalization (as they do) when our reporters are kept to much stricter standards?" he asked.

     My answer is yes, columns can and should be edited. I see nothing wrong and a lot right with correcting an unjustified generalization like the one that brought the protest on the Quinn column. One must be careful, of course, not to tamper with legitimately expressed opinions and points of view. But aside from that, I would edit a column in the same way I would edit a bylined analysis piece by a staff reporter.

Charlie Seib

Columnists and Conflicts

By Charles B. Seib

Chill gusts of post-Watergate morality are being felt on the golden summits where syndicated columnists dwell.

The issue: Should the columnists be expected to abide by the same conflict of interest standards most newspapers expect of their editorial staffs?

Syndicated columnists are a strange journalistic breed. They appear in many papers, but, in most cases, work for none. They are usually their own bosses, marketing their wares through sales, distribution and bill collecting enterprises called syndicates. A columnist and his syndicate usually split 50-50 the price a newspaper pays for the column, that price being based mainly on the paper's circulation.

A top syndicated columnist does very well; financially, he is a member of the elite of journalism. A superstar can make $75,000 or more from the column alone, and substantial additional amounts from such spinoffs as lectures, television appearances and books. At the level just below superstar, a columnist can clear as much as $40,000 from the column and match that by an aggressive pursuit of spinoffs.

They also have their problems. The pressure to produce on schedule and to high standards never lets up. There is always the threat of running dry or going out of style. Highly placed sources, on whom a column's success might depend, can become has-beens overnight. Since most syndicated columnists are not on any payroll, they must make their own provisions for sickness and old age.

All in all, though, it's a good life, with fame and fortune for those at the top and a comfortable living for many others. As long as the editors smile, that is. And some editors aren't smiling.

The National Conference of Editorial Writers, which includes a number of the editors who buy columns, and the National News Council, a watchdog over journalists' performance and threats to press freedom, have raised some ethical questions. And some of the editors have used their ultimate weapon—discontinuation of certain columns in their newspapers.

Here are some recent examples of the problems. These are cases that have come to my attention; undoubtedly they aren't the only ones. The order is alphabetical.

• Tom Braden, who writes on public affairs from Washington, strongly supported Nelson Rockefeller during the hearings on Rockefeller's financial largesse. It wasn't until later that he revealed—with some reluctance—that he had received over $100,000 in loans from Rockefeller back in the 1950s to finance the purchase of a newspaper.

• William F. Buckley, also a public affairs columnist, defended Rockefeller in the matter of the campaign book about Rockefeller's 1970 gubernatorial opponent, Arthur Goldberg. But Buckley did not tell his readers that he was chairman of the firm that published the book for the Rockefellers.

• Columnists Rowland Evans and Robert Novak, who write a joint public affairs column, run a profit-making seminar on the side. Twice a year about 65 businessmen come to Washington and pay $200 a head to attend. Public officials who figure in the Evans-Novak column speak at the seminars; in fact, they are the drawing cards.

• Ann Landers, who writes a personal advice column, accepted a free trip to China from the American Medical Association. Some editors felt that she didn't clearly disclose that AMA picked up the tab.

• Victor Lasky, best known as the author of the Goldberg book mentioned above, received $20,000 from Richard Nixon's Committee to Re-elect the President while writing a syndicated column. The $20,000 deal was a secret until it came out in Watergate testimony. And nine months then passed before Lasky's syndicate notified editors of it.

Defenses are entered in all the above cases. Braden asserts that a legitimate loan, properly repaid with interest, cannot be construed as an involvement amounting to conflict of interest. Buckley said that he assumed most people knew of his connection with the publishing house, but he has indicated that if he had it to do over again he would mention it.

Evans and Novak reject any suggestion that their column helps recruit public officials to appear at their seminars. They say they have criticized seminar participants in their column and have been kind to officials who have refused to appear.

Ann Landers' syndicate says that she adequately disclosed that the AMA paid for her China trip when she informed her readers that she went there as an AMA delegate.

Lasky maintains that, as a freelance writer, he had every right to make an undisclosed deal with CRP. He said he earned the $20,000 by writing speeches and gags for Martha Mitchell and that the CRP connection didn't influence his views, which were pro-Nixon in the first place.

There is something to be said for each of these defenses. But the fact remains that no self-respecting editor would permit a reporter on his staff to do any of the things listed and a self-respecting reporter would not do them in any case. (Which is not to say that some editors have not permitted such things and some reporters—and editors, for that matter—haven't done them.)

The offenses listed, if all can be called offenses, differ in degree. But they all show an insensitivity to the need to avoid even the suspicion of conflict of interest. That is what is bothering some editors. Through the NCEW they are pressuring syndicates to establish guidelines on conflict of interest. The response so far has been sparse.

The National News Council, prodded by NCEW, has warned syndicates and the writers and artists they distribute that "awkwardness for them is certain to grow unless there comes a general recognition that all communicators are under obvious obligation to live under the same standards they demand of those who hold public office."

Newspaper people are not usually receptive to written codes of conduct. They prefer to rely on personal and institutional integrity and the traditional standards of the news business. But few would quarrel with this from the code of ethics of the Society of Professional Journalists, Sigma Delta Chi:

"Journalists must be free of obligation to any interest other than the public's right to know. Gifts, favors, free travel, special treatment or privileges can compromise the integrity of journalists and their employers. Nothing of value should be accepted."

Is a free ticket to a distant country something of value? Does it impose an obligation? Is the agreement of a high official to appear at a money-making seminar a favor? Does a loan, although repaid with interest, amount to an obligation or favored treatment? Should a columnist feel obligated to reveal to his readers any circumstances that might lead to a suspicion of conflict of interest? Or should the editors and the readers be willing to rely on his assurance that he would never be influenced by favors or benefits?

Those questions almost answer themselves. As the news council said, journalists—including columnists—must be willing to live by the standards they expect of public officials. To do less—when the circumstances are in any way analogous—would be hypocritical.

—January 2, 1975

Technology and the News

The Coming of the Computer

By Robert C. Maynard

The late Norbert Wiener, frequently referred to as the father of the computer, made an observation once that is pertinent to the current ferment in the newspaper business over the use of technology. Wiener said that science is like a candy store, and if you have enough money, you may buy anything you want.

It would have been inconceivable to a lawyer practicing a generation ago that a time would come when he could merely press a few typewriter keys and have, within seconds, all the case law relevant to a particularly complicated area flash before him on a video screen. Yet, such information retrieval systems are becoming increasingly commonplace.

Journalism, like the law, has often been thought of as being tied to tradition in doing its business: slow to change, wedded to the past.

Now a series of technological developments threatens to bring the news business along quicker than many had ever imagined, indeed quicker than many journalists believe wise.

Most of the emphasis of the new technology has been on the production aspects of the business. The publishers and the craft unions are in protracted discussions all across the land over the loss of jobs to machinery and the problem of which unions will have jurisdiction over which aspects of the new technology.

Those arguments have been going on for some years and will only be solved through long and difficult bargaining and discussion. Technology might be able to eliminate jobs, but it doesn't replace the obligation of human beings to solve their problems with each other.

While those discussions go on, other aspects of journalism are increasingly affected by the potential capabilities of the computer. We are discovering we have a long way to go and much to learn before a smooth relationship between news and the computer becomes possible.

180

As in the law, research is indispensable to journalism. When an important news event occurs, whether a major fire or some dramatic political development, the reporter attempting to cover the event or the issue must first learn as much as possible of what has gone before.

The journalist's repository of the past, the morgue or library, is a place in which tons of yellowed newspaper clippings are stored. Orderly morgues are a blessing to a journalist in a hurry. Poorly organized ones have been known to drive otherwise stable souls to strong drink.

A small-town editor once was writing an editorial about Abraham Lincoln and attempted to put his hand on the pertinent clippings. He found nothing filed under what seemed to him to be the logical categories. "Lincoln"? No. "Presidents"? No. "Assassinations"? No. In exasperation he summoned his librarian back from lunch. "Deceased" was the right answer.

So, now the inheritors of Norbert Wiener's philosophy have come to the rescue of the journalist in a hurry. But, as the old mathematician warned, it hasn't been cheap.

For an expenditure so far of several million dollars, you can learn the date and subject of every clipping mentioning Abraham Lincoln in the library of the *New York Times*. And you can do it without shuffling through a single pile of yellowing, fading clippings.

Spotted around the newsroom are video display terminals. A reporter can ask the computer some very sophisticated questions, such as the dates of all the stories in which, for one example, the names of Willy Brandt, Richard Nixon and Alexei Kosygin appear together. The terminal will light up with the stories by date and give a few key words of what each story is about.

Any number of instances occur in which the ability to cross-reference public figures in a hurry would prove very useful to a journalist. The computer can make that possible, but the cost so far is nearly astronomical.

Besides, the system has a flaw that many reporters at the *Times* find vexing, to say the least. If you found that Brandt, Nixon and Kosygin have been mentioned in 12 stories, by looking at the dates and the two or three word digest, you might conclude that one story in particular is precisely what you need to make a good story better.

At that point, you press the button that ordinarily would cause the selected story to be displayed on the screen. As you sit there rubbing your palms in anticipation, the machine tells you the equivalent of "wait until tomorrow."

The reason is simple and human—too human for the taste of some reporters. The machine can tell the reporter all or most of what is available in the library, but if the reporter actually wants to see the story, a human being has to fetch it and lay it down before the camera's eye. If that human being is out to lunch, off for the day or otherwise occupied, you have to go to the morgue and fetch it, just as in olden days. For some time to come, it is fair to guess that much of the merging of journalism and computer technology will face flaws of that sort and of an even higher order of magnitude.

Newspapers are rushing around to the "hardware" manufacturers buying millions of dollars of research and equipment that either doesn't work at all or only works for part of the time, doing less than Norbert Wiener's minions promise for their machinery.

In a recent bulletin, the American Newspaper Publishers Association warned its members against paying cash for the new machinery. Always hold back some of the total sale price, the association warned, so that you can have time to make certain the equipment works before you pay for it.

While that is probably sound advice to anyone making a major purchase in this Nader-conscious age, it is especially good advice to newspapers. Some journalists, in fact, are openly debunking the new technology.

Eventually, the marriage between journalism and technology will probably work about as well as the rest of our gadgetry. Computer technicians will get the hang of journalism and tomorrow's journalist will have a better grasp of what makes computers work and therefore how to make them work for the news. But as the *Times* experience suggests, it isn't going to replace jobs nearly as quickly as some publishers hope—or as some workers fear.

—October 4, 1973

A Craft in Crisis: Printers and the Post

By William Greider

The following article, written in the fall of 1973 during a labor dispute at the Washington Post, *offers an inside look at the problems arising from changing technology in the news business.*

To explain the labor dispute which confronts the *Washington Post,* the tour might begin at the buff-brick entrance on 15th Street where a wonderful contraption is on display, all cleaned up and polished, red and silver, and impossibly complicated.

It is a Linotype machine, "the very heart of the newspaper production process," as the plaque says. With a good operator at the keyboard, it is a wonder to behold, whirling and clacking, smoking and thunking, a one-man foundry which casts molten lead into the lines of type that one by one become a newspaper.

But, now, the machine at the entrance is an object of nostalgia. For many people inside the building, it is a poignant symbol of encroaching loss.

Because the Linotype is obsolete or nearly so. The printing process is in revolution. The inventions which 90 years ago made mass-circulation newspapers feasible are now being eclipsed by computers. For newspapers, the new technology promises cheaper, faster production, more versatile and much more accurate. For hundreds of men and women who work at the *Post,* it approaches with a blunt message: Your skills, your jobs are no longer needed.

"It's a mental thing for the older fellows like me," says Robert Alt, a printer at work in the fourth-floor composing room. "To me, I've been doing this 22 years and, without hot type, it's not printing. I don't know what you call it, but it's not printing to me."

Up on the seventh floor, where the *Post's* managers are planning the future, Paul Tattersall, a young data-processing expert, describes the technology which is sweeping the newspaper industry.

"You are revolutionizing this business," he says with emphasis. "You are turning it inside out. You can't do that by executive fiat. You have to be very careful and patient. You run down a few unknowns, then you discover some new ones, then you run them down."

Tattersall has a small electronic machine waiting in storage on the seventh floor, an Optical Character Reader or scanner. It's about the size of an office water cooler and, when it is plugged in, it will do the work of about 115 keypunch operators on the fourth floor.

"Automation, we talk about this every day,' says Eugene Meuller, a printer and writer. "We're talking about people—humanity. How much further can they go? The upper echelons of the *Washington Post* have lost complete touch with the working people in this building. We're human beings, we got problems, we got families. We're not a bunch of wild-eyed radicals."

The OCR or scanner is just the beginning. In three or four years, if the technical problems can be worked out, the *Post* envisions a computer-centered production system which which would eliminate the last of the 37 Linotype machines now operating on the fourth floor. No more hot type. Employing electronic impulses, a computer's memory and photoelectric engraving, it will replace human dexterity—and fallibility. It will drastically shrink the number of people needed to print the newspaper.

"What we hope will happen," says John Waits, a *Post* executive, "is that as this progresses, as the numbers move down, there will develop a residual number to take care of the process. Just plain maintenance, for one thing. There will be a certain amount of button-pushing, and it's not unskilled button-pushing."

This managerial vision of the future, rational and inevitable, collides with the human aspirations of men and women who work here now, people like Aloysius O'Mahony, a printer since he was 14, a make-up expert, who assembles the loose lines of type into page format.

"I've devoted my whole life to printing, nothing else," O'Mahony says gravely. "I know nothing else. I love printing. It's an art."

A Collision of Values

Roughly speaking, these glimpses around the building describe the collision of values in the *Post*'s labor problems. The newspaper's managers are negotiating with the printers—Columbia Typographical Union No. 101—over a new contract, one which both sides hope will allow the future to happen, peacefully, without great suffering.

The stakes are enormous for both sides, because the *Post* management and the printers both regard this as a threshhold contract. The company hopes to clear away all of the restrictive work rules, including the print-shop featherbedding, which now prevent a quantum jump to the new technology. In exchange, it has offered a guarantee of lifetime jobs to 540 printers. The union wants to stake out the survival of the craft, establishing its jurisdiction over key points in the future production system, and also job security for several hundred more printers than the 540 men and women listed in the company's proposal.

"I don't think either side wants a hardline showdown," says Cecil Watts, a *Post* printer who is on the union's three-man bargaining committee. "But it's kind of like passing dynamite from hand to hand. Nobody wants to hold it for long."

The longer the company must wait the more it loses in the delay of cost-cutting techniques. The managers have vowed that, if necessary, they will attempt to continue publishing in the event of a strike. The union, on the other hand, could bargain itself into oblivion if it accepts a poor settlement. Both sides understand that once this watershed is past and the steady reduction of printers has begun their union will not again wield the leverage which it has now.

The situation at the *Post* is not unique. The *Washington Star-News,* though it is at a different stage in the changing technology, is bargaining with the typographical union on the same basic question of computer-controlled printing. In New York, the printers have been negotiating for nine months since their contract expired, wrestling with the same issues. Some nonunion newspapers, such as the *Los Angeles Times* and *Miami Herald,* have been free to plunge ahead with new techniques and a few unionized shops have taken tentative steps with the approval of the International Typographical Union (ITU).

At the *Post,* the negotiations are proceeding against a background of rancor, a series of scrapes between company and union in recent years. Over the last decade, the *Post* has spent a lot of money investing in various piecemeal automation techniques designed to speed up the production process. The results have been frustrating to both sides.

To the company, the aggravating reality is that production time and costs per page have gone up instead of down. It now takes more man-hours to put together a page of the *Post* than it did in 1966. Among other things, the managers blame the union work rules which prevent them from deploying the composing room manpower more efficiently, plus a latent spirit of non-cooperation among the workers.

But the printers see themselves as scapegoats for the failure of machines. As they see it, the step-by-step changes to speed up the process have robbed printers of their skill, their control over the product, their pride in quality, without any offsetting gain in efficiency. The management, they say, was hoodwinked by "the automation salesmen" and now, rather than admit that it was oversold, it blames the printers.

A Proud History

To grasp the full flavor of these differences, you have to understand the proud history which stands behind each of those printers. Generally, it is thought of now as a blue-collar craft, but printing is not like any other. Its members have a long tradition of intellectual importance and fierce individualism. When you meet a printer, he might be just a regular guy or he might be a closet poet or an over-the-hill jazz musician or something. It attracts people like that.

Among the first printers in the English-speaking world were priests. They set up a shop in Westminster Abbey and began printing Bibles with the new movable type invented by that German named Gutenberg. An assembly of printers is still called a "chapel." A lot of workers on the fourth floor at the *Post* have forgotten why—but some of them haven't.

In America, printers traveled across the continent with a special freedom because they possessed a unique skill, one that let them roam the frontier of civilization. Printers like Mark Twain traveled that way. The tradition of the "tramp printer" is still alive, but fading fast as employment shrinks. A man with an ITU journeyman's card could walk into a strange city's newspaper shop and sit down at a Linotype to work, no questions asked, so long as work was available.

That mystique has an important influence on the current troubles. A printer, even if he has no intention of tramping, may still think of it as an option—which affects his outlook toward the boss. George Moore, a *Post* printer for 12 years, describes the old individualism: "You always felt you could tell a guy to shove it and go down the street to work."

This outlook is expressed in the union's contract with the *Post* (and with a lot of other newspapers), a fierce insistence that the individual printer retains his freedom of choice. Newspapers like the *Post* have been trying for years to winnow out some of the work rules, but with only limited success.

On the fourth floor, for instance, only one man—the general foreman— has the right to discharge any printer. His action is subject to a referendum of all chapel members. If the printers overrule him, the case goes to arbitration.

The work force is divided into "regulars" and "subs." A regular, if he wishes, can skip his assigned shift and his place will be taken by a substitute, most of whom do not work a full week. But the *Post* is also obligated to hire any "subs" who report for work so long as the newspaper is behind on its "reproduction," the resetting of ads which have already appeared in the newspaper but were originally set in another shop. The *Post* is years behind.

"We don't have control over the manpower," says Ken Johnson, director of operations. "You can't expect them on a given shift or you wind up with more than you need."

John Waits, special projects manager, says the printers respond to the "live work" of getting out tomorrow's newspaper, but that enthusiasm is often diluted by the "repro" factor, which brings more workers onto the floor than are needed. "If you've got 10 people there to do the work of five people," he says, "there's a tendency to kind of make things come out even. That's human nature."

A Decline in Quality

To the printers, however, "repro" is a crucial guarantee of job security, an important bargaining chip which they intend to cash in during the current negotiations only if the price is right. The practice started long ago as a competitive weapon of publishers, as the printers like to note, and later emerged as the union's lever, a way of insuring that enough work is available to prevent seasonal layoffs. The printers argue that "repro" amounts to shared "featherbedding"—first by the company, which sells advertising at rates based on "repro" costs, then by the union, which gets the extra, unnecessary work.

In any case, the attitude of printers toward their work has soured considerably in recent years as new high-speed technology has reduced their control over the product. They do not agree on all of the reasons, but both managers and printers feel that the quality of printing in big-city newspapers has declined over the last generation, a hard thing for either to admit and not easy to explain.

"It's soul-destroying," says printer Harold Grainger, "to see the quality of some of the work that goes through here. There's a lot of 'railroading.' Let it go, close it out, never mind the corrections."

"Railroading" means a supervisor or foreman orders a printer to send the type forward without waiting for the proofreader's corrections. Managers concede that it happens sometimes. Sometimes, the fourth floor and the seventh floor blame it on the fifth floor—when reporters and editors miss their copy deadlines.

Here's one example of how the system has changed:

A good Linotype operator could cast six to eight lines a minute, but now most news copy goes to the keypunch operators who punch out a tape quickly that will drive the Linotype machine much faster than a man could —at 14 lines a minute. But before the tape goes to the Linotype, it must run through a computer which marks it for hyphenation and spacing, a decision which used to be the printer's. If you see the word "did" at the end of a line hyphenated "di-d," blame the computer. Each step that's been added, even though it's faster, has increased the opportunity for human error and mechanical failure.

Larry Wallace, the company's chief labor negotiator, describes the transition:

"The old-time Linotype operator, he set the type and he put his slug on there. It had his name on it and he took pride in an error-free galley. Now it's so impersonal. The keypunch operator punches that tape as fast as he can and it's gone. The average printer today doesn't feel the same sense of responsibility for errors, and it's not all his fault."

The bad feelings which developed on both sides complicate the bargaining, of course, even though many of the old points of conflict would be moot in the computer-oriented printing of the future. Based on their past experiences with automation, printers have a healthy skepticism about how well the new ideas will work. But, as the planners point out, the computer hook-up means something entirely different. It is not just conversion to photographic "cold type." The computer future would be one unified electronic system without all of the interlocking parts of men and machines.

Union Democracy

Another craft tradition which influences bargaining is the unique union which represents the printers. It is, perhaps, the most democratic of all unions, guided by a complex constitution which insures a voice for every member in even the smallest union decisions. The other day a referendum notice was posted on the chapel bulletin board at the *Post*: "Shall the Chapel pay Bro. Blum one day's pay at lobster rate?" Brother Blum lost, 325 to 239.

Printers take their union affairs so seriously that the ITU has two permanent political parties within it, the Independents and the Progressives, plus a third faction, independents with a small "i." As it happens, the Columbia local is headed by an Independent, President Ray Hall, while the ITU International officers are "Progs." Since the International must sanction any local strike, the internal politics could complicate the outcome.

Before the contract expired, representatives of the *Post* and the *Star-News* had already warned International officers that they are serious about seeing through their objectives this time.

"What we said was, now look, all the other papers around the country are using this equipment and we want it too," Wallace explained, describing a chance meeting between ITU and newspapers in Chicago in August, 1973. "We said we realize we will have to have an attrition agreement, but we want to be treated fair."

Just as union politics foreshadows the current negotiations, so does corporate politics. In recent years, the frustration has been mounting over the labor hang-ups and the rising production costs. Furthermore, the *Post* went to public stock ownership in 1971, which made the managers more budget-conscious and less tolerant of cost overruns. The newspaper's former president and former general manager departed. A new president, John Prescott, and Wallace were brought in from the Knight Newspapers, where both had experience with a long strike in Detroit.

Prescott promptly set a tougher tone for labor relations, including a $120,000 damage claim against the printer's union for an alleged "sick out" which crippled production one night and caused a loss in advertising.

"The *Post* does not feel that in the last 10 years it has stood up to the realities of its labor relations posture," Prescott says, "and it's going to be a different ball game. We're going to stand up to our responsibilities and we're going to be fair and reasonable."

Psych-War Tactics

In the last few months both sides have employed the psych-war tactics which often accompany collective bargaining. Company supervisors were sent off for training—so they could put out the paper in the event of a strike or lockout. A strange-looking wooden catwalk appeared in the alley between the *Post* building and the Pick-Lee Hotel next door. Union employees around the building call it the "rat walk." If there is a strike, supervisory employees could stay at the Pick-Lee and get to the *Post* without crossing picket lines out front.

The printers, on the other hand, have been accused of a slowdown, deliberately reducing the pace of work to prod management on the bargaining. Delays cost money, loss of advertising sometimes, fouled-up delivery.

Union officials deny that any slowdown was ordered, though individual printers acknowledge that some of their colleagues do lag at their work.

"Production may not be what it was prior to expiration of the contract, but production never is," says Cecil Watts of the union bargaining committee. "It is a morale factor. The company says it ought to get a full day's work, but when we go without a contract we're not getting a full day's pay."

Alarmed by an alleged slowdown, Prescott sent a warning letter to each composing room employee, promising that the kind of open disruptions which occurred during negotiations three years ago will provoke discharges this time. Union members were incensed that the letters were sent to their homes, and the local filed a complaint of unfair labor practices.

"They're trying to get at me through my wife and family," Howard Bradley complains. Anyway, production returned to normal even before the letter was distributed. Recently, the two sides were joined by an ITU representative for serious bargaining sessions.

The Attrition Issue

From the company's standpoint, the offer of lifetime jobs is a generous answer to the transition. Based on an annual attrition of 9 per cent from resignation or retirement, that agreement would gradually reduce the work force, but still guarantee retraining and work for the bulk of the *Post*'s printers.

"It's a tremendous commitment to retrain and build our system around 540 men," says Prescott.

"We're paying attention to the human factor," says Wallace. "We're not talking about putting 200 or 300 printers out of work."

The printers don't see it that way. For starters, they insist that the roster of 540 proposed by the company leaves out about 80 people who hold regular situations plus 15 apprentices. In addition, it offers nothing to another 185 printers on the "sub board," who work at the *Post* but usually only three or four days a week.

"What are we going to tell the other 200?" asks Charles Yerrid, a printer who is on the roster of lifetime jobs. "Bye-bye, we got ours?"

"It's a wedge," says Frank J. Antonelli, "to force us to throw in the 'repro.' It's a wedge to get us to think we're going to be out of jobs."

The *Post* managers, who deny the divide-and-conquer accusation, do not put a precise estimate on their future manpower needs. However, based on its proposal and if normal attrition continues, the newspaper obviously thinks it can get along 10 years from now with perhaps one-third of its present work force. Since printers earn about $13,000 a year, every 100 jobs eliminated represent at least $1.3 million in savings for the company.

Only the wisdom of Solomon—or perhaps collective bargaining—could sort out the claims and counterclaims on this issue. The managers say the union board has been "loaded up" with additional printers in the last year in anticipation of this settlement. The printers say "repro" would not be an issue if the *Post* had kept up with it over the years.

"We Don't Want Make-Work"

But one issue will not yield easily to a dollars-and-cents compromise —the radical redesign of newspaper printing. The future is not going to be simply more of the speed-up automation which printers have seen in the past, though some of them still speak of it in those terms.

Ultimately, according to the new concept, a reporter in the fifth-floor newsroom or a classified ad taker on the sixth floor will sit at a typewriter and automatically originate electronic impulses which a computer will organize and translate into a piece of film ready for the press. The computer will even organize the type into a whole page, replacing the human make-up artists. Someday, the experts think, the reporter's typewriter will be connected via the computer directly to the press itself.

"We're saying we have input jurisdiction wherever paper is put into the printers," Watts explains. "The company says we've got editors and reporters who do this."

That roughly describes the problem. The union would like to stake out rights to any job where copy is fed into the machine and, in some situations, the company is willing. But the managers insist that they cannot accept any new version of "featherbedding"—for instance, a system of printers simply retyping for the computer what reporters and ad takers have already typed.

"We do not intend to get into another form of reproduce," Prescott says.

In the long run, Cecil Watts agrees, phony jobs would be bad for printers. "We're not trying to featherbed," he says. "We want time off. We don't want make-work. We expect to be paid for going along with automation."

And some printers can look forward to the computer age and share in the excitement, even while they speak bitterly of the present.

"I see myself as a man who guides it," says Aloysius O'Mahony hopefully, "who makes the decisions about where it will go, who judges the final appearance. It's a process of art. It's not simply a mechanical process."

—October 28, 1973

190

Strike Coverage and Conflict of Interest

The Washington Post

Interoffice Memo

Messrs. Bradlee/Simons: 10/14/75

    The Post's coverage of its own strike has been
good--far better than is usual in this business.
Some of the credit must go to the spectacular way
the strike started; the pressroom vandalism made it
a dramatic story and also put the Post in a good
P.R. position. Nevertheless, a good--not great,
but good--job is being done.

    I was especially pleased to see on the budget
for tomorrow a story on the motivations of the
Guild people who cross the picket lines and those
who don't. That's the kind of story the Post would
be doing if some other public or quasi-public institution was involved. And therefore it is the
kind of story that should be done in the present
situation.

    It would be unrealistic to pretend that there
aren't special problems involved in covering yourself, particularly in a high-stake situation like
this. Credibility, for example. Even though the
reporting is exemplary, as it generally has been
in this instance, there is bound to be a suspicion
of conflict of interest. Also, there is bound to
be a certain softness, an over-acceptance of company statements, when the story is handled within
the shop.

    Perhaps there's an innovative way to deal
with all that. Maybe an outsider or team of outsiders could be hired to provide the coverage. Or
maybe a group of Post reporters and editors should
be detached to set up a strike bureau outside the
building. It's an interesting subject to kick
around.

(more)

If the Post's coverage so far has had a weakness, it is in the failure to dig into the broader aspects and effects of the strike.

What is going on at the Star, for example? Just what is happening to their circulation? (If this were a story about a government agency, would we be satisfied with anything as unspecific as our statements that their circulation has increased, with no figures?) Just what does the increased ad revenue mean to them in terms of that million-dollars-a-month deficit Allbritton reported?

What about reports that some of the Post trashers have gone to work in the Star pressroom? What is the feeling among Star Guildspeople about the Post picket line crossers? Are all the Star people back on a five-day week? Do they see this as the chance they needed? Have we tried to talk to Bellows about what he is doing to capitalize on the situation? It looks as though they are deliberately maintaining a large newshole; is that the case?

How do the newspaper readers feel? Are some of them discovering or rediscovering the delights of the Star? Are some pleased with the smaller Post? Certainly some effort to survey readers would be worthwhile.

In an October 3 story we reported that some ad agency spokesmen said retail sales and attendance at public events might decline. Has this happened? Whether it has or not, we should report on it. How do advertisers feel about the response to their ads in the Star? Is there any sentiment for giving the Star a bigger share of ad budgets even after this is over?

To get back to matters closer to home, what is being learned about the events of the night of October 1? Are we doing the kind of reporting on the grand jury sessions that we would be doing if the Post weren't involved? How many pressmen really

(more)

did the damage? Can we find out anything about advance planning? What is the insurance company's position on the possible return of the trashers to the pressroom after the strike is over? Is there reporting to be done on what is happening within the craft unions? The pickets are no longer abusive. Why?

I said earlier that there tends to be an over-acceptance of company statements. We have said a number of times that the Post is losing about $300,000 a day in ad revenues. Is this figure still valid? And to be meaningful, shouldn't it be adjusted by savings in newsprint and in salaries? I don't believe we have had anything on the costs of the outside printing, the helicopters, etc.? Wouldn't we be digging into such matters if the Post weren't involved?

And so on. Some of those items are too parochial, I am sure. And some may have been covered while I was away, although I think I have read all the stories. My main message is this: This is a big story, made bigger by the Post's special position in American journalism. It should be covered with the intensity and zeal for which this paper is noted.

Charlie Seib

Mortality and the Media

Why Newspapers Keep Dying

By Ben H. Bagdikian

> ### Death Notice
>
> On Wednesday, July 12, 1972, The Washington Daily News, at age 50, after a lingering illness. Survivors are The Evening Star, married to The News, July 12 at a deathbed ceremony, and The Washington Post. In lieu of flowers, the family requests jobs and contributions to the 600 former employees of the deceased.

Why do newspapers die? And why have competing papers been dying at an alarming rate since World War I?

The death of a newspaper is peculiar. There is a lot of romantic bunk about journalism from Brenda Starr on down. But it is a special business in an industrial age, the only major mass-produced industry with an intellectual product that has each item handcrafted and redesigned every day. It involves its creators in ways almost no other industry can so that the emotional shock of loss or separation is unique. For readers who liked or loved it, the loss of a paper can be like the death of a favorite relative.

But competitive newspapers fail for very unsentimental reasons. They suffer a terminal disease that has killed almost every face-to-face daily competition in the country. When death comes, a standard corporate requiem of "rising costs" and "unrealistic labor demands" is recited by the owners, and there are charges by employees and readers of callousness and conspiracy on the part of the cold-hearted villains who used the paper as a mere money-maker instead of a community institution.

It is true that costs are rising and it is true that there have been cold-hearted villains in the business. Frank Munsey was one of the early discoverers of how to make money killing newspapers and when he died in 1925 one of the great men in American journalism, William Allen White, wrote a classic obituary in his *Emporia* (Kan.) *Gazette*:

"Frank Munsey, the great publisher, is dead. Frank Munsey contributed to the journalism of his day the great talent of a meat packer, the morals of a money changer, and the manners of an undertaker. He and his kind have about succeeded in transforming a once noble profession into an 8 per cent security. May he rest in trust."

The Arithmetic of Advertising

There is no need to sympathize with the proprietors who sweet-talk their staffs and readers while guiding them into the corporate gas chamber. But unfortunately the death is usually from an impersonal disease and a simple one.

Daily newspapers make more than 70 per cent of their gross revenues from advertising. The goal of advertisers—who more and more sell standard brands in chain stores that cover an entire metropolis—is to get their message into every household of the area as cheaply as possible. It is cheaper for them to support one big paper than half a dozen small ones. So when one paper begins to dominate, it begins a stampede of advertisers that is the start of monopoly.

It is the process that killed the general circulation magazines—*Colliers, Saturday Evening Post, Look*—at the height of their circulations. They were all pitched at a general national audience, and television, with its even larger audiences, could do it cheaper per thousand.

It is why there were 2,300 dailies in the country in 1922 but 50 years later, with a population almost twice as large, with more real spending money and more reading ability, the total was only 1,750. In 1970, for the first time since records were kept, less than one paper a day was sold per family in America. This is not from less reading, but less buying of competing papers by the same family and the end of "Extra" and fewer multiple newsstand editions throughout the daylight hours by the same paper.

Newspaper production is intricate, ungainly and expensive. It requires a factory of large proportions in a metropolitan daily but once the thousands of plates are on the presses, each additional paper turned out is, in the manner of most assembly lines, cheaper to produce than the one before because the expensive preparation has already been done. Thus, the more copies turned out, the less it costs per copy.

That impersonal process affected the *Daily News*.

Minimum ad rates for the three Washington papers, before the death of the *Daily News*, were listed in the 1972 *Editor & Publisher Yearbook*. Under those rates, the same ad that cost the advertiser $27.20 to get his display before 1,000 readers of the *Post* cost him $35 for exposure to 1,000 readers of the *Star*, and $58.20 to get before 1,000 readers of the *News*. This is the result not of villainy but mass production. Like so much of the stress in the quality of life, it comes from each party's doing what seems best for himself.

The Social Consequences

But it is impersonal arithmetic with profound social consequences. It has contributed to the loss of community identity and loss of diversity in the news. In 1880 about 90 per cent of all urban places had their own daily papers and 61 per cent had more than one. Advertising was a small factor and each paper was small, the subscriber paying for most of the cost of the paper. Today fewer than 20 per cent of urban places have their own paper and fewer than 3 per cent competing ones.

There are less than 70 cities today with more than one newspaper management and only one, New York, with three. Over 1,500 have monopoly managements.

There can be some advantages to a newspaper monopoly. It reduces sensationalism. There is competition for the passing eye. Most papers are home-delivered so sensationalist displays don't "sell papers," as some critics simplistically assume.

A paper unafraid of competition can, if it will, work more carefully on its stories and take time to do comprehensive reports on central issues.

On the other hand, a paper unafraid of competition can also decide to suppress stories or avoid controversy or push only the hobbyhorses of its owners and editors.

Furthermore, when local competition dies, papers tend to shift to the cheapest news possible, and that is syndicated wire news. Staff-originated news costs 90 per cent more than syndicated material. A 1966 study showed that a monopoly paper suddenly faced with new competition increased its staff-written news by 24 per cent but after it defeated its new competitor it went back to its old practices.

The Readership Puzzle

If the arithmetic of advertising revenue is simple and brutal, there is another factor that is not so simple. The advertising money depends on circulation. But why do people buy a successful paper instead of its competitors?

It is not easy to answer, because papers are bought for many reasons by different people—for TV listings, porkchop prices, comics, sports and crossword puzzles as well as for news. But the general postwar pattern shows that failing papers were usually inadequate newspapers. The Hearst chain once boasted that it pitched its papers to the 14-year-old mind and the chain has been losing money and papers steadily.

Popular syndicated features are sometimes thought the salvation, but by themselves they have never saved a paper yet. When six former newspapers in New York—the *Journal*, the *American*, the *World*, the *Telegram*, the *Herald* and the *Tribune*—finally coagulated in the late *World Journal Tribune* the result was one of the most massive collections of popular, exclusive features in press history, but it wasn't enough to make a real newspaper.

Orvil Dryfoos, late publisher of the *New York Times*, was asked once what he thought made the crucial difference in the *Times'* successful competition against the *Herald-Tribune*. He said that during World War II, the *Trib*, hoping to bolster its financial position during a high-advertising period with rationed newsprint, decided to print as many ads as possible. The *Times*, knowing people would be hungry for news during the war, allocated more space to news. The *Times* made less money, but Dryfoos was convinced that the *Times* emerged from the war with reader loyalty the *Trib* never overtook.

A trustee of the parent group owning the *Wall Street Journal* was asked what event he thought catapulted that paper into a secure position in the top rank of American daily journalism. He said he thought it was the *Journal's* refusal to kill a story despite General Motors' public threat to cancel all its ads. "After that, everyone, including businessmen, knew that we were a paper with character."

A Slow Death

But a paper can cease to reflect the life in its community. The *Boston Transcript* was the essence of high-culture and power of the leaders of Boston before the Depression. It made money and a national reputation with good journalists. But when the aristocrats for which it was published lost their power in the 1930s, so did the *Transcript*, a relic of an obsolete past.

When competitive papers begin to lose their character or meaning for their community, it may be years before the sickness shows in the profit and loss statements. Death comes during crises—recessions, new media competition, a final loss of will by its owners. When the crisis comes it is too late to rebuild character and significance. An irony of American journalism is that so many dailies in so many places are drab, irrelevant imitations of each other but they survive because they are monopolies.

There should be a place for the second or third or fourth daily in big cities, but with mass ads there can't be. And with the race having only one winner, the fatal virus of second place may set in quietly years before some unhappy executive walks over to the bulletin board to tack up the death notice.

—July 23, 1972

Innocent Until Proven Guilty: Problems in Pre-Trial Publicity

FYI: Charles Manson and Media Irresponsibility

Written at the time of the Tate murder case, the following Washington Post *editorial puts forth the dangers to the freedom of the press from pre-trial publicity.*

A few days ago we talked about the difficulty the California courts will have in giving Charles Manson a fair trial in the Sharon Tate murder case. At that stage, it seemed to us, the news media and various public officials could share the blame for the potentially prejudicial publicity that had been spread about the shocking murders—the officials because they had talked too much about facts that should have been left for the trial, the news media for their failure to distinguish between accusation and fact.

Since then, For Your Information, the performance of the news media has gone from bad to worse. Last Sunday [December 14, 1969], for example, the *Los Angeles Times* and several other newspapers around the country and around the world published the account of one of Manson's followers, Susan Atkins, under her own byline. She sold the story of that horrible night in Bel Air for reasons best known to her, but presumably, in part, to raise money for her defense and in part to publicize her line of defense—that Manson had cast some sort of spell which compelled her and others to commit crimes. The story, to put it mildly, was grisly and almost beyond belief. She described the murders blow by blow to the point of saying which defendant knifed or shot which victim. It was not a denial of the charges against her but her own effort to place prime responsibility for the crimes on others.

This week, to cite a second example out of many possibilities, *Life* magazine went somewhat further and made its own judgment as to who was guilty. It began its article on the Tate case: "Long-haired, bearded little Charlie Manson so disturbed the American millions last week . . . that the victims of *his* blithe and gory crimes. . . ." (Our italics.) *Life* then went on to explain how Manson got the way he is and how he twisted the minds of his alleged accomplices.

Given these two stories—which are not the only two—it is impossible to avoid the charge that Manson and his band of strange followers have been tried in the press and found guilty. And it is difficult to believe that anyone who has read those accounts has not already formed an opinion about the guilt and the mental condition of the defendants. Yet the basic principle of American justice is that no one is regarded as guilty until that determination is made in a court of law and that every defendant is entitled to have a trial before a jury whose members have not prejudged the case. The publicity these and similar stories received will make it monumentally difficult to find an unbiased jury in California, where the case must be tried because the jury must be composed of people who are able to set aside what they have read and act only on the evidence before them.

The pity of it all is that these gross abuses of the rights of the defendants by the news media come just when the long and bitter fight between the legal profession and the editors and broadcasters was calming down. The judges and lawyers have been in battle array for years because of what they regard as media interference with the right of a fair trial. For their part, the editors and broadcasters have been up in arms over what they regard as the legal profession's effort to tell them what to print and say.

Now we have the Tate case, which seems to be a perfect example of news media irresponsibility. There is no public interest to be served by dissecting Charles Manson in public before his trial. There is no public interest to be served by publishing the self-serving statement of one defendant who is attempting to pin prime responsibility on another defendant. And there is a public interest which is not served by such actions—the need that the processes of justice not be fouled by unnecessary prejudicial pre-trial publicity.

The danger that the news media run in this kind of situation is that the courts, which are controlled by the legal profession, will find in such irresponsibility a justification for imposing legal restrictions on what can be published. The temptation to lawyers and judges to start down this road becomes stronger each time they confront the difficulties of providing a fair trial for defendants in a highly publicized case. And the Tate case is only one in a string of such situations. At the end of the road lie substantial dangers to freedom of the press, dangers that are far greater than any that might result from the exercise by our profession of an elementary respect for the principles of justice and of a reasonable amount of self-restraint.

—December 19, 1969

A Comic Strip Isn't a Court

By Robert C. Maynard

On Tuesday morning, May 29, 1973, the *Washington Post* and about a dozen other American newspapers incurred the wrath of hundreds of their readers by making the decision to omit, on grounds of fairness, a popular comic strip, "Doonesbury" by Garry Trudeau.

Between early Tuesday morning and mid-afternoon, the *Post* received no fewer than 500 telephone calls from disappointed readers wanting to know what had become of Doonesbury. The *Baltimore Sun* received enough telephone calls, according to one editor, to feel it was called upon to carry a news item on the deletion. The editor of the *Boston Globe* said his newspaper planned to do the same.

Doonesbury's well-earned popularity is based on the pithy way in which its characters sink their teeth into contemporary subjects. The strip is created with a sure-handed sophistication that is pointed even when it isn't funny.

The reason the Tuesday strip was dropped is that it was, in the opinion of the editors of the *Washington Post*, entirely too pointed and overstepped the bounds of decency, fairness and good judgment.

What Trudeau did was have his "WBBY" commentator give a little Watergate rundown which concluded with the judgment about a principal in the case as being "GUILTY! GUILTY, GUILTY, GUILTY!!"

Howard Simons, managing editor of the *Washington Post*, explained his decision to drop the strip:

"If anyone is going to find any defendant guilty, it's going to be the due process of justice, not a comic strip artist. We cannot have one standard for the news pages and another for the comics."

Tom Winship, editor of the *Boston Globe*, said he had great respect and regard for Doonesbury as a lively and intelligent strip. "It's a beautiful strip," he said, "but I have no trouble with this decision" not to run the installment.

It has long been recognized that cartoons are very much the creation of their authors and the points of view they express are granted a special license. Al Capp has been free to lampoon public figures and any number of strips have expressed a variety of political viewpoints, many of them quite contrary to the editorial stand of the newspapers in which they appear.

This is not the first instance in which editors of the *Washington Post*, for example, have exercised their prerogative to withdraw a cartoon. Indeed, one which an editor found racially offensive was withdrawn between the first and third editions. But that is a rare occurrence.

What gives the current Doonesbury controversy special status is that it is a stark case of the conflict of rights. Garry Trudeau clearly has a right to his opinion about Watergate. It can even be argued that the way he portrays his commentator, Mark, declaring a Watergate defendant "Guilty, Guilty, Guilty!!" suggests something of the extreme view that many take of the Watergate case.

For all that, other rights have their place. Those are the rights of a defendant to be considered innocent until proven guilty. It is that aspect of the matter which is so disturbing. Any number of readers and political figures have charged that the press has helped create a climate in which guilt is assumed on the part of the President and any number of his associates.

Responsible journalists have taken pains to make a distinction between finding that there is a probable cause to believe wrongdoing has occurred and a flat conclusion of guilt.

To many, it has seemed at times a distinction without any substantive difference. And, to be sure, there have been times when major news organizations have made assertions in the Watergate case which would have been far better left for the determination of a judicial body.

I am very much of the belief that in a free society, it is always dangerous to suppress expression. I am equally sure that in a nation of laws, it is profoundly dangerous for comic strip artists to ignore the fundamental right of defendants to be presumed innocent.

If I had to weigh those rights in the Doonesbury case, I'd say that Mark and his creator, Trudeau, must yield. It is even more profoundly so for the very reason that it is a cartoon appearing in the comic section. I'd like it never to be said that young readers received their first notions about fundamental rights from the comics and concluded that folk-hero characters are allowed to declare people guilty in advance of their trials.

Several of those who called felt they had a right to make up their own minds on the merits of the Doonesbury case. Sadly, that is the lesson of every decision of an editor to excise a given expression from the pages of any journal. Nonetheless, there is in my mind a line across which responsible expression cannot step without running the risk of excision. Trudeau, in my opinion, stepped across that line in having Mark speak as he did.

—May 31, 1973

Leaks and Liability

By David S. Broder

In commenting on President Nixon's August 15 [1973] formal speech on Watergate, the *Washington Post* editorially criticized "the curiously detached status—almost that of bemused spectator—which Mr. Nixon assumed for himself." It was "this studied sense of remoteness," the editorial said, that stripped all conviction from his statements deploring the transgressions committed by those in his employ.

Somehow that editorial came to mind when looking at the way leading newspapers handled Vice President Agnew's complaint that there was an effort "to indict me in the press" through calculated Justice Department leaks of kickback allegations.

Talk about curious detachment and a studied sense of remoteness! My favorite editorialists acted as if they had no kinship to the newspapers where these leaks had appeared.

The *Post*, which on August 13 reported that "informed sources" said several Maryland contractors had told the prosecutors of personal cash payments to Agnew, editorialized rather grandly that ". . . the Vice President is well within his rights to be powerfully annoyed. . . ."

The *Washington Star-News*, which on August 13 cited "reliable sources" as the basis for a similar story, now said editorially: "The Vice President is entirely correct in insisting that the Justice Department . . . find and stop the many sources of leaked information. . . ."

And the *New York Times,* which on August 16 named "sources close to the investigation" as buttressing its version of the payoff allegations, editorialized: "Vice President Agnew has every right to complain that his constitutional rights are being violated by leaks attributed to 'Justice Department sources'. . . ."

There hasn't been such a suspiciously conspicuous display of civic virtue since a San Francisco madam led her string of girls to the Red Cross blood bank during World War II.

All three papers washed their hands of responsibility for publishing the "leaks" by quoting Mr. Agnew's own statement that "the blame must rest with those who give this information to the press."

But that rationalization works only if those of us in journalism are going to set ourselves a low standard of conduct.

There are many reasons why the press ought to be wary of information leaked from criminal investigations. For one thing, the great lesson we supposedly learned from the McCarthy era was that responsible journalism requires that accusations against individuals not be delivered naked to the reader but be presented with due regard to the motives and credibility of the accuser.

The "sources close to the investigation" evasion makes this impossible. If the sources are, as Agnew suspected, on the government side, one has to wonder why a prosecutor with a genuinely strong case would risk it by premature publicity that could easily get him thrown out of court.

If, on the other hand, as the No. 2 man in the Justice Department says, the sources are "close to the investigation," because they are the very contractors who are under investigation, or their lawyers, then the reader should be told.

Those who relay leaked information forget that we as journalists have just as much stake in the probity of the criminal justice system as any other citizens. A while back, several hundred American newspapers published Jack Anderson's columns containing verbatim excerpts of Watergate grand jury testimony. The rationalization one heard from editors was that "somebody's going to publish it, whether I do or not."

Not a single editor I know argued that the grand jury system could survive repeated disclosure of confidential testimony. Not a single editor contended that the rights of accused persons can be protected if accusations made in that non-adversary forum are publicized. Nonetheless, the leaked testimony was published — and to hell with the consequences.

Now *Time* magazine, with its vast circulation, has told its readers that unnamed "Justice Department officials" believe Agnew's indictment is "inevitable," despite the fact that the prosecutor says not one scintilla of evidence has yet been given to the grand jury, which alone can determine that question. What does that imply about our system of justice? It implies that some journals, at least, think it is a farce and a fraud.

In this climate, when part of the press behaves as if any prominent politician accused of wrongdoing must be presumed guilty, what we need from our leading newspapers is not an attitude of lofty detachment, but the reassertion of a fundamental truth — that the burden of proving any one of us guilty falls entirely on the state, through a deliberately laborious process of indictment, prosecution and conviction at public trial in a court of law.

And that is a process in which the press interferes, not only at its own peril, but at hazard to the most important of everyone's fundamental rights.

— August 26, 1973

The British Press and Prejudicial Publicity

By Bernard D. Nossiter

Since October, 1972, the *Sunday Times* of London has had, set in type but never published, an important story questioning whether the Distillers Company negligently marketed thalidomide, the sedative that mutilates unborn children.

The article recalls that a test of the drug reported in the *British Medical Journal* some 15 years ago concluded that thalidomide can cause "definite antithyroid activity," that its workings are unknown and its use seems "unjustifiable" until more research is completed. Even so, Distillers decided to sell it through a drug company it has since sold off.

The unpublished *Sunday Times* piece also discloses that a doctor warned Distillers' Australian subsidiary of his "fears and suspicions" about the drug six months before the company took it off the market.

An American newspaper can publish these facts, but the *Sunday Times* cannot. Recently, five law lords from the House of Lords, Britain's highest court of appeal, ruled that publication would constitute contempt of court, prejudicing Distillers' right to a fair trial.

This decision comes nearly 12 years after the parents of thalidomide's victims — children born without arms and legs — began suing Distillers. It also comes as these suits are finally close to settlement out of court.

Thanks largely to other stories that the *Sunday Times* could and did publish, Distillers raised its original offer of compensation from less than $9 million to $52 million. Nearly all of the parents of the 400 mutilated children have agreed to this deal, and only a few details remain open.

Even though there is almost no chance of a trial and even though the litigation has dragged on so long, the law lords held that the case was still before the courts. Therefore, they reasoned, the suppressed *Sunday Times* article could damage Distillers' right to an uninfluenced trial. The decision illustrates one of the gravest handicaps under which the press operates here. Moreover, the lord justices gave five separate opinions, thereby compounding confusion over what constitutes contempt.

The most sweeping opinion came from Lord Justice Diplock. He held that comment on a pending case that inhibits anyone from going to court by holding him up to "public obloquy" violates the freedom to sue or defend a suit.

If Diplock had his way, the *Sunday Times* would have been prohibited from publishing even the first story in its campaign, a piece describing the drawn-out agony of parents and children and urging that Distillers had a moral obligation to make a bigger offer.

Lord Justice Reid delivered a more "liberal" opinion. "Fair and temperate criticism" of one party to a suit is not contempt, he said. But, he said, the suppressed *Sunday Times* article amounts to "prejudgment" of an issue — negligence — that might still come before the courts.

The law lords were not impressed by the fact that the thalidomide claims have been dragging on unsettled for more than 11 years. One, Lord Cross, even thought the affair was "in the early stages of litigation."

Nor were the lords concerned with the relative strength of the two parties — on one side, Distillers, a billion-dollar concern with a virtual monopoly over whiskey manufacturing here, and on the other, parents wrestling with enormous medical bills.

A lower jurisdiction, the court of appeal, held last winter that the suits were all but dormant and that the *Sunday Times* could print. As one commentator here observed, the court of appeal displayed "a concern for the real world." It was reversed by a House of Lords wrapped in "dry legalism."

The lords' decision touched off loud protests from most of the papers and from opposition members in Parliament. Jack Ashley, a deaf Labor M.P. who has campaigned strenuously for the victimized parents, called it "bizarre . . . astonishing . . . intolerable."

"The message from the House of Lords judgment is clear to all those perpetrating injustice," Ashley said. "If they issue a writ or institute proceedings, they will be carefully and legally protected from exposure by the British press. . . . The press is significantly censored, and the simple trigger mechanism which will spark off that censorship is available to any shyster who uses the law of contempt."

In a long letter to the (daily) *Times*, Harold Wilson, the Labor Party leader, expressed his concern over the ruling. "Parliament is hamstrung in its discussions of and decisions on matters of public importance if it cannot draw both on the facts and opinions freely published in the press. . . . Our debates (on thalidomide) were inspired and informed by the original article in the *Sunday Times*. . . . This decision . . . will not only inhibit the freedom of press comment; it will equally inhibit Parliament in both its legislative function and in its duty of holding the executive accountable to its authority."

If the lords have stated the law of contempt, Wilson concluded, Parliament must change it promptly.

The *Sunday Times* said it had no quarrel with the principle that protects litigants from newspaper comment once a case has been set for trial. But here there is no trial in prospect. The paper tartly observed that it had launched its campaign because of "the plain failure of the legal system to supply a remedy to the thalidomide children which was remotely acceptable."

Contempt, as Lord Reid noted, is a device to prevent interference with the administration of justice. But the rule is so strictly interpreted here that the press has been almost completely gagged in reporting another scandal, which has centered around bankrupt architect John Poulson, who until recently enjoyed Britain's largest practice. He has been accused of bribing officials in local government to award his firm big public building contracts.

The contempt rules are so harsh that, when Poulson and a prominent politician were charged recently, no newspaper here could use the word "bribe." They were limited to the precise language of the charge. Its words alleged that Poulson "conspired" with the politician "to corruptly make gifts or rewards to . . . (a) holder of offices in divers public bodies, to do acts in relation to the affairs, namely building projects of such bodies."

No paper could print when, where and how much Poulson paid, who got the money and what Poulson got in return. All this is routine coverage for the American press.

The (daily) *Times* of London even withdrew an editorial it had run in early editions before the charges were filed, and left the space blank in its final editions. The editorial had only urged the government to set up a tribunal examining all of Poulson's affairs.

The courts' heavy hand on the press could be changed if Parliament legislates on the subject. But, like so many of the judges, Prime Minister Edward Heath and his government are more concerned with newspaper abuses of freedom than with curbs on expression. The prospect for legislation reforming the grip of contempt is not rated very high.

—July 25, 1973

Privacy, the Public, and the Press

Trash

Judging from what we have read and the comments we have heard, there are numerous extenuating—or at least complicating—arguments that can be made concerning the *National Enquirer*'s foray into Mr. and Mrs. Henry Kissinger's trash. Evidently, for example, "everybody does it": Jack Anderson is known to have gleaned some of the columns that have run in this paper from a riffle through the late J. Edgar Hoover's trash; the F.B.I. (under J. Edgar Hoover) is known to have done its share of riffling through other people's trash; and we couldn't guarantee that over the years some reporter for this newspaper may not have done the same. Evidently, too, you can get lost in a whole lot of legal questions, which we gather have been resolved in favor of the scavengers: trash put out for collection seems to be owned by no one and to be fair game for anyone who wishes to appropriate it. And—if none of these complexities is sufficient to muddy the issue—it is possible to embark on a series of metaphysical journeys: How is this technique different, after all, from various other heists and journalistic appropriations of material people do not consider in the public domain? Is it not true that the public has a "right to know" all manner of detail about the lives of public figures? And on and on . . .

You will have perceived by now that we regard these intellectual exercises as being, well, so much garbage. For all we know, the right to publish the contents of the Kissingers' trash bags may be inherent in the First Amendment. But such arguments do not clarify the point; they obscure it. For the point, in our judgment, quite simply is that the *Enquirer*'s exercise in trash-picking outside the Kissinger home was indefensible—both as journalistic practice and as civilized behavior.

It is a question first of all of the way decent people behave in relation to each other, a question of how we permit one another to live. There are certain basic conditions, certain vulnerabilities, to all our lives—public and private figures alike—that we must be able to assume others will not take unfair advantage of. What Jay Gourley of the *National Enquirer* did is the moral and professional equivalent of, let us say, interviewing the six-year-old child of a public figure by way of acquiring some private information about that figure, or posing as a doctor in the presence of a sick and helpless public figure in order to pick up some "intimate" material about him. That these unacceptable techniques may bear some relationship to other "borderline" techniques of journalism does not seem to us in any way to justify them. We will be frank to say that, on the contrary, it merely suggests to us that those other techniques—to the extent that they take advantage of an unsuspecting victim—are themselves of dubious value and propriety.

But on any scale of journalistic practice, we would say that trash-picking belongs at the bottom. Mr. Gourley's "gleanings," for instance, as reported in this newspaper, purportedly revealed that "either Secretary of State Kissinger or his wife, Nancy, smokes Marlboro cigarettes, uses patent medicines and occasionally throws away the *New York Times* unopened." One could as readily conclude from the evidence that one of Secretary Kissinger's Secret Service agents smokes Marlboros, that his cook uses patent medicine and that those unopened *Timeses* collected on his doorstep while he and his wife were away last week on a vacation in the Caribbean, faithfully reading the *Times*.

Some scoop.

—July 10, 1975

Privacy and the Press

By Charles B. Seib

What happens when the public's right to know collides with the individual's right to be let alone? One thing that happens is considerable agonizing in newsrooms and editorial offices.

Privacy has become a popular topic in the continuing discussion of the powers and performance of the media. In such discussions, the focus is usually on the right of privacy of public figures, and there is a choice of sides available. One can argue that the press is too protective of its pals in public life, shrinking from tattling on the boozers on Capitol Hill, for example. Or one can argue that the gossip-hungry press has gone too far in depriving officials and other public figures of the decent personal privacy that is the right of every free man and woman. One can even argue—but few do—that the agonizing pays off and the press is generally doing a good job of balancing the conflicting interests of the public and the individual.

The privacy problem is by no means limited to public figures, however. It covers a spectrum as broad as society itself. And while the laws of libel and privacy set the broad bounds within which the media must operate, there are ethical, even moral, questions that go beyond the relatively simple one of whether a story is likely to produce a lawsuit.

Did the public have a right to know about Rep. Wilbur Mills' misadventures at the Tidal Basin and the other events that culminated in his hospitalization for alcoholism? Most newsmen would have no difficulty with that one. Mills was one of the most powerful men in Washington. His conduct drew police attention in a public place. Also, the fact that no arrest was made was in itself newsworthy. Further, it was reasonable to assume—after the Tidal Basin episode—that the excesses of his private life influenced his handling of public business. Therefore, publication was justified. Whether there was too much lip-smacking in the publication process is another question.

But suppose a congressman of Mills' stature has a mistress with whom he quietly spends about as much of the people's time as some of his colleagues spend at the poker table or on the golf course. Should the press report this breach of prevailing mores on the ground that the public has the right to know everything about the life of a public servant? Most newsmen would say no.

A rule of thumb sometimes used is that the misconduct must demonstrably affect a public man's performance of his job before it should be reported. Another is that something overt must happen—something on the record, like Mills' encounter with the police at the Tidal Basin.

A quite different instance in which the issue of privacy has been raised is the detailed, almost clinical, coverage of the mastectomies of Mrs. Ford and Mrs. Rockefeller. That one is fairly easy to handle. In the first place, there was no indication that privacy was sought or even desired; quite the contrary, in fact. Also, a public service was unquestionably rendered in that millions of women were alerted to the need for a regular check for breast cancer.

But here's a more difficult case: The adult son and daughter of a religious leader were arrested on serious drug charges. Both the *Post* and the *Star* identified the father in reporting the arrests. Several *Post* readers protested, saying it was unnecessary to drag the father into the story. The consensus among the *Post* editors involved was that the father's identity was a legitimate part of the story because it added human and social perspective. I concur in that conclusion, although not in total comfort.

Another tough case: Suppose a man of some prominence but not a public figure in any real sense dies under circumstances which, if published, would cause his family extreme anguish? This is one on which the editorial agonizing would be intense, with consideration given to the degree of the man's prominence and whether the circumstances of his death went beyond the bounds of private tragedy.

Often the journalist must decide whether to pursue a course that will exacerbate a wrong. For example, does a woman who has been raped have the right to have her name withheld from the news story? Most newsmen would say that she has—that except in quite unusual circumstances her right to privacy must supersede any counter-balancing right of the public to know all.

Last week, the Supreme Court handed down a decision in a case in which a father claimed that a television station illegally invaded his privacy by identifying, accurately, as his daughter a girl who was the victim of a multiple rape that resulted in her death. The station had learned the girl's name from an indictment made available to its reporter in the courtroom. In that circumstance, the court said the station had the right to use the name despite a state law against publishing a rape victim's identity.

The court made it clear, however, that it was rendering a narrow judgment and was not getting into the broader question of whether the First Amendment, which guarantees the freedom of the press, includes the right to publish anything that is true. But as Justice Byron White noted in the decision, there is a continuing "strong tide running in favor of the so-called right of privacy" in this country. More privacy cases can be expected.

In that decision, Justice White also referred to the collision between interests of individuals and the free press, both "plainly rooted in the traditions and significant concerns of our society." In collisions, injuries often occur. To minimize those injuries, the press must constantly weigh the potential for unfair invasion of privacy, carefully adjusting for its own competitive urges and a very human—and professional—appetite for gossip.

In 1890, two young Boston lawyers wrote for the *Harvard Law Review* an article which laid the foundation for our present legal approach to the privacy question. In that article, Samuel D. Warren and Louis D. Brandeis, who later became a distinguished Supreme Court justice, noted the threat of the then-new mass circulation newspapers to personal privacy. They charged that ''the press is overstepping in every direction the obvious bounds of propriety and decency,'' and then they stated what might be called a philosophical basis for a respect for individual privacy. They wrote:

''The intensity and complexity of life, attendant upon advancing civilization, have rendered necessary some retreat from the world, and man, under the refining influence of culture, has become more sensitive to publicity so that solitude and privacy have become more essential to the individual . . .''

Although written 85 years ago, those words have a contemporary ring. They might well be kept handy in the offices of the media, perhaps next to a small sign bearing the word ''compassion,'' as an antidote to the superficially attractive idea that everything that is true is publishable.

—March 8, 1975

Journalistic Gender

The Washington Post

Interoffice Memo

Messrs. Bradlee/Simons: 3/10/75

    Any ombudsperson dumb enough to use newsmen
in a column three times when he meant journalists
in general deserves all the mail I got this
morning.

                                    Charlie Seib

The Prouty-Butterfield Flap

By Charles B. Seib

The Alexander Butterfield-CIA story, which flared and then fizzled out in one brief week, provided a good—but not reassuring—case history of enterprise journalism as it is practiced on television today. There was a shoot-from-the-hip quality to it and a disturbing disregard for a man's reputation and for the public's need to make sense out of the strange doings in Washington.

The story had its beginning in an effort by two congressmen to defend their turf—namely the House investigation of the CIA. Reacting to a move to kill or restrict the investigation, they committed a little leak. They told reporters that they had learned of a CIA practice of "infiltrating" the executive agencies to the extent of placing an agent high on the Nixon White House staff.

The result was predictable. CIA Director William Colby called the story "vicious nonsense." Ron Nessen, the President's press secretary, said a mountain was being made of a molehill. And reporters set out on the trail of the alleged part-time spook on the old Nixon team.

The next day, July 11 [1975], shortly after 7 a.m., the two top network morning shows—the CBS, "Morning News" and the NBC "Today" show—came up with a name—the same name. They produced former Air Force Col. Fletcher Prouty, live on CBS and taped on NBC. Prouty said the high Nixon official with CIA ties was none other than Alexander Butterfield, who in 1973 started Richard Nixon's slide toward disgrace by disclosing the White House taping system.

Butterfield was a CIA "contact officer" in the White House, Prouty said. His source: E. Howard Hunt, a longtime CIA man who later was sent to prison for his connection with the Watergate burglary.

Just what is Butterfield supposed to have done for the CIA? That didn't come clear. On the CBS show, Prouty said Butterfield's function was "to open doors for CIA operations." On the NBC show he assented to a description of Butterfield as a "man with CIA connections." Imprecise descriptions to be sure, and far from identifying Butterfield as a CIA spy. But in the context, the implication was clear: Butterfield was the CIA's man right on the edge of the Oval Office.

Neither network provided a response from Butterfield or verification from any other source. NBC did couple a flat denial from Mrs. Butterfield with the Prouty charge. CBS put Prouty on the air without any denial, direct or indirect, but a half hour later reported that Mrs. Butterfield said the charge was "ridiculous." Both networks say they tried hard to locate Butterfield before the broadcasts, but without success.

The story hung there for two and a half days. Prouty elaborated on his charge, and it was widely carried in the print press, usually coupled with a CIA denial and with emphasis on Prouty's statement that he was not calling Butterfield a "spy." Then Butterfield, who had not been reached by reporters, astutely accepted an invitation to appear on the popular CBS show, "60 Minutes," that Sunday evening. There, before a prime time audience of around 20 million viewers, he indignantly denied Prouty's story. "Not a shred of truth," he said under questioning by Mike Wallace. At another point in the interview: "I have never been their designated contact man. That is absolutely false." Later: "I had no contact whatsoever with the CIA." And later: "I never did deal with the CIA in any way."

(Wallace says that Butterfield was not paid to appear on "60 Minutes," but his and his wife's fares—his from the West Coast and hers from Washington—and their hotel bills were paid by CBS.)

Since then, Hunt has denied he told Prouty that Butterfield was a CIA contact, and Sen. Church, who heads the Senate CIA investigation, has said no shred of evidence has been found to support the charge. Nevertheless, the Butterfields feel that his job search (he was eased out of his post as head of the Federal Aviation Agency last March) has been seriously hampered. And it is a fact of life that undoubtedly there will be some who will say, years from now, when his name comes up: "Oh, yes. He's the guy who scuttled Nixon for the CIA."

Prouty claims that he did not defame Butterfield—that he, after all, only called him a "contact officer." It is true that nowhere in the network transcripts is there the charge that Butterfield was a spy or an infiltrator. But consider this exchange between CBS reporter Daniel Schorr and Prouty:

SCHORR: Colonel Prouty, I guess you have no way of knowing whether President Nixon knew Alexander Butterfield, who worked in his office, was a CIA man?

PROUTY: I think that's one of the big problems. I would doubt Nixon or anyone else really knew it.

A strong implication that Butterfield was more than a contact man came again later in the CBS broadcast when Schorr and Bruce Morton of CBS were recapping the Prouty charge. Morton stated the question: "Did the CIA infiltrate the White House and other government agencies?" A tape of Colby's "vicious nonsense" denial was run, and then Morton said: "But earlier on this broadcast, a retired Air Force officer who handled liaison with the CIA told Daniel Schorr that a high-ranking White House aide during the Nixon administration was a CIA man." And then he and Schorr went into the Prouty material.

On the NBC broadcast, reporter Ford Rowan developed Prouty's assertion that during Butterfield's military career he was processed for assignment to CIA, which led to this exchange:

ROWAN: Is there any doubt in your mind that Alexander Butterfield was a man with CIA connections, who went to the White House staff, and his CIA connections persisted at the time he was on the White House?

PROUTY: No, I've never had any doubts about that.

At the end of the segment, Rowan did note that Prouty said he did not think that "Butterfield or any CIA man assigned to the White House" was asked to spy on the President.

Now, if Prouty was merely saying that Butterfield was a contact man, the man the CIA dealt with when it had something to take up with the White House (Butterfield's denial rejects even that role), why the rush by CBS and NBC to get the story before the public first thing Friday morning? And why the presentation of the Prouty revelation, if it can be called that, as a big development in the story about high-level CIA "infiltration" of the federal establishment?

In retrospect, it is clear that all concerned—Prouty and CBS and NBC—were careless in their handling of a man's reputation and of an important and complex story. Not only does it appear that unjustifiable harm was done to Butterfield, but a great disservice was done to the public in that the Butterfield story drew attention away from a very serious question: Just what has been the nature and extent of the CIA's involvement in the operations of other government agencies? That question is going to be hard enough to answer. Such distractions as the Butterfield caper don't make the job any easier.

Schorr and Rowan were asked for their afterthoughts on the Prouty broadcasts. Schorr defends the use of Prouty without supporting evidence on the ground that in an earlier situation Prouty's information stood up. Rowan defends his broadcast on the ground that he had received some support for Prouty's story from several other sources.

Conceding those points, one must still ask why they didn't take the time to check on Prouty's story more fully or at least wait for Butterfield's response.

Schorr said that although CBS learned the evening before the broadcast that NBC also had Prouty, competitive pressure was not a factor in the decision to go ahead. In fact, he said, that decision was made before he found out that Prouty had talked to Rowan. He noted, however, that Thursday was a dull news day and that the "Morning News" people were happy to get a good lead story for Friday morning.

Rowan conceded that competition was a factor in his pressing to get the story on the air. He said he didn't know that CBS had Prouty, but he thought ABC might have him. "In a situation like this," he said, "my thought is to get it on the air and see how it flies."

This one appears to have crashed.

—July 22, 1975

A Free Press and
the First Amendment

Seeking a Free Press: A Debt to George Seldes

By Colman McCarthy

The first day he went to work for the *Pittsburgh Leader*—long a deservedly dead newspaper—in 1909, George Seldes wrote a story about a street accident. "Stanislas Schmidt, aged 32, of 1811 Center Avenue, driver of a Silver Top Brewing Company delivery wagon, was slightly injured at 10 o'clock this morning at Penn Avenue and Liberty Street when his wagon was struck by a street car." Hours later, in rookie eagerness, he read through the first edition to find his story in print. There it ran: "Stanislas Schmidt, 32 years old, of 1811 Center Ave., driver of a beer delivery wagon. . ." Seldes immediately read the sign language of his newsroom. "Silver Top was not mentioned," he wrote years later. "Silver Top was a large advertiser. My education had begun."

Seldes did not spend a long time being tutored. In his day, the lessons of sell-out journalism were not complex, quick movements in the underbrush that the public seldom saw amid the grand foliage of The Latest News. Instead, Seldes, learning fast what the press should not be, stayed in the profession to be its critic, to say what the press should be. Many newsrooms today have reporters like Seldes, restive characters who play their typewriter by ear, pressure groups of one, their high standards for ethical journalism trussed firmly to the back of their conscience. Seldes went beyond this, and produced a large body of literature that is among our most insightful press criticism. A few resourceful newspapers now have internal critics—and print them, not just send them around to seminars—but anyone wanting to examine the art as it ran in the early editions ought to consume Seldes.

After surviving several years in Pittsburgh, Seldes went abroad to cover

World War I. Again, the young reporter found his copy being gutted, except now it was not a wary night editor striking out risky words but the military propagandist keeping the facts hidden in the first place. Seldes and other correspondents dined with generals and had tea with princes. "The journals (back home) that printed our stories boasted that their own representatives had been at the fighting front," Seldes wrote in *The Freedom of the Press.* "I now realize that we were told nothing but buncombe, that we were shown nothing of the realities of the war, that we were, in short, merely part of the great Allied propaganda machine whose purpose was to sustain morale at all costs and help drag unwilling America into the slaughter." Seldes described the deceits of the military but his dispiritment concerned the complicity of his own profession, which should have known better. "We all more or less lied about the war," he wrote. "On Armistice Day four of us took an oath on the battlefield that we would tell the truth the rest of our lives, that we would begin telling the truth in time of preparation of war, that we would do what was humanly possible to prevent the recurrence of another such vast and useless horror. Then we all went back to prosaic reporting in America."

For Seldes, it did not stay prosaic long. Too much was happening in American politics and industry during the 1930s and '40s — in the backrooms and boardrooms, the old twins — for him to be idle. But as a reporter, Seldes' deepest fascination was with the unreported news about the newsroom. Timid editors, publishers caring more for public relations than public service, predictable columnists, reporters too friendly with government press agents — all this, in Seldes mind, caused much of the American press to go to seed and come only part way back. "For myself all I can say is that I have never written a story which I knew to be untrue. Most newspapermen, I am sure, can make the same unqualified statement. But such statements are not enough. To them must be added the sin of omission. . . . In Europe I learned that any story derogatory to liberal and radical elements was sure to be published and all stories favorable to them would be played down or left out . . . (From Mexico) for some reason or another, it may have been due to lack of space, all stories giving the case against the Mexican government got either front page or prominent place while the charges . . . against American business interests got little or no space. When year after year similar experiences occur to a trained newspaperman he usually quits reporting both sides of a controversy. But he still publishes nothing but the truth."

After 20 years in the trade, Seldes wrote in 1929 *You Can't Print That,* a valuable book republished in 1968 by Scholarly Press, Grosse Point Woods, Mich. *Freedom of the Press* came in 1935 and examined the corrupting influences on American newspapers. It, along with *You Can't Say That,* has been reprinted by Da Capo Press (227 West 17th St., New York 10011). Other books, out of about a dozen, include *Iron, Blood and Profits, Can These Things Be!* and *Never Tire of Protesting* (Lyle Stuart).

Aside from his books, Seldes also wrote for 10 years—in the 1940s—a newsletter called "In fact." Many veteran reporters in Washington remember "In fact" and recall with affection its influence on their own careers.

One of the few who has written about Seldes in recent years is Nat Hentoff, whose press criticism in the *Village Voice* is in the tradition of Seldes, with much of the same clarity and bite. Hentoff notes that when Seldes criticized the foreign press for third-rate journalism his writing was well received, but "when Seldes began to take on American newspapers, he was, to put it mildly, largely shunned." Seldes has written letters to Hentoff telling of the shunning. "In the 10 years of its publication, 'In fact' never received a mention anywhere, with the exception of two or three small papers, notably the *Gazette & Daily* of York, Pa." Like the tireless researching of I.F. Stone, Seldes said that "In fact" had "many of its greatest scoops from official government documents."

Seldes, who, at this writing, is 82, could not help but be pleased with the reporters and editors who stuck with the Watergate story, bucking both government harassment and public indifference. The battle won this time by a free press is not isolated, though, but is part of the same war that Seldes fought in his generation. "In some of these episodes," Seldes wrote, "nothing but stupidity and ancient nonsense is at stake; but in others a new pattern begins to emerge: it is no longer nonsense and small town arrogance, it is self-evident violation of the civil rights of citizens by the forces elected or appointed to safeguard the Constitution, protect the minority, dispense 'equal justice under the law.' We come now to the forces which represent vested interests rather than the Bill of Rights."

One wishes that George Seldes was still in a newsroom, either climbing the walls with fury or tumbling them down in impatience. Many journalists lucky enough to work on newspapers guided by principled publishers and editors may be unaware of their fortunate and, indeed, minority position. From them, Seldes is owed a debt, payable by not only raking the muck but reseeding the ground after. This is the positive reform Seldes believed journalists capable of, beginning in-house.

It is a sadness that Seldes never received official honor for his press criticism, but much of it was directed at those who confer the honors. Better yet that he received another award, journalism's rarest; it is the prize grateful readers give when they read a piece and say: If this subject wasn't written about, the public would not know it.

—May 3, 1973

The Quizzing of TV Commentators

Spiro Agnew's Proposal

The following excerpts are from an appearance by then Vice President Spiro Agnew on "Kup's Show," WMAQ-TV, in Chicago, on October 20, 1970, as published in the Washington Post *October 26, 1970.*

Q. — I'd like to ask something about politics and TV. It was about a year ago in Des Moines that you made that speech attacking the TV commentators who came on after the President's Vietnam speech, and I remember you criticized one of them for even raising an eyebrow — and when you said that the President has a right to communicate with the people without having his thoughts characterized before they can even be digested. What I want to ask is: aren't you really saying there that these people have no right to analyze and interpret the President — which is generally thought to be one of the classic roles of the press?

A. — I thought — that the analysis is all right as long as it's balanced. Now, what happened in that case was that there was nothing but hostile criticism revealed to the public after that speech. I've really asked for more analysis, not less. I'd like to see more conservative commentators or people who reflect an opposite point of view. And that leads me to an interesting question I'd like to ask you both. I had a letter the other day suggesting that it would be a big benefit to the public if some of the premier news commentators, for example those that have had extremely wide exposure such as yourself or the network commentators, were examined by a group of people in government to explore in depth your opinions, your prejudices, if you will, if you have some, so that in the future the people who watch you would have a chance to know what underlying philosophy you have. Editorial comment must creep into talk shows to some extent . . . but I'm talking about the network commentators, people like Eric Sevareid and Howard K. Smith and people of that type. Don't you think it would be beneficial for the viewing audience to know what they believe, so that when they characterize certain things, that there be some understanding of what their underlying philosophy is . . .

Q. — Wouldn't you, Mr. Vice President, be criticized for government interference in the right of free speech? Anytime that government steps into any kind of an activity like this where free speech, or the press or commentators. . . ?

A. — No. I said people in government — public officials to examine these people — not in a sense of demanding an examination, but simply at their own free will — as I come here of my own free will to be questioned by you. Would you be willing to go on a program where some people in the Senate or the House questioned you? I mean simply an interesting probe into your convictions so that the people that watch Eric Sevareid, for example, would know where he stands on the issues he talks about. Don't you think that would be valuable? . . .

Q. — Well, would it be voluntary, or would you say we have a committee, and we want you to come down? That's not very voluntary . . .

A. — Now, I've got to clear that up, because I can see you're headed in the wrong direction on it. All I mean was nobody demanded that I come on your show. I would expect that nobody could demand that you would go on the kind of show I'm talking about. But I would think that if it would serve a useful purpose that you would be willing to appear on such a show, privately, not a government sponsored show, where the interrogation would be reversed. That's all I'm saying.

Q. —. . . I'm curious about this — do you think it would turn up anyone with any subversive connections?

A. — Boy, you fellows can really jump over 18 hurdles when you get on this subject. All I'm talking about is the people who are watching that tube have a right to know what your opinions are, if you happen to be a man who is telling the news every night, because you can select what parts of the news you want to emphasize and by your language you can convey a point of view that is not an editorial and yet is colored by your own viewpoints. Now, I think the people ought to know what those viewpoints are. That's all I am saying.

Q. — I'm fascinated by your proposal which I think is the first time you've made — at least the first time I've heard it — about having the commentators face some kind of a questioning. I wonder if you'd like to discuss that a little more . . .

A. — Yes, for example, we have some very widely followed shows — "Meet the Press," "Face the Nation," "Issues and Answers" — and talk shows such as yours. It would be very interesting to have a show — a panel type show where senators from either party, representatives, I suppose maybe a couple of governors — would sit down with someone who has a national reputation as a commentator, Frank Reynolds, someone like that, and just examine him in depth on where he stands personally on the issues he talks about every day.

Q. — Well, doesn't he make that clear in his commentary?

A. — I don't think he does, because he is allegedly reporting the news and not his own feelings.

Q. — Oh, he does commentary too, though.

A. — Well, when he gets into commentary he gives, to some extent, his views, on limited issues, but he's never been really probed. Neither have any of these people ever been probed.

Q. — Mr. Vice President, will you volunteer to be one of the interrogators on such a show, if one of the networks would set up such a show?

A. — After November I'd be glad to do it. I'll be pretty busy until then.

Eric Sevareid's Response

The following is a transcript from the Eric Sevareid CBS Evening News broadcast of October 21, 1970, as published in the Washington Post *October 26, 1970.*

The Vice President, Mr. Agnew, proposes that network commentators, like this one and brothers Smith and Reynolds down the street at ABC, "people of that type," he says, be publicly examined by government personnel. "The public has a right to know," he says, our opinions and prejudices.

The phrase, "people of that type" hurts a bit; we certainly don't think of Mr. Agnew as a type; we think he is an original.

What really hurts is the thought that maybe nobody's been listening all this time. If, after some 30 years of thousands of broadcasts, hundreds of articles and lectures and a few books, one's general cast of mind, warts and all, remains a mystery, then we're licked and we fail to see how a few more minutes of examination by government types would solve the supposed riddle.

Mr. Agnew wants to know where we stand. We stand — or rather sit — right here, in the full glare. At a disadvantage as against politicians; we can't cast one vote in committee, an opposite vote on the floor; can't say one thing in the North, an opposite thing in the South; we hold no tenure, four years or otherwise, and can be voted out with a twist of the dial.

We can't use invective and epithets, can't even dream of impugning the patriotism of leading citizens, can't reduce every complicated issue to yes or no, black or white, and would rather go to jail than do bodily injury to the marvelous English language.

We can't come down on this side or that side of each disputed public issue because we're trying to explain far more than advocate and because some issues don't have two sides; some have three, four or half a dozen and in these matters we're damned if we know the right answers. This may be why most of us look a bit frazzled while Mr. Agnew looks so serene.

Another reason may be that we have to think our own thoughts and write our own phrases. Unlike the Vice President, we don't possess a stable of ghostwriters. Come to think of it, if there are mysteries around, unseen spirits motivating the public dialogue, maybe that's the place that could use the glare of public scrutiny — that stable of anonymity.

Finally, at the risk of sounding a bit stuffy, we might say two things. One, that nobody in this business expects for a moment that the full truth of anything will be contained in any one account or commentary, but that through free reporting and discussion, as Mr. Walter Lippmann put it, the truth will emerge.

Second, that the central point about the free press is not that it be accurate, though it must try to be; not that it even be fair, though it must try to be that; but that it be free. And that means, in the first instance, freedom from any and all attempts by the power of government to coerce it or intimidate it or police it in any way.

FYI: The Post's Opinion

For Your Information, we would like to add a few brief thoughts of our own about this business of bias or slant, or whatever you may choose to call it, in the news. Just to begin with, it exists; it is a problem if for no other reason than because extremely few people are free of prejudice. This includes newsmen; it also includes readers and viewers; people who claim to see a bias are usually seeing it out of some bias of their own.

The question is what to do about it and, as Eric Sevareid suggests, there are some checks and balances built into a free, competitive press, not the least of which is that the whole thing, the total product, is out there for inspection every day—which is not quite the way it works in government. So the customer can judge for himself. This is no guarantee, of course, that what appears is comprehensive or accurate or objective, which is what seems to trouble Mr. Agnew, and the fact is, of course, that there can be no guarantee; all anybody can do is try to be right and fair and let the public judge, because there are no absolute standards or measurements which everybody would accept.

This, in a nutshell, is what's wrong with the Vice President's approach — the idea that he or anybody else in government should be entrusted with the role of arbiter of Truth, that he can identify biases and prejudices and rub them out, and leave us with some pure, unvarnished version of The News. To the extent that he proposes to do this by a sort of intellectual — or philosophical — saliva test, conducted in the format of a TV panel show, there is no great harm in the idea if he or others in government want to play newsman-for-a-day. But it is a little silly to think that there is any real protection for the innocent viewer to be found in this kind of Show Biz—if only because there is no insurance that a TV newscaster would be any more candid or forthright in the role of interviewee than a public official.

What is a little sinister about this, then, is not the idea itself but the thinking behind it, because the thinking leads in all logic to a far deeper interference by the government in the news business, a far more fundamental reversal of roles. This has the look, in other words, of the thin edge of a very dangerous wedge, when it is seen in the context of all the other things the Vice President has had to say about news monopolies and elitist East Coast conspiracies and all the rest.

Mr. Agnew is not the first government official, of course, to cringe under the heat of public criticism, nor the first to look for ways to turn it down, off—or, better yet, around. But he is, perhaps, the first to display so powerful an impulse to move right up against, if not beyond, the bounds that have for so long protected freedom of expression in this country from interference or control by the government.

—October 26, 1970

A Warhol Movie and Britain's Media Health

By Bernard D. Nossiter

A TV film about Andy Warhol and his pop art playmates was kept off the little screen in London recently by two eminent Appeals Court judges who had not seen it. They were acting at the request of a man who compiles trivia and who also had not seen it.

Lord Denning and Justice Lawton cited as "evidence" of indecency previews from three of the more lurid papers. The *News of the World, Sunday Mirror* and *Daily Express* had all licked their lips over one scene in particular. It is said to show a large lady dipping her bared breasts in paint and applying them to a canvas.

The judges held that the part-time board which oversees commercial television here had neglected its duty by failing to look at the film. This conveniently ignored the review made by the board's full-time executives charged specifically with that task.

The temporary injunction was issued on the plea of a private citizen, one Ross McWhirter, a former sports writer who says he read law at Oxford. McWhirter and his twin brother Norris publish the enormously successful *Guinness Book of Records* and he told me he was acting from a profound sense of "the rule of law." He had read, he said, that the film shows "some woman with fat, pendulous breasts painting with her nipples."

"This is an insidious movement," he suggested, a kind of naked camel's nose under the decent home viewer's tent. "It will be another part of her anatomy later on," he warned, if the television folk get away with it.

As it turns out, eminent justices and McWhirter have all been the unwitting instruments of Jimmy Vaughan, a promoter who owns the distribution rights to Warhol's feature film, *Trash*. Vaughan, trying to draw attention to the movie, urged the *Sunday Mirror* to ask for an advance showing of the television thing and the outcome has made Warhol a household name here.

One point in this little story has already been made by Mr. Bumble who long ago observed that "The law is a ass." But another is the fierce concern here for free, adult and unfettered media.

The night the TV film was cancelled, television stations were flooded with angry phone calls and the overwhelming majority were protesting interference with their right to judge what was and was not indecent. Lord Shawcross, head of one of the commercial television companies, defended the judges and was promptly slapped down by a mass petition from his own staff.

The British may be the world's best authors of letters to the editor and

223

the columns of every serious daily were filled with angry and sarcastic missives.

A handful read like that of a *Telegraph* reader in Hereford who praised McWhirter for his "fight against ever-declining standards." But the vast majority sounded more like a *Times* reader from Cheshire who wound up: "Sir, I am sick and tired of people who think they have the right to decide what is good for me; please may I make these decisions myself?"

The BBC satire, "Up Sunday," weighed in with a skit showing three be-wigged judges, two of them engrossed in the bare breasts and buttocks that regularly feature in the three censorious newspapers. The third judge was a dummy.

A few days later, the real life Appeal Court judges finally watched the Warhol film, made clear they did not like what they saw, but reluctantly lifted their injunction on the grounds that it was the business of the Independent Broadcasting Authority to determine what shall and shall not be seen on commercial television. The IBA, a part-time body of establishment types, then let the film be shown and Britain easily survived the experience.

The real point, then, is the vitality of all this, the enormous concern shown over what was seen by most as a threat to free expression in the temporary suppression of a marginal film. Given this kind of climate, it does not seem that the media here have much to worry about.

In fact, there are plenty of recent incidents to demonstrate that media and government conduct a running battle not wholly unlike that in the United States.

Last fall, the *Sunday Times*, boldest of the established papers, ran a story based on a confidential document showing that the government was considering closing down nearly half of the nation's rail tracks. The paper had consulted the *Railway Gazette,* a trade journal, for help.

The government responded by sending some Scotland Yard detectives to search the *Gazette* office and question editors and writers there and at the *Sunday Times*. A *Gazette* editor charged that his telephone had been tapped and one of his reporters had been threatened by the police with information that could have been acquired only by tapping the reporter's phone.

The outcry this touched off, in Parliament and elsewhere, persuaded the government to drop any plans for prosecution. But it still has not answered the charges of phone tapping and blackmail.

Again, the government, at the urging of Distillers Company, persuaded the High Court to suppress a *Sunday Times* story that questioned Distillers responsibility for the thalidomide catastrophe. The Court was afraid the newspaper was pressuring the whiskey company, a fear the court conveniently subdued when Distillers' bankers applied even more powerful pressure.

[The government was compelled to call off its legal dogs in the railway case but succeeded in winning an appeal to Britain's highest court that suppressed the thalidomide story. Both incidents have left behind the unpleasant suggestion that the government can and will use its power against organs that offend.]

Harold Wilson, the Labor Party leader, gave the press and individual reporters a bad time when he was prime minister. But not long ago, he delivered an eloquent speech on behalf of a free press and warned that some of its greatest dangers come from the spinelessness of the media themselves.

There is more than a little to this, too. Every national and big provincial paper here has an important writer who is briefed daily and in private by the prime minister's press spokesman. These writers, the "Lobby correspondents," then write insider stories with no attribution, purveying the government's line as if it were revealed truth.

When Premier Edward Heath was selling Common Market entry to an unconvinced electorate, one technique was the "media breakfasts." Each week leading figures from the press and television gathered with key ministers and civil servants to plan how best to promote the policy. This is a degree of collaboration that would appall most American journalists, even "friendly" reporters on a specialized beat.

The BBC itself, still the world's television pacemaker, is not beyond reproach. It is accepting money from British Petroleum, one of the seven oil giants, to produce a series on ecology. One film deals with Alaska and never mentions the threat of an oil pipeline to Alaska's environment, a pipeline that BP wants to help build.

In sum, the media here as everywhere are subject to the seduction of insiderism, money, flattery, interest and all the other wiles of power centers wise in the ways of manipulation. But there is enough diversity and rivalry, and above all, an influential public that cares, to ensure that someone is likely to blow a whistle and prevent seduction from becoming rape. The forces—above all, government, any government—that would curb and inhibit the media are typically on the defensive in Britain. This, perhaps, is the key point that distinguishes the situation here from the United States at the beginning of 1973.*

—February 2, 1973

---

*Author's note: Before James McCord came clean with Judge Sirica.

Justice Stewart's View of the Press

For the last decade, and most particularly for the last few years, the American press has been at the center of the political storms that have swept the country. What the press did, or did not do, in its coverage of Vietnam, Watergate and the Johnson and Nixon administrations has been the topic of uncounted speeches and articles. Perhaps not since the days of the abolitionists before the Civil War has the press—its strengths and shortcomings—been the center of so much public debate.

In much of that debate, or so it seemed to us, the issues were never squarely joined. Many of the critics of the press seemed to start from the proposition that the traditional role of the American press was to be supportive of the government and that it had embarked on a new course by adopting an antagonistic view of two Presidents and their policies on at least two major national issues. The defenders of the press (and we, of course, are among them) started from the view that the press was doing what it was always supposed to be doing—querying, testing, probing all policies and decisions of government. The real difference in the last decade from prior decades, at least as we saw it, was that the executive branch of government had never before lied to the American people so consistently and so demonstrably as it did about Vietnam and Watergate.

The real issue in this debate, the one that rarely was joined, is the proper role of the press in American political life. Is the press, as Thomas Macaulay wrote, a fourth estate, given special protection by the First Amendment and charged by those who founded this country with providing an additional check on the official power of the three branches of government? Or has the press created this role for itself, pushed its First Amendment right beyond that intended by the Founders, and arrogantly assumed a larger place in political life than it should hold? The starting point in such a debate should be the Constitution and the views of the men who wrote it. Today we print an extract from a speech on that subject delivered recently by Supreme Court Justice Potter Stewart. It is a remarkable speech because it is rare for a Justice to address a live public issue so squarely and so consisely. While we do not agree with everything that Justice Stewart says, particularly with his and the Court's view of the right to access to information, his speech seems to us to be a more substantial contribution to public understanding of the government-press conflict than almost anything else that has been said by a government official in the recent past.

—November 11, 1974

226

The Role and Rights of the Press

By Potter Stewart

Mr. Stewart is an associate justice of the U.S. Supreme Court. This article is excerpted from an address given at the Yale Law School Sesquicentennial Convocation. It is reprinted with permission.

It was less than a decade ago—during the Vietnam years—that the people of our country began to become aware of the twin phenomena on a national scale of so-called investigative reporting and an adversary press—that is, a press adversary to the executive branch of the federal government. And only in the two short years that culminated last summer in the resignation of a President did we fully realize the enormous power that an investigative and adversary press can exert.

The public opinion polls that I have seen indicate that some Americans firmly believe that the former Vice President and former President of the United States were hounded out of office by an arrogant and irresponsible press that had outrageously usurped dictatorial power. And it seems clear that many more Americans, while appreciating and even applauding the service performed by the press in exposing official wrongdoing at the highest levels of our national government, are nonetheless deeply disturbed by what they consider to be the illegitimate power of the organized press in the political structure of our society. It is my thesis that, on the contrary, the established American press in the past 10 years, has performed precisely the function it was intended to perform by those who wrote the First Amendment of our Constitution. I further submit that this thesis is supported by the relevant decisions of the Supreme Court.

Surprisingly, despite the importance of newspapers in the political and social life of our country, the Supreme Court has not until very recently been called upon to delineate their constitutional role in our structure of government.

Our history is filled with struggles over the rights and prerogatives of the press, but these disputes rarely found their way to the Supreme Court. The early years of the Republic witnessed controversy over the constitutional validity of the short-lived Alien and Sedition Act, but the controversy never reached the Court. In the next half century there was nationwide turmoil over the right of the organized press to advocate the then subversive view that slavery should be abolished. In Illinois a publisher was killed for publishing abolitionist views. But none of this history made First Amendment law because the Court had earlier held that the Bill of Rights applied only against the federal government, not against the individual states.

With the passage of the Fourteenth Amendment, the constitutional framework was modified, and by the 1920s the Court had established that the protections of the First Amendment extend against all government— federal, state, and local.

The next 50 years witnessed a great outpouring of First Amendment litigation, all of which inspired books and articles beyond number. But, with few exceptions, neither these First Amendment cases nor their commentators squarely considered the Constitution's guarantee of a free press. Instead, the focus was on its guarantee of free speech. The Court's decisions dealt with the rights of isolated individuals, or of unpopular minority groups to stand up against governmental power representing an angry or frightened majority. The cases that came to the Court during those years involved the rights of the soapbox orator, the nonconformist pamphleteer, the religious evangelist. The Court was seldom asked to define the rights and privileges, or the responsibilities, of the organized press.

In very recent years cases involving the established press finally have begun to reach the Supreme Court, and they have presented a variety of problems, sometimes arising in complicated factual settings.

In a series of cases, the Court has been called upon to consider the limits imposed by the free press guarantee upon a state's common or statutory law of libel. As a result of those cases, a public figure cannot successfully sue a publisher for libel unless he can show that the publisher maliciously printed a damaging untruth.

The Court has also been called upon to decide whether a newspaper reporter has a First Amendment privilege to refuse to disclose his confidential sources to a grand jury. By a divided vote, the Court found no such privilege to exist in the circumstances of the cases before it.

In another noteworthy case, the Court was asked by the Justice Department to restrain publication by the *New York Times* and other newspapers of the so-called Pentagon Papers. The Court declined to do so.

In yet another case, the question to be decided was whether political groups have a First Amendment or statutory right of access to the federally regulated broadcast channels of radio and television. The Court held there was no such right of access.

Last term the Court confronted a Florida statute that required newspapers to grant a "right of reply" to political candidates they had criticized. The Court unanimously held this statute to be inconsistent with the guarantees of a free press.

It seems to me that the Court's approach to all these cases has uniformly reflected its understanding that the free press guarantee is, in essence, a *structural* provision of the Constitution. Most of the other provisions in the Bill of Rights protect specific liberties or specific rights of individuals: freedom of speech, freedom of worship, the right to counsel, the privilege against compulsory self-incrimination, to name a few. In contrast, the free press clause extends protection to an institution. The publishing business is, in short, the only organized private business that is given explicit constitutional protection.

This basic understanding is essential, I think, to avoid an elementary error of constitutional law. It is tempting to suggest that freedom of the press means only that newspaper publishers are guaranteed freedom of expression. They *are* guaranteed that freedom, to be sure, but so are we all, because of the free speech clause. If the free press guarantee meant no more than freedom of expression, it would be a constitutional redundancy. Between 1776 and the drafting of our Constitution, many of the state constitutions contained clauses protecting freedom of the press while at the same time recognizing no general freedom of speech. By including both guarantees in the First Amendment, the Founders quite clearly recognized the distinction between the two.

It is also a mistake to suppose that the only purpose of the constitutional guarantee of a free press is to insure that a newspaper will serve as a neutral forum for debate, a "market place for ideas," a kind of Hyde Park corner for the community. A related theory sees the press as a neutral conduit of information between the people and their elected leaders. These theories, in my view, again give insufficient weight to the institutional autonomy of the press that it was the purpose of the Constitution to guarantee.

In setting up the three branches of the federal government, the Founders deliberately created an internally competitive system. As Mr. Justice Brandeis once wrote: "The [Founders'] purpose was, not to avoid friction, but, by means of the inevitable friction incident to the distribution of the governmental powers among three departments, to save the people from autocracy."

The primary purpose of the constitutional guarantee of a free press was a similar one: to create a fourth institution outside the government as an additional check on the three official branches. Consider the opening words of the free press clause of the Massachusetts Constitution, drafted by John Adams:

"The liberty of the press is essential to the security of the state."

The relevant metaphor, I think, is the metaphor of the fourth estate. What Thomas Carlyle wrote about the British government a century ago has a curiously contemporary ring:

"Burke said there were Three Estates in Parliament; but, in the Reporters' Gallery yonder, there sat a Fourth Estate more important far than they all. It is not a figure of speech or witty saying; it is a literal fact—very momentus to us in these times."

For centuries before our Revolution, the press in England had been licensed, censored, and bedeviled by prosecutions for seditious libel. The British Crown knew that a free press was not just a neutral vehicle for the balanced discussion of diverse ideas. Instead, the free press meant organized, expert scrutiny of government. The press was a conspiracy of the intellect, with the courage of numbers. This formidable check on official power was what the British Crown had feared—and what the American Founders decided to risk.

It is this constitutional understanding, I think, that provides the unifying principle underlying the Supreme Court's recent decisions dealing with the organized press.

Consider first the libel cases. Officials within the three governmental branches are, for all practical purposes, immune from libel and slander suits for statements that they make in the line of duty. This immunity, which has both constitutional and common law origins, aims to insure bold and vigorous prosecution of the public's business. The same basic reasoning applies to the press. By contrast, the Court has never suggested that the constitutional right of free *speech* gives an *individual* any immunity from liability for either libel or slander.

In the cases involving the newspaper reporters' claims that they had a constitutional privilege not to disclose their confidential news sources to a grand jury, the Court rejected the claims by a vote of five to four, or, considering Mr. Justice Powell's concurring opinion, perhaps by a vote of four and a half to four and a half. But if freedom of the press means simply freedom of speech for reporters, this question of a reporter's asserted right to withhold information would have answered itself. None of us—as individuals—has a "free speech" right to refuse to tell a grand jury the identity of someone who has given us information relevant to the grand jury's legitimate inquiry. Only if a reporter is a representative of a protected *institution* does the question become a different one. The members of the Court disagreed in answering the question, but the question did not answer itself.

The cases involving the so-called "right of access" to the press raised the issue whether the First Amendment allows government, or indeed *requires* government, to regulate the press so as to make it a genuinely fair and open "market place for ideas." The Court's answer was "no" to both questions. If a newspaper wants to serve as a neutral market place for debate, that is an objective which it is free to choose. And, within limits, that choice is probably necessary to commercially successful journalism. But it is a choice that government cannot constitutionally impose.

Finally the Pentagon Papers case involved the line between secrecy and openness in the affairs of government. The question, or at least one question, was whether that line is drawn by the Constitution itself. The Justice Department asked the Court to find in the Constitution a basis for prohibiting the publication of allegedly stolen government documents. The Court could find no such prohibition. So far as the Constitution goes the autonomous press may publish what it knows, and may seek to learn what it can.

But this autonomy cuts both ways. The press is free to do battle against secrecy and deception in government. But the press cannot expect from the Constitution any guarantee that it will succeed. There is no constitutional right to have access to particular government information, or to require openness from the bureaucracy. The public's interest in knowing about its government is protected by the guarantee of a free press, but the protection is indirect. The Constitution itself is neither a Freedom of Information Act nor an Official Secrets Act.

The Constitution, in other words, establishes the contest, not its resolution. Congress may provide a resolution, at least in some instances, through carefully drawn legislation. For the rest, we must rely, as so often in our system we must, on the tug and pull of the political forces in American society.

Newspapers, television networks and magazines have sometimes been outrageously abusive, untruthful, arrogant and hypocritical. But it hardly follows that elimination of a strong and independent press is the way to eliminate abusiveness, untruth, arrogance or hypocrisy from government itself.

It is quite possible to conceive of the survival of our Republic without an autonomous press. For openness and honesty in government, for an adequate flow of information between the people and their representatives, for a sufficient check on autocracy and despotism, the traditional competition between the three branches of government, supplemented by vigorous political activity, might be enough.

The press could be relegated to the status of a public utility. The guarantee of free speech would presumably put some limitation on the regulation to which the press could be subjected. But if there were no guarantee of a free press, government could convert the communications media into a neutral "market place of ideas." Newspapers and television networks could then be required to promote contemporary government policy or current notions of social justice.

Such a constitution is possible; it might work reasonably well. But it is not the Constitution the Founders wrote. It is not the Constitution that has carried us through nearly two centuries of national life. Perhaps our liberties might survive without an independent established press. But the Founders doubted it, and . . . I think we can all be thankful for their doubts.

—November 11, 1974

A Kind of Epilogue

A DEW Line on the News

By Philip Foisie

Every year or so, the editors of the Washington Post *leave the pressures of the news and the newsroom behind them for several days and escape to some secluded spot to think about their newspaper—where it has been and where it ought to be going. Such a meeting took place in January, 1974, at Port Deposit, Md. The following article by the* Post's *assistant managing editor for foreign news was presented at that meeting as the basis of a discussion on newsgathering in the '70s.*

As recently as last October, Saudi Arabia and Kuwait were the butt of our jokes about camels and airconditioners and I, for one, had never heard of William Simon. A few months later, service stations in the Washington area were closing on Sunday. It was not the first surprise of 1973, only the latest. The Yom Kippur war was totally unexpected, as was the Russian wheat deal—both the deal itself and its effect on the farm and in the supermarket. And on and on, back through the months of last year.

I think this says something important about today's world, which is fast becoming more interdependent and less predictable, and about the way we newsmen have been looking at the world. During our occasional lapses into self-congratulation, we have the illusion that we are on top of the major news. I believe that in fact we are surprised more often than we ought to be and need to be. I think I know why.

For example, there are a number of clearly discernible trends that will probably endure at least through the '70s and that point the way to an explosion of major developments abroad. Increasingly, those developments will have a dramatically sudden and sometimes decisive impact on the way Americans live. We know what the trends are (they are almost cliches) and every now and then we write a story about them. But we are not using our knowledge of the trends consistently enough and wisely enough to plan our coverage, to focus on the news.

We become so preoccupied with that important part of our file—recording what happened "today" and close at hand—that we fail to see enough of the big ones coming up over the horizon.

The series by one of our science correspondents many months ago was the first major takeout on the energy crisis to appear in American newspapers. But what good is it to boast that we were first when we didn't really follow through?

We are not inventing enough of the right questions. We have not established a Distant Early Warning system of news intelligence. We have not developed the knack of identifying and writing regularly about problems before they become crises, especially when those problems first appear at a distance, are hard to tell and hard to explain to the reader, and generally fail to conform to our definition of "news."

There can no longer be any doubt that economics, finance, trade and technology are absolutely central to the very quality of our everyday lives and to our government's policies, yet many of us still suffer from an archaic bias against giving good display to these gray and dismal sciences. This is why these days such publications as *Business Week,* the *Petroleum Intelligence Weekly,* and the *Financial Times* of London, to name just a few, are often closer to the cutting edge of what it's all about than we are.

As a paper with a heavily political focus in a very political town, and with a special penchant for personal style, we tend to jump on major stories only when they have entered the political arena, and then it is often much too late. The point has been made that our government—especially this administration—doesn't have a DEW line either.

If the national desk had Nixon announcing a committee to study an aluminum shortage ("it happened today" and "who's going to head it?") or if the metropolitan desk learned that an Alexandria scrap dealer was offering $1 a pound for used beer cans, those stories might well make page one, and should. If, a few months earlier, our foreign editor, Lee Lescaze, offered a story that Surinam and Jamaica were involved in an effort to organize bauxite-producing countries into an "OPEC" [Organization of Petroleum Exporting Countries], I doubt very much that it would be considered ("Surinam, for God's sake!") and a part of the blame would be the foreign desk's for not selling it hard enough or explaining its significance. We are not as good at anticipatory journalism as we need to be these days.

We still think too much in terms of "hard" news and "soft" news and let the first crowd a bit too much of the second off page one. I think we should now talk more about "hardware" and "software" news. Hardware news is about money, material, technological breakthroughs—the things that matter most in today's world, and it is frequently "soft" in the sense that it doesn't have a news peg. Our "hard" news can frequently be "soft-ware"—which I would define as press conferences, official statements, communiques, and other contrived events in which leaders posture or pass diplomatic signals or generally try to cope with words with the hard facts of life they find themselves confronting. I think we need more "hard-ware" stories on page one. Nixon cannot talk oil out of shale; science and industry must find a way.

Finally, we are surprised too often by the turn of events because we listen too much to conventional wisdom and talk too much to conventional sources. We had Saudi Arabian Oil Minister Zaki Yamani's threat of employing oil as a weapon first, last April, and heard it all again from Pete Petersen* long before the dam broke, but we didn't believe it because we were assured Yamani didn't mean it. "What are the Saudis going to do with the oil if they don't sell it to the West?" We forget that we live in an increasingly outlandish world, and we must learn to think more about the unthinkable. But there were sources whom we are not accustomed to tapping who did see it coming. When our diplomatic correspondent, Murrey Marder, went to Chicago on the grain story, for example, he was astonished to discover how much he could learn about his beat from dealers in the commodities markets.

Here are a few of the trends that I think will govern news developments through the '70s. Most of them appear not to be easily reversible, and some of the curves can be plotted with almost statistical precision, failing some unexpected solution not now in sight.

Trend No. 1—*the limit of resources*, a logical place to begin in the midst of the oil crisis. Next will be the metals crisis. Fertilizer is a problem already, and as population grows and water becomes scarcer, famine will increase. And so on. We have entered the Era of Shortages (and at the very time when much of the world is becoming accustomed to affluence or is anticipating it: the conflict could be very violent). C. Fred Bergsten of Brookings Institution refers to the "cruel problem of compound arithmetic where infinite appetites compete for finite resources."

Where raw materials are involved, oil has set the pattern and other shortages will probably occur even more quickly. The effect of shortages falls unevenly on nations, and the United States is more fortunate than most, but the U.S. cannot remain an island of prosperity in a sea of world recession or depression.

Trend No. 2—*limits on growth*. Little is being heard from the ecologists these days, it's true, and in any event the problems are to some extent less visible in the more affluent parts of the world that appear to be edging toward zero population growth. The effect of some environmental pollu-

---

*Former Secretary of Commerce Peter Petersen, who was on a presidential mission to explore problems with U.S. allies on matters of trade.

tion may be slowed to some extent, also. But basically the problem won't go away just because we are paying less attention to it. We are in danger of treating this trend as though it were merely a fad.

The population explosion, with its own special awesome compound arithmetic, will be an increasingly big story. The U.N. has designated 1974 as Population Year and there'll be a lot of hoopla, including an international population conference in Bucharest in August. We must be all over this story during the next few years, and focus especially on that part of the story that concerns urban disaster areas like Tokyo, Djakarta, Calcutta and Lagos.

Trend No. 3—*the limits of power.* The so-called "superpowers" are increasingly less powerful; the term itself is outmoded. The U.S. is a superpower only in terms of nuclear firepower. In almost every other respect, the U.S. (and Russia) is witnessing an erosion of its ability to work its will on the world, even on its own allies. It will have to bargain harder and more often with weak "third world" countries. It will find it increasingly difficult to negotiate favorable trade and monetary agreements and to protect its currency from camel money. It will have to pay a high price this year and next to keep those overseas bases that advancing technology has not rendered obsolete. It will have to worry like hell about the spread of nuclear weapons. Some dominoes will fall as we sit idly by behind the Nixon Doctrine.

Who would have thought in 1903, or even in 1963, that the U.S. would even contemplate a formula for surrendering sovereignty over the Canal Zone?

We will be following the skirmishes in the New Economic War that some in the "third world"—taking advantage of shortages— now feel emboldened to wage, and I do not mean that the U.S. is powerless in the struggle. It has two big weapons—technology, which everyone including the Russians wants, and the fact that along with Canada it produces about 85 per cent of the world's grain. But in terms of U.S. influence, it is likely to be downhill for some time to come. Allende would have fallen anyway, whatever was our role.

A resort to gunboat diplomacy in the Persian Gulf would test the validity of this trend, but I'm with those who say that it's not do-able without the Russians, and probably even with the Russians.

Trend No. 4—*the spread of terror.* There has been an incredible change in the quality of political violence, and there will probably be more violence as well. It is the age of the urban guerrilla, of the big scare, of premeditated outrage. New technology aids the desperate causist; corporations, cities, even governments have been held virtual hostage for hours or days. A rumor that a terrorist planned to infest a region's water supply with germ warfare caused near panic in parts of Germany precisely because, today, it is plausible.

Terrorism is becoming fashionable, possibly a last gasp of the youth in revolt, an earlier trend that apparently was short-lived. It is also becoming profitable. The Ford settlement in Argentina was extraordinary, and the apparently uncontrollable wave of kidnappings and extortion may bring down Peron if death does not overtake him first. Terrorism has also become multinational and disciplined. A Santa Barbara waitress, a Moroccan, a Pakistani, arrested in London with suspected links to the IRA that could be supplying them with Russian weapons brought in on an East German freighter?

Terror in support of a genuine cause is designed to draw attention to that cause, and as one bizarre innovation follows another we cannot help but comply. But we should give less space and play to the merely bizarre and bloody (the shootout at Rome airport) and more to the incidents that are more significant in terms of menace to a vulnerable society (terrorists armed with anti-aircraft) and in terms of unsettling effect (the hijacking that led to the closure of the Jewish transit camp in Austria).

One of the shortages in the world is patience. We have under-reported and underestimated the extent to which desperate men will use desperate means. We must pay more attention this year to oppressed minorities and esoteric wars, the little wars that threaten to involve the U.S. and the world in big consequences. This violence is well-bankrolled. It doesn't matter all that much how many are being killed in Mozambique and Rhodesia; the U.S. will be increasingly affected as long as those wars continue.

I see other major trends as well. The world is becoming more interdependent. Increasingly, what happens in one country affects others more quickly and more deeply. Even the U.S. cannot solve many of its major new problems without the cooperation of many other countries, as the forthcoming Law of the Sea conference will demonstrate. And in a number of cases, relatively comparable societies abroad have already reached where we appear to be heading and have things to teach our readers. If this country must eventually turn away from growth, Norway is well worth watching. Hence the need for what some of our best reporters call "comparative journalism."

The world is also becoming increasingly authoritarian, not in the sense of governments moving to the left or right on the political spectrum (that trend has about run its course) but in the sense of governments moving more into the center of people's lives. The invasion of privacy, for example, will be an increasingly important story in the '70s.

Finally, the news is becoming increasingly complex. Or, to put it more precisely, we journalists must become increasingly aware of the growing impact of science and technology on the lives of men and nations. It is not merely that an explosion of scientific discovery and technological innovation is altering the course of events as never before; scientists are also providing new tools with which we can better understand what is happening and why.

236

The great advance of electronic warfare since 1967 made the Yom Kippur war a very different kind of war from its predecessor, for example. The SALT negotiations cannot be covered well until we better understand nuclear technology and find a way to explain it to our readers. And can we focus on the coming food crisis without listening to those climatologists who warn that a drastic climate change is taking place throughout the world that will have a literally chilling affect on mankind in the not-so-distant future?

I think the *Post* must use these trends more methodically to line up our sights on the news. We should reach out more for the news, and not wait until it comes to our doorstep, until it "happens." We counterpunch too much, as does our government, I'm told.

Contributors

Ben H. Bagdikian

Noted press critic and former ombudsman for the *Washington Post,* Ben H. Bagdikian was born in Marash, Turkey in 1920 and naturalized a U.S. citizen in 1926. He began his newspaper career as a reporter for the *Springfield* (Mass.) *Morning Union* in 1941 after graduation from Clark University. Since then he has worked as a reporter, columnist, foreign correspondent and chief Washington correspondent for the *Providence Journal;* as a contributing editor of the *Saturday Evening Post;* as project director on a study of future U.S. news media for the Rand Corporation. In 1970 he came to the *Post.*

At the *Post,* Mr. Bagdikian was, first, assistant managing editor for national affairs and later ombudsman, taking over Richard Harwood's role. He left the *Post* in August 1972 to return to freelance criticism.

Mr. Bagdikian has written articles for many magazines and is also the author of several books, among them *The Information Machines: Their Impact on Men and the Media* (Harper & Row, 1971) and *The Effete Conspiracy and Other Crimes by the Press* (Harper & Row, 1972).

Benjamin C. Bradlee

A New Englander, born in Boston, Benjamin C. (for Crowninshield) Bradlee was named executive editor of the *Washington Post* in September 1968 after serving nearly three years as managing editor. His association with the newspaper, however, goes back to 1948, when he served three years as a *Post* reporter covering federal courts. The State Department drafted him in 1951 to be a press attache for the U.S. embassy in Paris.

In 1953 he joined *Newsweek* magazine's Paris bureau and was European correspondent for four years. It was a job that took him all over Europe and the Middle East, including coverage of the Anglo-French invasion of Suez and the Algerian rebellion, Cyprus and Morocco.

Mr. Bradlee came back to Washington in 1957, first as a *Newsweek* political correspondent, later as Washington bureau chief. He began intensive coverage of presidential campaigns, touring with Kennedy and Nixon in the 1960 campaigns. He had become a close friend of Sen. John Kennedy, who was his next door neighbor in Georgetown, and later wrote *That Special Grace,* published by Lippincott in 1964, and *Conversations With Kennedy* (W. W. Norton, 1975).

Mr. Bradlee, 52, was educated at St. Mark's School, Southboro, Mass., and Harvard College (class of '43), where he received an A.B. degree.

David S. Broder

Political correspondent and columnist for the *Washington Post,* David S. Broder was awarded the Pulitzer Prize for "distinguished commentary" in May 1973, and in 1972 was rated as America's most respected political reporter in an American University survey of 100 leading political journalists.

Before joining the national reporting staff of the *Post* in 1966, Mr. Broder covered national politics for the *New York Times* (1965-66), for the *Washington Star* (1960-65) and for *Congressional Quarterly* (1955-60).

He is a frequent contributor to magazines such as *Harper's* and *Atlantic Monthly,* and is the author of *The Party's Over: The Failure of Politics in America* (Harper & Row, 1972).

Born in Chicago Heights, Ill., in 1929, he received his bachelor's degree and master's in political science from the University of Chicago, served two years in the U.S. Army and began his newspaper career on the *Bloomington* (Ill.) *Pantagraph.*

Kenneth Crawford

In a journalism career spanning more than 50 years, Kenneth Crawford has covered administrations from Coolidge to Nixon and events ranging from the Southern Illinois gang wars and Mississippi flood in the late 1920s to the invasion of France. He landed with the first wave in Normandy on D-Day.

Born in Wisconsin in 1902 and educated in public schools and Beloit College, he began his career working as correspondent and bureau manager for United Press in several Midwest bureaus, and later in Washington, D.C., and Buffalo, N.Y. In Buffalo, he left UP to become political editor of the now-defunct *Buffalo Times.*

Mr. Crawford returned to Washington in 1933 as correspondent for the *New York Post* and seven years later became Washington bureau manager of the experimental newspaper *PM.* During World War II he covered the war for *Newsweek* in North Africa, Italy, the Middle East, England and France.

In 1944, he returned once again to Washington as a correspondent for *Newsweek,* then became bureau chief and later a political columnist for the magazine. He retired in 1971 but continues to write columns for the *Washington Post.*

Philip Foisie

Philip Foisie, *Washington Post* assistant managing editor for foreign news who discusses here the need for a more distant focus on the news, was born in Seattle, Wash., in 1922. During World War II, he served with Army

Intelligence in the China-Burma-India Theater. Soon after graduation from Harvard College in 1947, he returned to the Far East, working in Shanghai with the United Nations Relief and Rehabilitation Administration and later with the *China Press* as city editor.

Returning to the United States in 1949, Mr. Foisie worked successively with the *San Francisco Chronicle;* the *Press Democrat* of Santa Rosa, Calif.; and the *Louisville Courier-Journal.*

He joined the *Washington Post* as cable editor in 1955, served as foreign editor from 1960 to 1968, when he became assistant managing editor, with continuing responsibility for the foreign news coverage of the *Post*. In this role, he is also responsible for the *Post's* involvement in the *International Herald Tribune* in Paris and in the *Los Angeles Times-Washington Post* News Service.

Philip L. Geyelin

Washington Post Editorial Page Editor Philip L. Geyelin, who joined the *Post* in 1967 and was awarded a Pulitzer Prize in 1970 for "general excellence" in editorial writing, has been a Washington journalist for more than 20 years.

For the *Wall Street Journal*, Mr. Geyelin covered the 1948 Dewey campaign, the White House, the Eisenhower and Stevenson campaigns. From 1956 to 1960 he served as the *Journal's* chief European correspondent, covering events in Suez, Lebanon, Berlin, Baghdad and the fall of the Fourth French Republic. And as the *Journal's* diplomatic correspondent in Washington until 1967, he traveled to Vietnam, Cuba, the Dominican Republic and Europe. His coverage of these major international stories earned an Overseas Press Club Citation in 1966.

A graduate of Yale University and a veteran of the U.S. Marine Corps, Mr. Geyelin, 53, is also the author of the thoughtful study *Lyndon B. Johnson and the World,* published by Frederick A. Praeger Inc. in 1966.

Meg Greenfield

The author of the parody here on presidential campaign coverage, Meg Greenfield has been deputy editorial page editor of the *Washington Post* since 1970. She came to the *Post* editorial page staff in 1968 after working for *Reporter* magazine for 11 years, first as a researcher and later as its Washington correspondent and editor.

A 1952 summa cum laude graduate of Smith College, Miss Greenfield, 45, studied at Cambridge University on a Fulbright scholarship before joining *Reporter.*

William Greider

A national staff writer for the *Washington Post* since November 1968, William Greider, 39, was graduated from Princeton University in 1958 and soon afterward joined the *Wheaton* (Ill.) *Daily Journal* as a reporter and later became managing editor. In 1962 he went to the *Louisville Times* as a reporter and from 1966 to 1968 served as Washington correspondent for the *Courier-Journal & Times*.

Richard Harwood

Early in 1970, at a time of great controversy over the media, veteran newsman Richard Harwood was appointed assistant managing editor of the *Washington Post* and the newspaper's first ombudsman. His duties included writing "The News Business" column for the editorial page, responding to consumer complaints, and offering internal criticism of the daily paper in the form of memoranda to the executive and managing editors. Many of these memos are published here for the first time.

Now editor of the *Trenton Times*, Mr. Harwood, 50, served with the U.S. Marine Corps in World War II and then worked successively for the *Nashville Tennessean, Louisville Times* and *Courier-Journal & Times* before joining the *Post* in 1966 as national correspondent and later foreign correspondent in Vietnam.

A graduate of Vanderbilt University and both a Nieman and Carnegie Fellow, Mr. Harwood is the co-author with Haynes Johnson of *Lyndon,* a biography of President Johnson (Praeger, 1973). He has been a contributor to several other books. Among his journalistic awards are the Sigma Delta Chi medal for national reporting and two George Polk awards —for national reporting and for criticism.

Stephen D. Isaacs

A national staff reporter of the *Washington Post,* Stephen D. Isaacs admits his speaking fee is considerably lower than those of the reporters and columnists he writes about here. In fact, as city editor and metropolitan editor of the *Washington Post* for about six years, he used to speak for nothing quite frequently in Washington.

A 1959 graduate of Harvard, Mr. Isaacs has been with the *Post* for 15 years and has held jobs ranging from police reporter to copy editor to chief of the New York bureau. Now 38, he is the author of a *Washington Post* book tentatively titled *Jews and Political Power,* which will be published by Doubleday & Company in September 1974.

Haynes Johnson

An assistant managing editor of the *Washington Post,* Haynes Johnson has had a long and distinguished journalistic career. Both he and his father Malcolm won Pulitzer Prizes for reporting. In addition, Mr. Johnson is the author or co-author of seven books about contemporary American life. The *Columbia Journalism Review* has called him "as fine a writer and reporter as the craft knows."

As a journalist, he has worked for the *Wilmington* (Del.) *News-Journal,* the *Washington Star* and the *Post.* And he has served in a number of capacities—city reporter, copy editor, night city editor, national reporter and on special assignments in America and overseas.

Mr. Johnson, 44, a native of New York, earned a bachelor's degree in journalism from the University of Missouri and a master's in American history from the University of Wisconsin.

Robert C. Maynard

Now a member of the editorial page staff of the *Washington Post,* Robert C. Maynard was associate editor/ombudsman of the *Post* for more than a year, beginning November 1, 1972.

Before assuming the ombudsman duties, Maynard served for five years as the newspaper's national correspondent, covering politics, race relations, labor and Congress. For a brief period, he was the *Post*'s White House correspondent.

Mr. Maynard joined the *Post* in 1967 after working for six years on the *York* (Pa.) *Gazette & Daily,* where he was night city editor and urban affairs reporter. While on the York newspaper, Mr. Maynard was chosen as a Nieman Fellow and spent a year at Harvard studying music, art history, urban politics and economics.

Born in 1937 in Brooklyn, N.Y., to Barbadian parents, he attended the public schools of New York City before deciding on a career in journalism. He began his first newspaper job at the age of 16 on the now-defunct black weekly, the *New York Age.*

Colman McCarthy

Colman McCarthy, 37, says he began in journalism as a fourth-grader when he put out a one-page class newspaper. It folded when he went on to fifth grade, but ever since Mr. McCarthy has been writing.

A graduate of Spring Hill College in Mobile, Ala., Mr. McCarthy came to the *Washington Post* in 1968 and contributes columns and editorials to the editorial page.

Mr. McCarthy also has written for the *New Republic, Saturday Review, Rolling Stone, Reader's Digest* and the *Jewish Digest.* In 1973 Houghton Mifflin published his book *Disturbers of the Peace* and Acropolis published *Inner Companions* in 1975.

Bernard D. Nossiter

Bernard D. Nossiter, the *Washington Post*'s London bureau chief who writes here about Britain's media health and problems with prejudicial publicity, has been with the *Post* since 1955. Previously, he worked as a reporter for the *Worcester* (Mass.) *Telegram,* the *Wall Street Journal, Fortune* magazine and the *New York World Telegram & Sun.*

A 1947 magna cum laude graduate of Dartmouth College with a master's in economics from Harvard, Mr. Nossiter, 49, did economic affairs reporting for the *Post* for nine years.

Charles B. Seib

Charles B. Seib became the *Washington Post*'s fourth ombudsman November 15, 1974, succeeding Robert Maynard in the role of internal critic, consumer (reader) complaint respondent, and columnist on the media. His column appears regularly in the *Post* editorial pages and is syndicated to other newspapers by the Washington Post Writers Group.

Before moving to the *Post*, Seib had been managing editor of the *Washington Star-News* and its predecessor, the *Washington Star,* for six years. He began his career at the *Star* in 1954, and has also worked for the *Allentown* (Pa.) *Chronicle*, the Associated Press, the *Philadelphia Record*, International News Service and the Gannett News Service.

Seib, 56, was born in Kingston, New York, and is a graduate of Lehigh University.

Jules Witcover

A member of the national staff of the *Washington Post* since January 1973, Jules Witcover was a Washington correspondent for 20 years for the Newhouse Newspapers and later the *Los Angeles Times.* He has been a regular contributor to the *Columbia Journalism Review* on the performance of the Washington press corps and has written articles for numerous national magazines.

Mr. Witcover, 48, is also the author of four books on national political figures, including *A Heartbeat Away: The Investigation and Resignation of Vice President Agnew,* written with *Post* reporter Richard M. Cohen and published by Viking Press in April 1974.

Suggested Reading

Books

A Free and Responsive Press, Twentieth Century Fund, 1973.

Alsop, Joseph and Stewart, *The Reporter's Trade,* Reynal, 1958.

Alsop, Stewart, *Center: People and Power in Political Washington,* Harper & Row, 1968.

Aronson, James, *The Press and the Cold War,* Bobbs-Merrill, 1970.

Bagdikian, Ben H., *The Effete Conspiracy and Other Crimes by the Press,* Harper & Row, 1972.

Bagdikian, Ben H., *The Information Machines: Their Impact on Men and the Media,* Harper & Row, 1971.

Balk, Alfred and James Baylon, *Our Troubled Press—10 Years of the Columbia Journalism Review,* Little, Brown and Company, 1971.

Barron, Jerome A., *Freedom of the Press for Whom?,* Indiana University Press, 1973.

Bernstein, Carl and Bob Woodward, *All the President's Men,* Simon & Schuster, 1974.

Crouse, Timothy, *The Boys on the Bus,* Random House, 1973.

Diamond, Edwin, *The Tin Kazoo: Television, Politics, and the News,* MIT Press, 1975.

Epstein, Edward J., *News From Nowhere: Television and the News,* Vintage, 1974.

Ghiglione, Loren, *Evaluating the Press,* New England Daily Newspaper Survey, 25 Elm Street, Southbridge, Mass. 01550.

Hohenberg, John, *The News Media: A Journalist Looks at His Profession,* Holt, Rinehart and Winston, 1968.

Krieghbaum, Hillier, *Pressures on the Press,* Thomas Y. Crowell Company, 1972.

Liebling, A.J., *Mollie and Other War Pieces,* Ballantine Books, 1964.

Liebling, A.J., *The Press,* Ballantine Books, 1964.

MacDougall, Curtis D., *The Press: A Critical Look From the Inside,* Dow Jones Books, 1972.

MacDougall, Curtis D., *Newsroom Problems and Policies,* Dover, 1963.

Mayer, Martin, *About Television,* Harper & Row, 1972.

Mencken, H.L., *A Gang of Pecksniffs, and Other Comments on Newspapers, Publishers, Editors and Reporters,* edited and introduced by Theo Lippman Jr., Arlington House, 1975.

Minor, Dale, *The Information War,* Hawthorne Books, 1970.

Minow, Newton, John Bartlow Martin and Lee M. Mitchell, *Presidential Television,* a Twentieth Century Fund publication, Basic Books, November 1973.

Newman, Edwin, *Strictly Speaking: Will America Be the Death of English?* Bobbs-Merrill, 1974.

Pollard, James E., *The Presidents and the Press: Truman to Johnson,* Public Affairs Press, 1964.

Pride, Armistead S., comp., *The Black Press: A Bibliography,* Association for Education in Journalism, School of Journalism, Ad Hoc Committee on Minority Education, University of Minnesota, 1968.

Reston, James, *The Artillery of the Press,* Harper & Row, 1967.

Rivers, William L., *The Adversaries: Politics and the Press,* Beacon Press, 1970.

Scammon, Richard and Ben Wattenberg, *The Real Majority,* Coward-McCann, 1970.

Schramm, Wilbur, *Responsibility in Mass Communications,* Harper and Brothers, 1957.

Seldes, George, *Freedom of the Press,* Da Capo Press, 1971.

Seldes, George, *You Can't Do That,* Da Capo Press, 1972.

Seldes, George, *You Can't Print That,* Scholarly Press, 1968.

The Rights of Fair Trial and Free Press, American Bar Association, Chicago, 1969.

Stop the Presses, I Want to Get Off! Tales of the News Business From the Pages of (MORE) Magazine, edited and introduced by Richard Pollack, Random House, 1975.

Tebbel, John, *The Media in America: A Social and Political History,* Thomas Y. Crowell Company, 1974.

Thornbrough, Emma Lou, *T. Thomas Fortune: Militant Journalist,* Chicago Press, 1972.

Wolseley, Roland E., *The Black Press, U.S.A.,* Iowa State University Press, 1971.

Writing in Style, from the Style section of *The Washington Post,* distributed by Houghton Mifflin/Boston, 1975.

Articles and Reports

Bagdikian, Ben H., "The Little Old Daily of Dubuque," *The New York Times Magazine,* Feb. 3, 1974.

Barron, Jerome A., "Access to the Press—A New First Amendment Right," *Harvard Law Review,* Vol. 80, No. 8, June 1967.

Bickel, Alexander M., "The 'Uninhibited, Robust and Wide-Open' First Amendment," *Commentary,* November 1972.

Booth, Wayne C., "Loathing and Ignorance on the Campaign Trail: 1972," *Columbia Journalism Review,* Nov./Dec. 1973.

Duscha, Julius, "A Free and Accessible Press," *Progressive,* January 1974.

Duscha, Julius, "After Watergate: The Press Still Under Pressure," *The Bulletin,* Nov./Dec. 1973.

Epstein, Edward Jay, "A Reporter at Large—The Panthers and the Police: A Pattern of Genocide?" *The New Yorker,* Feb. 13, 1971.

"Freedom of the Press, *Current,* December 1972.

Gruenstein, Peter, "Release Politics: How Congressmen Manage the News," *Progressive,* January 1974.

Harwood, Richard L., "A Question of Relevancy," Fifth A. J. Liebling Memorial Lecture delivered at the 1971 International Labor Press Association convention in Miami Beach, Nov. 15, 1971.

Isaacs, Norman E., Benno C. Schmidt Jr. and Fred W. Friendly, "Beyond Caldwell," *Columbia Journalism Review,* Sept./Oct. 1972.

Johnson, Haynes, "The Newspaper Guild's Identity Crisis," *Columbia Journalism Review,* Nov./Dec. 1972.

"Junketing Journalists," *Time,* Jan. 28, 1974.

"Mass Media and Violence," a staff report to the National Commission on the Causes and Prevention of Violence, U.S. Government Printing Office, 1969.

Mintz, Morton, "Auditing the Media: A Modest Proposal," *Columbia Journalism Review,* Nov./Dec. 1972.

Morris, John G., "This We Remember," *Harper's,* September 1972.

Moynihan, Daniel P., "Presidency and the Press," *Commentary,* March 1971.

Pincus, Walter, "Usable Press: Unidentified News Sources and Their Motives," *The New Republic,* Oct. 20, 1973.

Rosenthal, A. M., "Save the First Amendment," *The New York Times Magazine,* Feb. 11, 1973.

"Setting the Record Straight: Accuracy and Corrections by the News Media, *Newsweek,* Jan. 28, 1974.

Watson, Denton L., "Time for a New Black Press," *The Crisis,* November 1972.

Welch, Susan, "The Press and Foreign Policy: The Definition of the Situation," delivered at the American Political Science Association convention in Los Angeles, September 1970.

Witcover, Jules, "How Well Does the White House Press Perform?" *Columbia Journalism Review,* Nov./Dec. 1973.

31